OFFICIAL ENCYCLOPEDIA OF
FOOTBALL

★ ★ ★ ★ ★ ★ ★ ★ ★ ★ ★   ★ ★

OFFICIAL ENCYCLOPEDIA OF
FOOTBALL

Don R. Smith

GALLERY BOOKS
An Imprint of W. H. Smith Publishers Inc.
112 Madison Avenue
New York City 10016

First published in the UK in 1989 by
The Hamlyn Publishing Group Ltd.,
a division of The Octopus Publishing
Group

This edition published in 1989 by Gallery
Books
An imprint of W.H. Smith Publishers Inc
112 Madison Avenue
New York
New York 10016

ISBN 0-8317-6304-3

Produced by Mandarin Offset

Printed and Bound in She Kou.

Photographic Acknowledgements

All of the photographs in the book were obtained from the libraries of NFL Properties Inc, and the Pro Football Hall of Fame:

Charles Aqua Viva, 10 right
Eric Lars Bakke, 146
John E. Biever, 74
Vernon Biever, 10 above, 70, 86 far right, 103 above, 127, 156
David Boss, 19, 62/3 above left, 132
Clifton Boutelle, 53
George Brace, 105
Peter Brouillet, 91 opposite bottom
Bill Cummings, 111, 139
Jonathan Daniel, 63 above
Bruce Dierdorff, 84
Brian Drake, 26 right, 83
Dunn/Focus West, 102/3
Emmons & Brockway, 8
Malcolm Emmons, 26 above, 36, 78 below, 90 right
Nate Fine Photos, 78 right
James F. Flores, 99, 118
Larry Fullerton, 14, 31
Mike Gaines (artist), 11

George Gellatly, 88
Richard Gentile, 170
George Gojkovich, 62, 130, 158/9 above left, 171
Green Bay Press Gazette, 69 left
Rod Hanna, 43, 154
Chris Hopkins (artist), 86 right
Paul Jasienski, 15
Al Kooistra, 18
LeFebvre-Luebke, 84
Richard Mackson, 143 above
Tal Makita, 167
John McDonough, 122/3 above left, 142
Perry McIntyre, 110
Mike Minardi, 151 above
Al Messerschmidt, 35, 65, 76 bottom, 151 left
P. R. Miller, 27
New York Jets, 48, 105
NFL Photos, 4/5, 9, 22 above, 24, 29, 39, 53, 54, 58, 59 above, 64, 67, 68, 72, 73, 115 left, 133 above left, 133 above, 138, 153, 164
Darryl Norenberg, 42 below right
PRM, 40, 47, 55 above left, 79, 94, 174
Pro Football Hall of Fame, 44, 46, 52, 61, 82, 85, 93, 106, 115 below, 121, 123 above, 127, 136
Richard Raphael, 39
Kevin W. Reece, 147 left
Russ Reed, 20
Frank Rippon, 41, 56

Fred Roe, 161
Bob Rosato, 6/7, 131
George Rose, 103 left, 126
Ron Ross, 59 above left
Manny Rubio, 2/3, 23 below left, 66 above, 116, 170
Robert B. Shaver, 71, 98, 106/7
Owen Shaw, 174
Barton Silverman, 96
Carl Skalac Jr., 139, 149
Chuck Solomon, 55 above, 66 right, 123
Jay Spencer, 172
Paul Spinelli, 1, 82
R. H. Stagg, 119
Vic Stein, 48
Stewart/Focus West, 135
Tony Tomsic, 3, 23 below, 34, 37, 69 far left, 134/5, 147 above, 155, 162
Corky Trewin, 56, 87, 159 above
United Press, 145
United Press International, 150
Ron Vesely, 30/1, 95
Ed Webber, 75, 114
Herb Weitman, 145 left, 158, 166
Wide World Photos, 16/7
Lou Witt, 91
Bill Wood, 42 below
Michael Zagaris, 22 right, 91 opposite top
John Zimmerman, 137

INTRODUCTION

Pro football in the 1980s has become one of the world's most popular sports. One recent Super Bowl was viewed live by 127 million people in 59 nations and then seen on replay by 300 million Chinese. National Football League preseason games played overseas each year give the sport truly international appeal.

In the 97 years since the first football player was openly paid to play in 1892, the lifeblood of pro football has been the enthusiasm of tens of millions of fans who have thrilled at the deeds of many of the 20,000 who played in an estimated 12,000 games, many so dynamic in scope that they never will be forgotten.

Each decade has had its magic memories – Pudge Heffelfinger, Jim Thorpe, the flying wedge, the dropkick in the early years . . . Bronko Nagurski, Sammy Baugh, the 73-0 game, the man-in-motion in the maturing stages . . . Otto Graham, Bert Bell, the All-America Football Conference, "the Greatest Game Ever Played" in the post-World War II seasons . . . Joe Namath, Vince Lombardi, the merger, the Super Bowl when pro football had its own "war" in the 1960s . . . Monday night football, NFL Players Association, Roger Staubach, Joe Montana, blitz, bomb, and ball control in the modern era.

Here, in one volume for the first time is the *NFL's Official Encyclopedia of Football* – a glossary of 591 players, teams, leagues, terms, and assorted subjects from every era of the sport. Designed for fans of every age and every team, the *NFL's Official Encyclopedia of Football* will rekindle the enthusiasm of long-time fanatics and explain for newcomers the captivating mystery that is pro football.

A

Abramowicz, Dan

b. Steubenville, Ohio, 13 July 1945.

Dan Abramowicz, a 6-1, 195-pound graduate of Xavier University, was an obscure seventeenth-round draft choice of the New Orleans Saints in 1967. Given little chance to make the team, he instead developed into the Saints' top pass receiver, and in 1969 led the NFL with 73 receptions. He played with New Orleans until 1973, when he was traded to San Francisco, and he ended his career with the Buffalo Bills. When he retired after the 1975 season, Abramowicz had a career total of 369 receptions for 5,686 yards and 39 touchdowns. He also caught at least one pass in each of the last 105 games of his career, an NFL record at the time.

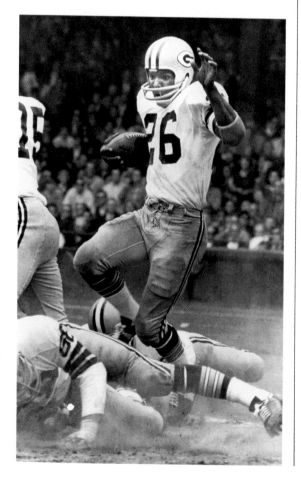

Herb Adderley's 60-yard interception return for a touchdown in Super Bowl II was the only interception run back for a score in the first 10 games.

Adderley, Herb

b. Philadelphia, Pennsylvania, 8 June 1939.
Hall of Fame: 1980

A first-round draft pick of the Green Bay Packers in 1961, Herb Adderley began his pro career as a halfback but shifted to cornerback late in his rookie season. He soon developed into an outstanding defensive back. In nine years with the Packers, the 6-1, 200-pound Michigan State graduate won all-pro honors four times and played in five Pro Bowls, five NFL championship games, and Super Bowls I and II. In the second Super Bowl, he scored on a 60-yard interception return.

In 1970, Adderley moved to the Dallas Cowboys, with whom he played in Super Bowls V and VI. He retired after the 1972 season with 48 career interceptions, which were returned for 1,046 yards and seven touchdowns. He also returned 120 kickoffs for 3,080 yards and two touchdowns.

AFC vs. NFC

In 1970, the AFL-NFL merger created a 26-team National Football League consisting of two 13-team conferences, the American and National Football Conferences (the addition of expansion teams Seattle and Tampa Bay in 1976 created the current 14-team conferences). The NFC won the interconference series in 1970 and 1971, but has won only one season series since – 1981. The AFC has won 12 and tied four series. Overall, the AFC has a 444-388-8 winning record in regular-season games with the NFC. The AFC also holds a 12-11 edge in the Super Bowl series and a 450-435-14 advantage in pre-season games since 1970. The NFC leads the AFC 11-8 in the Pro Bowl series.

All-America Football Conference

On June 4, 1944 representatives from Buffalo, Chicago, Cleveland, Los Angeles, New York, and San Francisco met in a St. Louis hotel room to form the All-America Football Conference. Brooklyn and Miami also entered before the league began play in 1946. The new league's founder was Arch Ward, the *Chicago Tribune* sports editor who had started the College All-Star game. Jim Crowley was named commissioner. The AAFC eventually succumbed, but only after a costly and competitive four-year struggle. Unlike previous NFL rivals, the AAFC left a lasting mark on pro football, being the first league to travel by air. The new league lured away more than 100 former NFL players with fat contracts. The AAFC signed 40 of the 66 members of the 1946 College All-Star team, and NFL teams were forced to increase salaries.

By 1949, the AAFC was faced with a unique, unsolvable problem. The Cleveland Browns had become too good for the rest of the league. The Browns won all four AAFC championships and amassed a sensational 52-4-3 record. Fans throughout the league, including Cleveland, simply were losing interest. NFL Commissioner Bert Bell established terms to end the financial bloodshed. Cleveland, San Francisco, and Baltimore would be admitted into the NFL, and the players from other AAFC squads would be divided among the established NFL teams.

The eight teams in the AAFC in 1946 included the Brooklyn Dodgers, Buffalo Bisons, Miami Seahawks, and New York Yankees in the Eastern Division, and the Chicago Rockets, Cleveland Browns, Los Angeles Dons, and San Francisco 49ers in the Western Division. Miami disbanded after the season but was replaced by the Baltimore Colts in 1947. Buffalo changed its name from Bisons to Bills. That alignment remained in place in 1948, but in 1949 the New York and Brooklyn franchises merged, and Chicago changed its name from Rockets to Hornets. In the final AAFC game, Cleveland defeated San Francisco 21-7 for the 1949 championship.

Allegheny Athletic Association

Thanks to the meticulous record-keeping of O.D. Thompson, the manager of the Allegheny Athletic Association football team, pro football has a genuine "birth certificate." It is a tattered expense accounting sheet of an AAA game played with the Pittsburgh Athletic Club on November 12, 1892, which contains the notation: "game performance bonus to W. Heffelfinger for playing (cash) $500." The AAA expense sheet is the earliest evidence of a direct cash payment to anyone for playing football.

The Allegheny Athletic Association football team existed for only seven seasons, from 1890 to 1896, but left its lasting mark on history with its professional philosophy. Its first venture in the pro ranks was a big success. The AAA team defeated the PAC 4-0, and the expense sheet shows a $621 profit for the game. The next

week, the team paid $250 to another player – Ben (Sport) Donnelly – to perform against Washington and Jefferson College. In 1893, the team had three players under $50-per-game contracts for the entire season.

George Allen's 69 victories with Washington place him second in successes behind Joe Gibbs. His 49 victories with the Los Angeles Rams rank him third behind Chuck Knox and John Robinson.

Allen, George

b. Detroit, Michigan, 29 April 1918.

In 12 seasons as a head coach with the Los Angeles Rams from 1966 to 1970 and the Washington Redskins from 1971 through 1977, George Allen compiled a 116-47-5 record. His .705 winning percentage ranks fourth among pro football coaches. In both cities, Allen transformed losing teams into winners. Neither had a losing season during Allen's tenure. Allen was NFL Coach of the Year in 1967 when the Rams won the Coastal Division with an 11-1-2 record.

Allen, who attended Alma College, Marquette University, and the University of Michigan, moved to the Redskins in 1971. Adopting a "Future Is Now" theme, he made numerous trades, sacrificing future draft choices for veterans who could help immediately. In 12 seasons in the NFL, he made 131 trades, 81 of them while with the Redskins. Under Allen, Washington qualified for the NFC playoffs five times in seven years. In 1972, the Redskins defeated Dallas 26-3 for the NFC championship but lost to Miami in Super Bowl VII. Allen returned to the Rams for the 1978 season but was released after two preseason games.

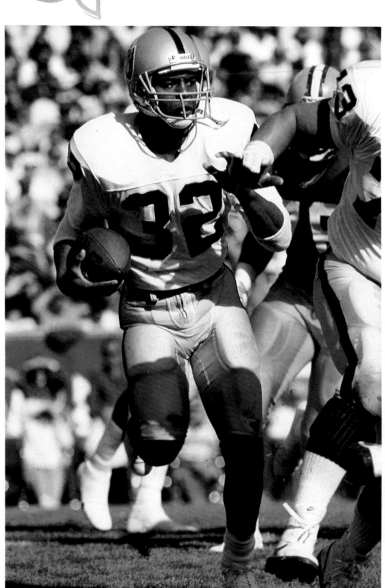

Allen, Marcus

b. San Diego, California, 26 March 1960.

Marcus Allen, the 1981 Heisman Trophy winner and consensus All-America from the University of Southern California, was the first-round draft choice of the Los Angeles Raiders in 1982. The 6-2, 205-pound running back, who is still active, led the Raiders in rushing in each of his first seven seasons. Allen rushed for an NFL-leading 1,759 yards in 1985 and added 555 yards on receptions en route to 2,308 combined net yards. Two years earlier, against Washington in Super Bowl XVIII, Allen won most valuable player honors by rushing for 191 yards. His 74-yard touchdown run that broke the game open is a Super Bowl record. Allen's career record included 6,932 yards rushing, 3,470 yards on 368 receptions, and 78 touchdowns.

Alley-Oop

A play first made famous by Y.A. Tittle and R.C. Owens of the San Francisco 49ers in the late

Above: Marcus Allen has been the one consistent factor in the Los Angeles Raiders' offense since he joined them in 1982.

Right: Lance Alworth leaps high to catch a pass. In nine seasons with the Chargers he averaged more than 1,000 yards in receptions every year.

1950s. Tittle would throw a high pass toward the end zone that was too high for anyone to catch except Owens, who had exceptional leaping ability.

Alworth, Lance

b. Houston, Texas, 3 August 1940.
Hall of Fame: 1978

In 1962, Lance Alworth, flashing a smooth and graceful form that earned him the nickname "Bambi," joined the San Diego Chargers, with whom he was destined to become the premier pass receiver of the American Football League. More than any other player, he epitomized the exciting, wide-open offensive approach that made the Chargers the glamour team of the AFL. The 6-0, 184-pound sprinter from the University of Arkansas caught at least one pass in 96 consecutive games. He was all-AFL seven years, a seven-time AFL All-Star game selection, and a unanimous choice for the all-time all-AFL team. He became the first AFL player to be elected to the Pro Football Hall of Fame.

Alworth was an All-America halfback in college, but he made use of his 9.6 speed in the 100-yard dash, great leaping ability, and sure hands to excel as a flanker in the AFL.

After nine seasons with the Chargers, he was traded to the Dallas Cowboys in 1971. That year, Alworth caught the first touchdown pass in the Cowboys' 24-3 Super Bowl VI victory over Miami. He retired following the 1972 season. In 12 pro seasons, he recorded 542 receptions for 10,266 yards and 85 touchdowns.

American Bowl

In response to the NFL owners' 1985 resolution to stage at least one international preseason game each year, the American Bowl was inaugurated in Wembley Stadium in London, England, on August 3, 1986. In the first game, the Chicago Bears defeated the Dallas Cowboys 17-6 before a sellout crowd of 82,699. The NBC national telecast produced a 12.4 rating and a 36 percent share in the United States, making it the second-highest-rated daytime preseason game. The audience of 10,650,000 viewers was the highest ever for a preseason game. The American Bowl series results:

Date	Teams, Score	Attendance
8-3-86	Chicago Bears 17, Dallas Cowboys 6	82,699
8-9-87	Los Angeles Rams 28, Denver Broncos 27	72,786
7-31-88	Miami Dolphins 27, San Francisco 49ers 21	70,500

American Football Conference

With the completion of the AFL-NFL merger in 1970, the National Football League was split into two conferences, the American Football Conference and the National Football Conference.

The 10 teams from the American Football League were joined by three teams from the National Football League – Baltimore, Cleveland, and Pittsburgh – to form the 13-team AFC. The Baltimore (moved to Indianapolis in 1984) Colts, Boston (moved to New England in 1971) Patriots, Buffalo Bills, Miami Dolphins, and New York Jets made up the AFC Eastern Division. The Cincinnati Bengals, Cleveland Browns, Houston Oilers, and Pittsburgh Steelers made up the AFC Central Division. The Denver Broncos, Kansas City Chiefs, Oakland (moved to Los Angeles in 1982) Raiders, and San Diego Chargers made up the AFC Western Division. In 1977, the Seattle Seahawks became the fourteenth AFC team and a permanent member of the Western Division.

In the 19 seasons since 1970, AFC champions hold a 10-9 edge over the NFC champions in Super Bowl competition. The championship summary:

Miami Dolphins	(5)	1971, 1972, 1973, 1982, 1984
Pittsburgh Steelers	(4)	1974, 1975, 1978, 1979
Oakland (Los Angeles) Raiders		
	(3)	1976, 1980, 1983
Denver Broncos	(3)	1977, 1986, 1987
Cincinnati Bengals	(2)	1981, 1988
Baltimore Colts	(1)	1970
New England Patriots		
	(1)	1985

The American Bowl in London is contested annually by two specially invited teams. It is an extra preseason game, played a day after the Hall of Fame game, and has played to sellout crowds every year. Philadelphia and Cleveland played in 1989.

American Football League 1

Red Grange, the fabled "Galloping Ghost" halfback from the University of Illinois, gave the National Football League a huge promotional boost when he joined the Chicago Bears on Thanksgiving Day, 1925. He then embarked on a coast-to-coast barnstorming tour with the Bears that attracted massive pro football crowds for the first time.

In 1926, Grange's manager, C.C. (Cash and Carry) Pyle, informed the Bears that Grange would not play for them unless they gave him a five-figure salary and one-third ownership of the team. The Bears' co-owners, George Halas and Dutch Sternaman, refused. Pyle then leased Yankee Stadium in New York and petitioned the NFL for a franchise. Tim Mara, who just a year earlier had founded the New York Giants, balked. Pyle countered by threatening to organize a new league, then following through on his threat.

Pyle created the New York Yankees franchise, with Grange as its key figure, as the flagship team for his American Football League. The Rock Island (Illinois) Independents defected from the NFL to join the new league and seven new teams – the Philadelphia Quakers, Cleveland Panthers, Chicago Bulls, Boston Bulldogs, Brooklyn Horsemen, Newark Bears, and a road team named the Los Angeles Wildcats – also were admitted.

Several NFL players defected to the new league. Giants coach Bob Folwell resigned to join the Quakers, and Joey Sternaman, brother of the Bears' co-owner, formed the Chicago Bulls. Politician and former Princeton athlete Bill Edwards was hired as AFL commissioner at a salary of $25,000. In contrast, NFL president Joe Carr was paid $2,500 in 1926.

But Pyle's grandiose plans were not matched by AFL fan support, which was minimal outside of New York City. Cleveland and Newark quickly folded, and the Brooklyn Horsemen merged with the NFL Brooklyn Lions. By sea-

son's end, only the Yankees, the Quakers, and the traveling Wildcats still were operating. The Quakers finished first with a 7-2 record. Grange's Yankees were second with a 9-5 mark.

Because the AFL no longer existed, no peace agreement was necessary. But as a concession to Pyle and Grange, the NFL accepted the Yankees franchise for the 1927 season. The Yankees played in 1927 and 1928 before going out of business.

American Football League 2

In 1936, 10 years after the first American Football League folded, a second AFL came into being. The league existed for only two years and never had more than six teams operating at one time. The Boston Shamrocks, New York Yankees, Pittsburgh Americans, and Rochester Tigers played both seasons. The Brooklyn Tigers and Cleveland Rams competed only in 1936, while the Cincinnati Bengals and Los Angeles Bulldogs were active only in 1937. The Shamrocks were scheduled to play a championship game with the Rams in 1936, but refused to travel to Cleveland because they were owed pay for past games. Boston had the best regular-season record (8-3), so it was declared the champion. In 1937, the Los Angeles Bulldogs won with a perfect 8-0 record.

In spite of its short existence, the second AFL did make a mark on pro football history. The Rams' franchise was the forerunner of the Cleveland Rams team that began play in the NFL in 1937. The Bulldogs were the first Los Angeles team that did not play all of its games on the road. The team did make a long swing through the East but played its last two games in Gilmore Stadium in Los Angeles. Also, an AFL game in Miami is credited with laying the groundwork for the building of the Orange Bowl.

Ken Strong, the New York Giants' ace halfback and kicker, bolted to the New York Yankees, and, in turn, was blackballed by the NFL for several years. Another big name, Morris (Red) Badgro, became the player-coach at Rochester. Sid Gillman, later a famous coach and general manager, experienced his only pro football play with the 1936 Cleveland Rams.

American Football League 3

Of all the leagues in history that challenged the NFL, the third American Football League was the most poorly conceived. The AFL was organized in 1940, with the Columbus Bullies, Milwaukee Chiefs, Boston Bears, New York Yankees, Buffalo Indians, and Cincinnati Ben-

★ ★ **AFL Champions,** 1960-1969 ★ ★
(Home team in bold)

1960	**Houston Oilers** 24, Los Angeles Chargers 16
1961	Houston Oilers 10, **San Diego Chargers** 3
1962	Dallas Texans 20, **Houston Oilers** 17 (two overtimes)
1963	**San Diego Chargers** 51, Boston Patriots 10
1964	**Buffalo Bills** 20, San Diego Chargers 7
1965	Buffalo Bills 23, **San Diego Chargers** 0
1966	Kansas City Chiefs 31, **Buffalo Bills** 7
1967	**Oakland Raiders** 40, Houston Oilers 7
1968	**New York Jets** 27, Oakland Raiders 23
1969	**Kansas City Chiefs** 17, Oakland Raiders 7

gals. Five of the six teams operated again in 1941, although the New York team changed its name to the Americans. Boston did not play. The Columbus Bullies won championships each year, going 8-1-1 in 1940, and 5-1-2 in 1941.

The third AFL signed very few NFL players. Its principal gate attractions were two recently graduated college stars, John Kimbrough of Texas A&M and Tom Harmon of Michigan. Both played with the New York Americans. Later in the year, a game in Cincinnati was forfeited because the Bengals did not have enough players. Manpower shortages created by the involvement of the United States in World War II made further play impossible in 1942. However, there was nothing in the league's two-year existence to indicate any other eventual outcome.

American Football League 4

On August 14, 1959, a young Dallas, Texas, businessman named Lamar Hunt, and representatives from five other cities organized the American Football League, the fourth league to adopt that name. Dallas, Denver, Houston, Los Angeles, Minneapolis, and New York were charter members. Buffalo and Boston joined a short time later. In November, World War II hero and former South Dakota governor Joe Foss was named commissioner. In January, 1960, Minneapolis dropped out of the AFL and was replaced by Oakland. The AFL planned one major rules innovation – the option of a two-point conversion by running or passing after a touchdown.

Few gave the AFL any chance of success, but the new league got a big boost when the American Broadcasting Company signed a five-year television contract that assured national exposure and much-needed income for the costly player signing war with the NFL that lay ahead. The AFL began play in 1960 with the Boston Patriots, Buffalo Bills, Houston Oilers, and New York Titans in the Eastern Division, and the Dallas Texans, Denver Broncos, Los Angeles Chargers, and Oakland Raiders in the Western Division. In 1961, the Chargers transferred to San Diego. In 1963, the Texans moved to Kansas City, where they became the Chiefs. The badly mismanaged Titans were taken over by the AFL in 1962 but resurfaced under new ownership as the Jets in 1963.

The demise of the Titans marked the low point in AFL history. In 1963, the AFL signed eight number-one draft choices, and in January, 1964, Foss announced a five-year, $36 million TV contract with the National Broadcasting Company that would start in 1965. That year, the Jets moved into new Shea Stadium, and record

crowds added to the AFL's growing credibility. While the AFL did sign a certain number of outstanding stars, the NFL honestly could claim it had signed the lion's share of coveted players in the early 1960s. But in January, 1965, Sonny Werblin, the Jets' owner, dropped a bombshell by signing Joe Namath, a highly touted quarterback from the University of Alabama, to a reported $400,000 contract. Without a doubt, Namath's signing marked the turning point in the AFL-NFL war. Merger talks soon began and the war officially ended on June 8, 1966.

The NFL and AFL agreed on seven major points: (1) Pete Rozelle would be the commissioner of pro football; (2) the leagues would play a world championship game; (3) all existing franchises would remain at their present sites; (4) a combined draft would be held; (5) two franchises would be added by 1968, one in each league – the money from each to be paid to the NFL; (6) AFL clubs would pay an indemnity of $18 million to the NFL over a 20-year period; and (7) inter-league preseason games would be played in 1967 with a single league schedule to commence in 1970.

On August 5, 1967, the Denver Broncos gave the AFL its first victory over an NFL team by defeating the Detroit Lions 13-7 in a preseason game. In 1968, the Cincinnati Bengals became the AFL's second expansion franchise, the first being the Miami Dolphins in 1966. The NFL-champion Green Bay Packers won the first two Super Bowl games, over Kansas City and Oakland, but upset victories by the New York Jets in Super Bowl III and the Kansas City Chiefs in Super Bowl IV gave the AFL a 2-2 tie in the AFL-NFL portion of the Super Bowl series. In just 10 years, the American Football League provided the impetus for the most dynamic period of growth in the history of any sport.

American Professional Football Association

Pro football was in a state of disarray as the 1920s approached. Teams were loosely organized and players moved freely from one team to another. The Columbus Panhandles once noted they had played against Knute Rockne, the famous Notre Dame coach who moonlighted as a pro end on Sundays, six times on six different teams one season.

A league in which all members would operate under the same rules appeared to be the answer. Four teams from Ohio held a preliminary organizational meeting in Canton, Ohio, on August 20, 1920. A month later, on September 17, representatives of 10 teams from four states met again in Canton to formally organize the

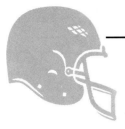

American Professional Football Association. The charter members were the Akron Pros, Canton Bulldogs, Cleveland Indians, Dayton Triangles, Decatur (Illinois) Staleys, the Hammond (Indiana) Pros, Muncie (Indiana) Flyers, Racine (Chicago) Cardinals, Rochester (New York) Jeffersons, and the Rock Island (Illinois) Independents. Four other teams, the Buffalo All-Americans, Chicago Tigers, Columbus Panhandles, and Detroit Heralds joined the league sometime during the year. On October 3, the first game matching two APFA teams was played, with Dayton defeating Columbus 14-0, with Lou Partlow of Dayton scoring the first APFA touchdown.

Formation of a league did not bring about immediate order to the pro football chaos. A league membership fee of $100 was established but no team ever paid it. Schedules still were made haphazardly with league and non-league teams. Akron, Canton, and Buffalo all claimed the 1920 championship.

Jim Thorpe, who was elected the APFA president because he was the best-known name in pro football, proved to be a mere figurehead. He was replaced by Joe Carr in 1921. Carr's first item of business was to award the 1920 APFA championship to Akron. In 1922, the APFA changed its name to the National Football League.

Ken Anderson drops back to pass. His accuracy was such that his completion percentage was regularly among the best in the AFC. He ranks fourth among retired players under the passer-rating system now in force.

Anderson, Ken

b. *Batavia, Illinois, 15 February 1949.*

Ken Anderson, a 6-3, 212-pound quarterback from Augustana College in Illinois, was the third-round draft pick of the Cincinnati Bengals in 1971. In his 16-season career that ended in 1986, Anderson led the NFL in passing four times – in 1974, 1975, 1981, and 1982. Anderson completed more than 60 percent of his passes in seven different seasons. He passed for more than 3,000 yards in both 1975 and 1981, when he led the Bengals to their first AFC championship. In Cincinnati's losing effort in Super Bowl XVI, Anderson completed 25 of 34 passes for 300 yards and two touchdowns. In a game against Houston on January 2, 1983, he completed a then-NFL-record 20 consecutive passes. His lifetime record shows 2,654 completions for 32,838 yards, 197 touchdowns, and an 81.8 passing rating.

Atkins, Doug

b. *Humbolt, Tennessee, 8 May 1930.*
Hall of Fame: 1982

During 17 seasons as a defensive end with three teams in the National Football League, Doug Atkins, a 6-8, 275-pound man-mountain,

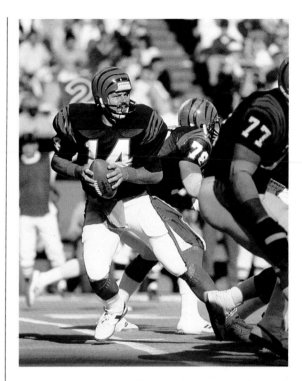

earned acclaim as a devastating pass rusher. Atkins began his pro career as a first-round draft choice of the Cleveland Browns in 1953. In 1955, he was traded to the Chicago Bears, for whom he became the ringleader of a powerful defensive unit for the next 12 years. He finished his pro career with the New Orleans Saints from 1967 to 1969.

Atkins was particularly dangerous when he was angered, so opponents carefully avoided antagonizing him. Even when no rancor was involved, the University of Tennessee graduate specialized in making life miserable for opposition quarterbacks. One of his favorite tricks was to throw a blocker at his quarterback. Another was to hurdle over a blocker to get at a passer. Atkins was a three-time all-pro pick and a veteran of eight Pro Bowls.

Atlanta Falcons

In the mid-1960s, with the AFL-NFL war at a fever pitch, both leagues cast eager eyes at Atlanta as a possible expansion city. In anticipation of a pro team but with no firm assurances, Atlanta Mayor Ivan Allen, Jr., broke ground for the $18 million Atlanta-Fulton County Stadium on April 15, 1964. At the urging of NFL Commissioner Pete Rozelle, pollster Louis Harris conducted a poll that revealed that Atlanta citizens overwhelmingly favored the NFL over the AFL.

On June 30, 1965, Rankin M. Smith, a 41-year-old executive vice president of an insurance company, was awarded a franchise for approximately $8.5 million. Two months later, the club was officially named "Falcons" when a Georgia schoolteacher supplied the name in a contest. The new team set an NFL record by selling 46,000 season tickets that year.

In the spring of 1966, the Falcons made Tommy Nobis, the highly touted linebacker from Texas, their first draft pick. Atlanta lost its season opener to the Los Angeles Rams 19-14 on September 11, but head coach Norb Hecker's Falcons did win three games, which equaled the first-year record for an NFL expansion team. Norm Van Brocklin eventually succeeded Hecker as coach in 1968, guiding the Falcons to their first two winning seasons, 7-6-1 in 1971 and 9-5 in 1973. In 1977, the Falcons reached another milestone when their rugged defense, led by defensive end Claude Humphrey, established an NFL 14-game record by allowing just 129 points.

In 1978, the Falcons reached the playoffs for the first time and defeated Philadelphia 14-13 in the wild-card game. But they lost to Dallas a week later. Paced by Steve Bartkowski's pass-ing and William Andrews's running, the 1980 Falcons, under coach Leeman Bennett, won their only NFC Western Division championship with a 12-4 record. However, they once again lost to Dallas in the divisional playoff round. Atlanta's only other playoff appearance came in the 1982 championship tournament. The Falcons lost to Minnesota in the first round.

During the 1980s, the Falcons' offense featured center Jeff Van Note and tackle Mike Kenn (perennial Pro Bowl players), wide receiver Alfred Jenkins, hard-running Gerald Riggs, and Billy (White Shoes) Johnson, an excellent receiver and the NFL's all-time kickoff return leader.

Members of the Hall of Fame:
None
Championships Won:
NFC Western Division: 1980
Overall Record:

NFL Regular Season	126	205	5	.382
NFL Postseason	1	3	0	.250
Total	127	208	5	.381

The Atlanta Falcons' defense gang tackles Denver's Tony Dorsett. In week 3 of the 1988 season, they stopped the San Francisco 49ers' offense and scored an upset victory in Candlestick Park.

Steadily increasing attendance has been a hall-mark of the National Football League ever since official records first were kept in 1934. Per-game average attendance figures at selected intervals follow:

1934 8,211	1965........47,286
1940 19,328	1970........52,381
1944 20,393	1975........56,116
1950 25,356	1980........59,787
1955 35,026	1981........60,745
1960 40,106	1986........60,663

In the American Football League, average attendance grew from 16,538 in 1960 to 40,620 in 1969.

Backfield

The area behind the line of scrimmage where the running backs line up and the quarterback passes. Also the collective term for those players.

Badgro, Morris (Red)

b. Orillia, Washington, 1 December 1902.
Hall of Fame: 1981

A graduate of the University of Southern California, Morris (Red) Badgro first played pro football with the New York Yankees in 1927. He then tried major league baseball for two seasons before returning to the NFL in 1930 with the New York Giants. Excellent on both offense and defense, he was named all-pro three of six years with the Giants. The 6-0, 190-pounder scored the first touchdown in the first regularly-scheduled NFL championship game in 1933. The next year, he tied for the league receiving title with 16 receptions. Badgro played a final season with the Brooklyn Dodgers in 1936 and, at 78, he became the oldest person ever elected to the Pro Football Hall of Fame.

Ball

The NFL football is manufactured by the Wilson Sporting Goods Company and bears the signature of Commissioner Pete Rozelle. It is an inflated rubber bladder filled with 12½ to 13½

Audible

A change of the play shouted in code by the quarterback at the line of scrimmage. Usually prompted by defensive alterations employed by an opponent.

pounds of air, enclosed in a pebble-grained leather case of natural tan color. It is in the form of a prolate spheroid, has a long axis of 11 to 11¼ inches, a long circumference of 28 to 28½ inches, a short circumference of 21¼ to 21½ inches, and weighs 14 to 15 ounces.

Ball Control

Ball control is a strategy that enables the offensive team to maintain possession of the football for the longest period of time. An ideal ball-control team will feature a strong running game complemented by an effective but not heavily used passing game. Ball control also is a tactic attempted by most teams who are leading near the end of a game. The theory is that the longer the offensive team maintains possession, the less time the opponent has to generate a scoring drive.

Barney, Lem

b. Gulfport, Mississippi, 8 September 1945.

A second-round draft pick of the Detroit Lions in 1967, Lem Barney starred as a cornerback with the Lions for 11 seasons. The 6-0, 190-

pound Jackson State graduate intercepted 10 passes to lead the NFL in his rookie season. He wound up his career with 56 interceptions, which he returned for 1,079 yards and seven touchdowns. Barney, who played in seven Pro Bowls, accounted for 1,312 yards on punt returns and 1,274 yards on kickoff returns in his career. He was named all-pro in 1968, 1969, and 1972.

Battles, Cliff

b. Akron, Ohio, 1 May 1910; d. 27 April 1981.
Hall of Fame: 1968

Cliff Battles, a Phi Beta Kappa scholar who was a triple-threat star at West Virginia Wesleyan, made a lasting mark as one of the first great breakaway runners. He led the NFL in rushing as a rookie with the Boston Braves in 1932. A year later, the 6-1, 201-pound speedster became

the first pro to gain more than 200 yards in one game.

The Braves, who changed their team name to Redskins in 1933, moved to Washington in 1937. Battles enjoyed his finest season in 1937. He won his second league rushing title and played a major role in the Redskins' first NFL championship season. Battles was named all-pro in 1933, 1936, and 1937, and accumulated 3,622 rushing yards in six years. While still at peak form, he retired after the 1937 season because his salary of $3,000 had been frozen for six years and Redskins owner George Preston Marshall refused to discuss a raise.

Baugh, Sammy

b. Temple, Texas, 17 March 1914.
Hall of Fame: 1963

When Sammy Baugh, an All-America from Texas Christian University, became the number one draft pick of the Boston (Washington) Redskins in 1937, pro football was played mostly on the ground, with the forward pass usually being thrown only as a last resort. When he retired 16 seasons later, the game had evolved into a far more crowd-pleasing show that featured the forward pass as a regular and valued part of the attack. More than any other player, the 6-2, 180-pound string bean was responsible for this remarkable offensive evolution.

Baugh used his brilliant passing abilities to lead the Redskins to the 1937 NFL championship. In the finale against the Chicago Bears, he threw three long touchdown passes to assure a 28-21 victory. In 16 seasons, Baugh won six individual league passing titles and also earned all-pro honors six times.

Making Baugh's record even more remarkable is the fact that he played his first eight seasons as a Single-Wing tailback and his last eight as a T-formation quarterback. Baugh also was one of history's finest punters and an outstanding defender before free substitution rules turned him into an offensive specialist. In 1943, he intercepted four passes in one game and led the NFL with 11 interceptions.

Baugh led the NFL in punting four years. His 45.1-yard career average still ranks as the best ever. In 1943, he became the first player to achieve an unusual "triple crown" by winning individual titles in passing, punting, and interceptions. In 16 seasons, he completed 1,693 of 2,995 passes for 21,886 yards and 186 touchdowns, all records at that time.

Baugh was named as the first head coach of the New York Titans in 1960, leaving after the following season, and in 1964 he was coach of the Houston Oilers.

"Slinging Sammy" Baugh throws downfield for Washington in a game at New York. Known mainly as an offensive threat, Baugh was also the first player to intercept four passes in a single game.

Baughan, Maxie

b. Forkland, Alabama, 3 August 1939.

Linebacker Maxie Baughan played with the Philadelphia Eagles from 1960 to 1965 and then with the Los Angeles Rams from 1966 to 1970. He concluded his career with the Washington Redskins from 1971 to 1974. Baughan, a 6-1, 230-pounder played in eight Pro Bowls and missed a ninth because of injuries. A two-time all-pro choice, he intercepted 18 passes in his career. Baughan was a second-round draft choice of Philadelphia in 1960. He is head coach at Cornell University.

Bednarik, Chuck

b. Bethlehem, Pennsylvania, 1 May 1925.
Hall of Fame: 1967

A two-time All-America at the University of Pennsylvania and the Philadelphia Eagles' bonus draft pick in 1949, Chuck Bednarik became the NFL's last authentic "iron man" during his 14 seasons in pro football. Rugged and durable, a bulldozing blocker and bone-jarring tackler, the 6-3, 230-pound Bednarik missed only three games in 14 years. He played center on offense and linebacker on defense at a time when most pros were playing on just one unit.

Starting in 1950, Bednarik was named all-pro seven straight years, once as a center and six times as a linebacker. He also starred in eight Pro Bowls. In 1960, at 35, Bednarik responded to a team emergency by playing both ways in the latter stages of the 12-game season. He concluded the remarkable year with a 58-minute performance in the Eagles' NFL championship game victory over Green Bay, making a game-saving tackle of Jim Taylor in the final seconds.

Bell, Bert

b. Philadelphia, Pennsylvania, 25 February 1985;
d. 11 October 1959. Hall of Fame: 1963

Bert Bell, who was elected Commissioner of the National Football League in January, 1946, quickly displayed the strong, far-sighted leadership the league desperately needed to successfully combat unprecedented problems that loomed in the immediate future. Bell created a "war plan" for the challenge of the All-America Football Conference. He rejected any plan that would leave the AAFC intact, and eventually presided over a "merger" after the 1949 season that erased all but three AAFC teams.

Just before the 1946 NFL championship game, Bell set the stage for strong anti-gambling codes by suspending Merle Hapes of the New York Giants because he had neglected to

report a bribe offer he didn't accept. Bell also established a far-sighted television code that permitted only road games to be televised back to home cities unless all tickets had been sold in advance. He later angered NFL owners when he recognized the NFL Players' Association "in the best interests of pro football."

Bell established the Philadelphia Eagles' franchise in 1933 and kept it alive through the 1930s in spite of financial losses. He moved to the Pittsburgh Steelers as a part-owner in 1940, a status he maintained until his election as Commissioner. Bell died of a heart attack while watching an NFL game between the Eagles and Steelers in Philadelphia's Franklin Field Stadium.

Bell, Bobby

b. Shelby, North Carolina, 17 June 1940.
Hall of Fame: 1983

An all-state prep quarterback in North Carolina and an All-America tackle at the University of Minnesota, versatile Bobby Bell began his pro career with the Kansas City Chiefs of the American Football League in 1963 as a defensive end. In his third season, Bell was shifted to outside linebacker, where he became a star of unusual magnitude. The 6-4, 225-pound Bell was named all-AFL/AFC eight consecutive years as a linebacker – after he had been selected all-AFL as a defensive end. He also played in the last six AFL All-Star games, the first four AFC-NFC Pro Bowls, and Super Bowls I and IV. Bell was picked for the AFL's all-time team in 1969. In 12 seasons with the Chiefs from 1963 to 1974, he intercepted 25 passes for 479 yards and six

An official game ball. It is produced by the Wilson Sporting Goods Company, which has been the sole manufacturer of the NFL game ball since 1941.

touchdowns. Bell was the first Chiefs player to be elected to the Pro Football Hall of Fame.

Bench Area

The coaching, support staff, and substitute players of both teams are assigned to clearly marked bench areas on opposite sides of the field. The bench area is confined to a 36-yard wide region between the two 32-yard lines. It is located behind the six-foot wide white border that rims the field and is bordered by a solid yellow restraining line.

Berry, Raymond

b. Corpus Christi, Texas, 27 February 1933. Hall of Fame: 1973

Raymond Berry lacked the speed and height normally associated with a pro football end but he combined unusual jumping ability, excellent hands, a scientific approach to pass receiving, and endless hours of hard work to excel for 13 seasons with the Baltimore Colts. When he retired after the 1967 season, the 6-2, 187-pounder who had experienced only mild success as a football player at Southern Methodist University, ranked as the NFL's top career pass-catcher with 631 receptions for 9,275 yards and 68 touchdowns.

Berry blossomed into stardom when quarterback Johnny Unitas joined the team in 1957. Berry caught almost 600 passes from Unitas during the next 11 seasons. He was a game-saving hero many times but he was at his absolute best in the 1958 NFL title game, when the Colts defeated the New York Giants 23-17 in overtime: Berry caught 12 passes for 178 yards and one touchdown. In 1958, 1959, and 1960, he led the NFL in receiving, earned all-pro honors, and played in three of his five Pro Bowls. In 1961, he recorded a career-high 75 catches. He became head coach of the New England Patriots in 1984, and in 1986, he led the Patriots to Super Bowl XX, becoming the first team to win three playoff games on the road.

Bethea, Elvin

b. Trenton, New Jersey, 1 March 1946.

A two-year NAIA All-America at North Carolina A&T, Elvin Bethea was a third-round draft pick of the Houston Oilers in 1968. The 6-2, 252-pound defensive end played 16 seasons, longer than any other Oilers player. He led Houston in sacks six times, including a career-high 14½ in 1976. Bethea was selected to play in the 1969 AFL All-Star game and in seven AFC-NFC Pro Bowls in the 1970s. He retired after the 1983 season.

How meticulous is Raymond Berry about receivers running correct routes? When he was an assistant coach at Dallas and was showing receivers a particular route, he noticed that they kept going out of bounds. He insisted the practice field was kept narrow, and was proved correct when it was measured.

Bidwill, Charles W. Sr.

b. Chicago, Illinois, 16 September 1895;
d. 19 April 1947.
Hall of Fame: 1967

In 1932, long-time Chicago Bears fan Charles Bidwill, Sr., arranged for the necessary financial backing to keep the team from going bankrupt. A year later, Bidwill bought his own home-town team, the Cardinals, for $50,000. The Cardinals, cross-town rivals of the Bears, were big losers both on the field and at the box office every year, but Bidwill's faith in the future of pro football never wavered.

The end of the Second World War brought the challenge of the rival Chicago Rockets in the new All-America Football Conference to "Blue Shirt Charley," so named because he always wore a blue shirt. But Bidwill stunned the AAFC by signing Charley Trippi, a heralded All-America from Georgia, to a then-unprecedented $100,000 contract.

The signing of Trippi marked the final step in the formation of the Cardinals' "Dream Backfield" – Paul Christman, Pat Harder, Marshall Goldberg, and Trippi. The quartet (with Elmer Angsman replacing Goldberg on offense) led the Cardinals to the NFL championship in 1947 and a Western Division title in 1948. But Bidwill was not around to see his team's finest triumphs. Stricken suddenly by pneumonia, he died in 1947 at 51.

Biletnikoff, Fred

b. Erie, Pennsylvania, 23 February 1943.
Hall of Fame: 1988

Many scouts thought Fred Biletnikoff, an All-America at Florida State, was too small and too slow to play professional football. But the 6-1, 190-pounder proved the experts wrong by catching 589 passes for 8,974 yards and 76 touchdowns in a 14-year career as a wide receiver with the Oakland Raiders, for whom he played from 1965 to 1978. Biletnikoff utilized fluid moves, deceptive speed, great hands, and a work ethic rarely matched in modern-day pro football to reach stardom. A constant worrier, he chewed his fingernails and developed several ulcers, but he was consistently effective on the playing field.

Biletnikoff was a four-time all-AFL/AFC pick and the NFL receiving champion in 1971. He played in two AFL All-Star games, four AFC-NFC Pro Bowls, nine AFL/AFC championships, and Super Bowls II and XI. In Super Bowl XI, he caught four passes for 76 yards and won Most Valuable Player honors.

Bingaman, Les

b. MacKenzie, Tennessee, 3 February 1927;
d. 20 November 1970.

Les Bingaman began his pro football career as a 6-3, 250-pound middle guard with the 1948 Detroit Lions. When he concluded his seven-year tenure in 1954, the University of Illinois graduate had ballooned to 335 pounds. Rated as one of the NFL's premier middle guards, he was an agile team leader who won all-pro honors four consecutive years from 1951 to 1954. Bingaman was the Lions' co-captain in 1950 and again in 1953.

Blanda, George

b. Youngwood, Pennsylvania, 17 November 1927. Hall of Fame: 1981

George Blanda's astounding 26-season, 340-game career was divided almost equally among three teams. With the Chicago Bears from 1949 to 1958 (interrupted when he played one game for the Baltimore Colts in 1950), he

George Blanda played in more games than anybody before him and it is unlikely that a player will ever make 300 appearances again. His 2,002 points is an equally impregnable record.

was the regular quarterback for just two seasons. He retired in 1959 because the Bears had decided to use him as a kicking specialist only. The emergence of the American Football League in 1960 gave him a new opportunity with the Houston Oilers. For seven years in Houston, Blanda was a big-yardage quarterback who led the Oilers to the first two AFL championships. When Houston waived him after the 1967 season, he moved to the Oakland Raiders, with whom he excelled for nine more years as a backup quarterback and a kicker.

Blanda, a 6-2, 215-pound graduate of the University of Kentucky, earned lasting fame during a five-game stretch in 1970 when he led the Raiders to four victories and one tie with last-second touchdowns or field goals. The heroics started with a three-touchdown passing outburst against Pittsburgh. The next week, his 48-yard field goal with three seconds left tied Kansas City. He then threw a scoring pass and kicked a 52-yard field goal in the last 96 seconds to defeat Cleveland. Next came a touchdown toss that defeated Denver, followed by a game-ending field goal that upended San Diego. That year, at 43, he was named the AFC Player of the Year.

Blanda wound up his career with 2,002 points – far more than any other player. He attempted 4,007 passes, completing 1,911 for 26,920 yards and 236 touchdowns. Blanda retired in August, 1976, just a few months shy of his 49th birthday.

Blindside

The area outside a quarterback's vision. Also to tackle a quarterback from his blindside as he sets up to pass.

Blitz

A rush at the quarterback involving linebackers and/or defensive backs.

Blizzard Bowl

On December 19, 1948, the day of the NFL championship game between the Philadelphia Eagles and Chicago Cardinals, a raging blizzard completely obliterated the playing area at Shibe Park in Philadelphia. NFL Commissioner Bert Bell decided that even though the 10-yard first-down chain would be used, there would be no measuring. The referee would be the final judge of all first downs. The sidelines were marked with ropes tied to stakes, and the officials' white penalty flags were invisible in the snow. Early in the fourth quarter, Steve Van Buren plowed through the snow from the 5-yard line for the only score. Philadelphia won 7-0.

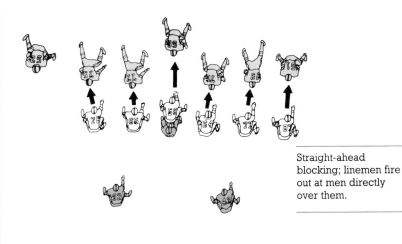

Straight-ahead blocking; linemen fire out at men directly over them.

Blocking

Blocking is the legal effort by an offensive player to obstruct a defensive opponent from stopping the passing or running plays of the offensive team.

PASS BLOCKING is the obstruction of an opponent by the use of that part of his body above the knees. The blocker's hands (open or closed) must be kept inside his elbows and may be thrust toward the opponent as long as the contact is with the opponent's body below the neck.

RUN BLOCKING is an aggressive action by a blocker to keep an opponent from tackling the ball carrier. Contact may be made with the head, shoulders, hands, and/or outer surface of the forearm.

Blount, Mel

b. Vidalia, Georgia, 10 April 1948.
Hall of Fame: 1989

Mel Blount was an All-America at both cornerback and safety at Southern University when he was drafted by the Pittsburgh Steelers in 1970. His hard hitting play in the NFL is largely responsible for the change in bump-and-run rules that eliminated downfield contact, limiting it to within five yards of the line of scrimmage.

He played 200 games in his 14 seasons and intercepted at least one pass in every season, leading the NFL with 11 in 1975. Blount was named all-pro in 1975, 1977 and 1981, as well as earning five trips to the Pro Bowl. The 6-3, 205-pound defensive back played in all four of the Steelers' Super Bowls and six AFC championship games.

In total, Blount made 57 interceptions, returning them for 736 yards and two touchdowns, and recovered 13 opponents' fumbles for two touchdowns. On kick-off returns, he averaged more than 25 yards per carry, totaling 911 yards in 36 attempts.

Bomb

A long pass completion.

Bootleg

A deceptive move by the quarterback on which he fakes a handoff, then hides the ball against his hip and runs around one of the ends.

Bradshaw, Terry

*b. Shreveport, Louisiana, 2 September 1948.
Hall of Fame: 1989*

Louisiana Tech quarterback Terry Bradshaw was the Pittsburgh Steelers' first round pick in the 1970 NFL draft. The 6-3, 210-pounder became the trigger man of a powerful offense that won four Super Bowl championships from 1974 to 1979. Bradshaw, a damaging ball carrier when forced to run, accounted for 30,246 offensive yards during his 14-year career. Bradshaw's career totals show 2,025 pass completions for 27,989 yards and 212 touchdowns. He

Right: Terry Bradshaw was an inspirational leader on the field. The longest pass of his career was caught by backup quarterback, Mark Malone, who had lined up as an extra tight end. The play covered 88 yards.

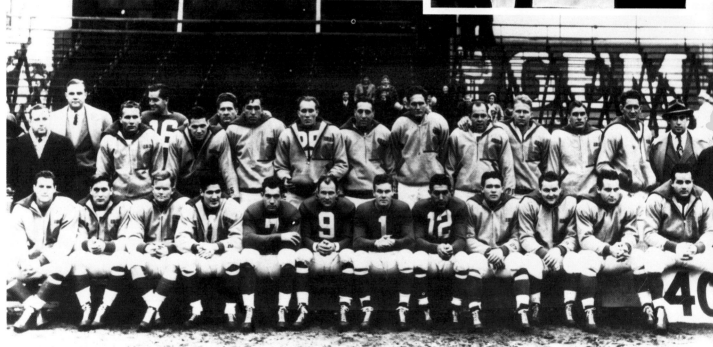

also rushed for 2,257 yards and 32 touchdowns. He twice led the NFL in touchdown passes, with 28 in 1978 and 17 in the strike-shortened 1982 season. In Super Bowl XIII, Bradshaw threw four touchdown passes to lead a 35-31 victory over the Dallas Cowboys. Bradshaw, who was chosen as the Most Valuable Player in Super Bowls XIII and XIV, passed for a record 932 yards and nine touchdowns in four Super Bowls. His 3,833 yards and 30 touchdown

Above: The Brooklyn Dodgers line up for a team photo in 1938. As the Tigers in 1944, Brooklyn lost all its games, a feat not repeated for more than 30 years.

passes in 19 postseason games are also NFL records. Bradshaw, who was all-pro in 1978 and all-AFC in 1979, was picked for three Pro Bowls.

In his first year of eligibility, Bradshaw was elected to the Hall of Fame.

Brooklyn Dodgers

In 1930, John Dwyer, a Brooklyn businessman, purchased the Dayton Triangles NFL franchise, moved it, and renamed the team the Brooklyn Dodgers. In both 1940 and 1941, the Dodgers, powered by tackle Frank (Bruiser) Kinard and quarterback Clarence (Ace) Parker, finished just one game behind the NFL Eastern Division champions. In 1944, the team changed its name to Tigers. In 1945, Brooklyn and Boston merged, played games in both cities, and were known simply as "The Yanks." In December, the Brooklyn franchise withdrew to enter the new All-America Football Conference.

Brown, Jim

b. St. Simons, Georgia, 17 February 1936.
Hall of Fame: 1971

A superb all-around athlete who could have excelled in several sports, Jim Brown earned lasting fame as a 6-2, 232-pound fullback who amassed unprecedented yardage during his nine years with the Cleveland Browns from 1957 to 1965. Brown, a consensus All-America at Syracuse University, was Cleveland's first-round draft pick in 1957. He immediately became the most dominating figure in the National Football League.

As a rookie, Brown won the NFL rushing title and was named both Rookie of the Year and Player of the Year by one major publication. He was a unanimous all-pro pick eight times, and won eight league rushing championships. He rushed for more than 1,000 yards for seven years. In 1963, he set a season record of 1,863 yards rushing that lasted 10 years. Brown played in nine consecutive Pro Bowls and was

the game's most valuable back three times. He closed his career with a three-touchdown outburst in the 1966 Pro Bowl. He was selected as the NFL's Most Valuable Player in 1958 and 1965.

Brown stunned the sports world in 1966 with the announcement he was retiring, even though he was just 30 years old and at the peak of his career. In nine seasons, he never missed a game and compiled an amazing record – 12,312 yards, 106 touchdowns rushing, and 126 total touchdowns. All were career records. His two rushing records have been surpassed only by Chicago's Walter Payton, who played 13 seasons and carried the ball 1,479 more times, and Tony Dorsett of Denver during the 1988 season.

Brown, Larry

b. Clairton, Pennsylvania, 19 September 1947.

A 5-11, 195-pound power-running halfback from Kansas State, Larry Brown was an eighth-round draft pick of the Washington Redskins in 1969. Brown rushed for 888 yards, fourth-most in the NFL, as a rookie, then won the NFL rushing championship with 1,125 yards in 1970 and the NFC championship with a career-high 1,216 yards in 1972. Brown had career totals of 5,875 yards rushing and 2,485 yards on 238 pass receptions. He scored 55 touchdowns, 35 by rushing and 20 on receptions. In 1973, he led the NFL with 14 touchdowns. Brown was named all-pro in 1970 and 1972, and was selected for four Pro Bowl games. Slowed by a knee injury, he retired after the 1976 season.

Below left: Mel Blount always stayed close to his receiver. His size, combined with athletic ability, made him one of the most accomplished defensive backs in the history of the NFL. He was elected to the Hall of Fame in his first year of eligibility.

Below: Arguably the greatest running back of all time, Jim Brown's rushing average stands up to any comparison. His final career figures are even more remarkable, considering he played only nine seasons.

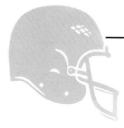

Brown, Paul

b. Norwalk, Ohio, 7 September 1908.
Hall of Fame: 1967

Paul Brown was an exceptionally successful coach at all levels of football, including Massillon, Ohio, High School, Ohio State, and the Great Lakes Naval Training Station. While Brown was at Great Lakes, Mickey McBride, the owner of the new Cleveland team in the All-America Football Conference, offered him $20,000 a season plus 15 percent of the profits to make the jump to pro football. Brown quickly began to line up an imposing cast of playing talent. He also hired a full-time staff, began measuring a player's learning capabilities by the use of intelligence tests, and started grading players on the basis of extensive film studies. All were innovations in the pro football world.

Brown's tactics produced immediate divi-

Roosevelt Brown's solid play on the Giants' offensive line earned him bids to 10 consecutive Pro Bowls, as well as all-pro selections from 1956 to 1963.

dends. The Cleveland Browns won all four AAFC titles and their 52-4-3 record was so superior to the rest of the competition that fans throughout the league simply lost interest. Brown's teams were equally successful when they moved to the National Football League in 1950. The Browns won seven divisional titles in eight years, and NFL championships in 1950, 1954, and 1955. Brown, who left Cleveland after the 1962 season, compiled a 158-48-8 record in 17 seasons as the team's head coach.

A year later, he returned to an active role as head coach and general manager of the new Cincinnati Bengals team. Brown gave up coaching in 1975, and with a career record of 170-108-6, he ranks sixth on the all-time coaching victories list. He continues in the general manager's role today.

Brown, Roosevelt

b. Charlottesville, Virginia, 20 October 1932.
Hall of Fame: 1975

Roosevelt Brown, a star tackle from Morgan State College, was selected in the twenty-seventh round of the 1953 draft by the New York Giants. He was 6-3 and weighed 255 pounds but he knew little about playing football. He did have one advantage – he didn't know he could be cut. He thought that signing his $2,700 contract meant he had made the team.

Giants head coach Steve Owen saw enough potential in Brown to keep him in camp. Within weeks, Brown had won a starting offensive tackle job. Brown played for 13 years with the Giants and was a unanimous all-pro pick eight consecutive years from 1956 to 1963. He played in nine Pro Bowls.

Brown, Willie

b. Yazoo City, Mississippi, 2 December 1940.
Hall of Fame: 1984

Grambling State College graduate Willie Brown began his pro football career as a struggling free agent, but he finished among the elite with his election to the Pro Football Hall of Fame in his first year of eligibility in 1984. The 6-2, 190-pound defensive back was first signed by the Houston Oilers in 1963 but was cut during summer training camp. Brown then moved to the talent-thin Denver Broncos, for whom he became a starting cornerback in his sixth game as a rookie. He earned all-AFL honors in his second season and was an established star by the time the Broncos traded him to Oakland in 1967.

Blessed with all the skills of a perfect defensive back – speed, size, mobility, aggressiveness, determination, and a keen football sense –

Brown developed into pro football's premier cornerback during his 12 seasons with the perennially-contending Raiders. He was named to the all-time AFL team in 1969 and won all-AFL/AFC acclaim seven times. He played in five AFL All-Star games, four AFC-NFC Pro Bowls, nine AFL/AFC championship games, and Super Bowls II and XI. In Super Bowl XI, he scored on a 75-yard interception return to wrap up a 32-14 Oakland triumph over Minnesota. His 16-season record showed 54 interceptions for 472 yards and two touchdowns.

Buchanan, Buck

b. Gainesville, Alabama, 10 September 1940.
Buck Buchanan, a 6-7, 274-pound defensive tackle from Grambling State College was a first-round draft choice of the Kansas City Chiefs in 1963. For the next 13 years, Buchanan was a leading force on the Chiefs' perpetually dominating defense. He missed only one game in his 181-game pro career. Buchanan was a virtually unanimous all-AFL choice from 1966 to 1969 and an all-AFC pick in 1970. He was out-standing in Super Bowl IV, when the Chiefs bottled up the Minnesota Vikings offense to score a 23-7 upset.

Buffalo Bills

Ralph C. Wilson, a Detroit businessman who had long desired a pro football team of his own, was granted a franchise in the new American Football League in 1959. The city of Buffalo, eager to return to pro football after an 11-year hiatus following the demise of the All-America Football Conference, agreed to increase the capacity of War Memorial Stadium from 22,500 to 36,500.

Enthusiasm for AFL football ran high in Buffalo and 100,000 Buffalo residents turned out to cheer the Bills in a welcome-home parade before the first-ever AFL preseason game on July 30, 1960. The Bills lost that game to the Boston Patriots, then lost the regular-season opener to the New York Titans and finished third in their division. In mid-1961, Buster Ramsey, the team's original head coach, was replaced by Lou Saban, who had just been fired by Boston.

Saban carefully began a building program that produced AFL championships in both 1964 and 1965. Quarterback Jack Kemp (now a member of President George Bush's Cabinet), and fullback Carlton (Cookie) Gilchrist provided the offensive glitter while Billy Shaw, an offensive guard, and Tom Sestak, a talented defensive tackle, gave the Bills excellent line strength. Both Shaw and Sestak were named to the all-time all-AFL team. Saban left after the 1965 sea-

son but, with Joe Collier as head coach, the Bills won a third consecutive Eastern Division title in 1966.

Saban returned for a second term in 1972 and almost immediately transformed the Bills from tail-enders into contenders. A key element in Buffalo's turnabout was the sensational running of O.J. Simpson, who, in 1973, became the first back in history to rush for more than 2,000 yards in one season (2,003). That was also the year the Bills moved into 80,020-seat Rich Stadium in suburban Orchard Park. Season ticket sales passed 46,206, the listed capacity of the vacated War Memorial Stadium. In spite of an improved record, the Bills reached the playoffs just once during Saban's second tenure. They won a wild-card spot in 1974 but lost to the Super Bowl-bound Steelers in the first round of the playoffs.

With Chuck Knox as head coach and rookie running back Joe Cribbs carrying for 1,185 yards and catching 52 passes, the Bills won their first AFC Eastern Division championship in 1980 with an 11-5 record. Once again, they suffered a first-round playoff loss, this time to San Diego. In 1988, with bright new stars such as quarterback Jim Kelly, defensive end Bruce Smith, and linebackers Shane Conlan and Cornelius Bennett providing new punch to the lineup, the Bills went 12-4 and won their second division crown. Coach Marv Levy's team defeated the Houston Oilers in the divisional playoffs, but lost to the Cincinnati Bengals in the AFC championship game.

Members of the Hall of Fame:
(1) O.J. Simpson

Championships Won:
AFL: 1964, 1965
AFL Eastern Division: 1964, 1965, 1966
AFC Eastern Division: 1980, 1988

Overall Record:

AFL Regular Season	65	69	6	.485
NFL Regular Season	111	167	2	.400
AFL Postseason	2	2	0	.500
NFL Postseason	2	4	0	.333
Total	180	242	8	.428

Bump-and-Run

A pass-defense technique in which the pass defender bumps the receiver as he comes off the line, then stays with him downfield.

Buoniconti, Nick

b. Springfield, Massachusetts, 15 December 1940.
Nick Buoniconti joined the Boston Patriots of the American Football League as a thirteenth-round draft choice in 1962. Many people considered him too small to be a professional

middle linebacker, but the 5-11, 220-pound Notre Dame graduate became the core of the Patriots' defense for the next seven seasons. In 1969, he was traded to Miami, where he played until 1974. He sat out one year, then returned to play in 1976. Buoniconti proved to be a dynamic defensive leader of the Dolphins' team that enjoyed a perfect season in 1972 and won Super Bowls VII and VIII.

Buoniconti played in six AFL All-Star games, five as a Patriot and the sixth as a Dolphin. He twice was selected to play in the Pro Bowl in the 1970s. Buoniconti was named to the all-time AFL team in 1969.

Butkus, Dick

b. Chicago, Illinois, 9 December 1942.
Hall of Fame: 1979

Dick Butkus became obsessed with a determination to play pro football while he was still in grade school. Through junior high, high school, and the University of Illinois, where he was a two-time All-America, his burning desire never flickered. Once he joined the Bears as a number one draft pick in 1965, he immediately developed another all-consuming desire – to be the best.

Playing with maniacal efficiency, the 6-3, 245-pound Butkus quickly established himself as the premier middle linebacker in pro football. Challenged only by his brilliant teammate, half-back Gale Sayers, for Rookie of the Year honors, Butkus was voted all-pro six times and was picked for eight Pro Bowls in nine seasons. Butkus displayed instinct, strength, leadership, meanness, and a consuming desire to pursue and tackle. Still, he was a clean player who was totally devoted to his career, and admitted he played every game as though it were his last.

Eventually, injuries took their toll on Butkus. In 1970, a badly damaged right knee didn't totally respond to surgery. Three years later, he limped off an NFL field for the last time. In nine seasons, Butkus registered 47 takeaways – 22 interceptions and 25 opponents' fumble recoveries.

Above: Dick Butkus redefined the term hard hitting. As a linebacker he had a nose for the ball and would stop at nothing, as long as it was within the rules, to get the ball carrier.

Right: Jim Kelly led the Buffalo Bills against Cincinnati in the 1988 AFC championship game. Buffalo set two records in 1988: the earliest clinching of a division title (week 10) since the 16-game schedule started in 1978, and the highest cumulative regular-season attendance (622,793).

★ ★ ★ ★ ★ ★ ★ ★ ★ ★ ★ ★ ★

Campbell, Earl

b. Tyler, Texas, 29 March 1955.

The Heisman Trophy winner in 1977, fullback Earl Campbell, a 5-11, 233-pound All-America from the University of Texas, was the first player selected in the 1978 NFL draft. In his rookie season with the Houston Oilers, he rushed for an NFL-leading 1,450 yards. He was the Rookie of the Year, the NFL's Most Valuable Player, and a unanimous all-pro. Campbell rushed for a career-high 1,934 yards in 1980. He rushed for more than 100 yards 40 times in his career and played in five Pro Bowls. In 1984, Campbell was traded to the New Orleans Saints, with whom he finished his career a year later. In eight seasons, he rushed for 9,407 yards and gained 806 yards on 121 receptions.

Canadeo, Tony

b. Chicago, Illinois, 5 May 1919.
Hall of Fame: 1974

A graduate of little-known Gonzaga University, Tony Canadeo joined the Green Bay Packers as a seventh-round draft choice in 1941. A two-way star who could do almost anything on a football field, the 5-11, 195-pound Canadeo amassed 8,682 combined net yards in 11 seasons with the Packers. He averaged 5.8 yards every time he touched the football, a remarkable statistic for the era in which he played.

Canadeo's career in Green Bay was divided into a pre-war segment when he played quarterback for a contending team, and a post-war period when he became a heavy-duty running back for a losing team. He earned all-pro honors as the Packers' regular passer in 1943. Six years later, in 1949, he became only the third player in pro history to rush for more than 1,000 yards, and he made the all-pro team a second time.

Canadian Football League

Although organized pro football in Canada had its roots in a rugby-style game dating back to 1891, the modern Canadian Football League had its start in 1948 when CFL teams began adding American college stars to their rosters. The Grey Cup game is the CFL equivalent of the Super Bowl.

Canadian football is played much like American football, but there are several rules variations. In the CFL, there are 12 men on each team, the field is 110 yards long, and a team is allowed only three downs to make a first down. A one-point "rouge" is scored when a team punts over the opponent's end zone.

The Canadian Football League has enjoyed remarkable stability. The British Columbia (Vancouver) Lions, organized in 1954, is the league's youngest franchise. The current CFL membership consists of the Hamilton Tiger-Cats, Ottawa Rough Riders, Toronto Argonauts, and Winnipeg Blue Bombers in the Eastern Division; and the Lions, Calgary Stampeders, Edmonton Eskimos, and Saskatchewan (Regina) Roughriders in the Western Division. The CFL season begins in July and ends in November.

Cannon, Billy

b. Philadelphia, Mississippi, 2 August 1937.

Billy Cannon, the Heisman Trophy winning halfback at Louisiana State University in 1959, signed contracts with both the Los Angeles Rams of the NFL and the Houston Oilers of the new AFL. The Oilers had to go to court to establish the validity of their contract. The 6-2, 220-pound Cannon was an important part of the Oilers' championship seasons in 1960 and 1961, leading the AFL with 948 yards rushing in 1961.

In 1964, Cannon was traded to the Oakland Raiders, who later converted him into a tight end. He was one of 19 players who played in all 10 AFL seasons, and he finished his career with the 1970 Kansas City Chiefs. Cannon was all-AFL as a halfback in 1961 and as a tight end in 1967. He played in two AFL All-Star games. In 11 seasons, he rushed for 2,449 yards and caught 236 passes for 3,656 yards.

Earl Campbell was for many years the hub of the Houston offense. Amongst retired players, only Jim Brown had a higher season's rushing average than Campbell's 1,175-yard yearly rate.

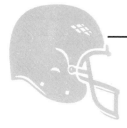

Canton Bulldogs

The Canton Bulldogs became a pro team in 1904, ceased operations after a gambling scandal in 1906, then returned in 1912 to become the leading team in the pre-league days of pro football. The Bulldogs, who added the fabled Jim Thorpe to their roster in 1915, claimed unofficial world championships in 1916, 1917, and 1919. They became a charter member of the American Professional Football Association, the direct forerunner of the National Football League, in 1920. In 1922 and 1923, new player-coach Guy Chamberlin led the Bulldogs to two consecutive NFL championships. The Bulldogs disbanded in 1927.

Cappelletti, Gino

b. Keewatin, Minnesota, 26 March 1934.

Gino Cappelletti played football at the University of Minnesota in the early 1950s and joined the Boston Patriots of the new AFL in 1960. With the Patriots, the 6-foot, 190-pounder was both a place-kicker and a wide receiver. From 1960 to 1969, he scored an AFL-record 1,100 points and caught 292 passes for 4,589 yards and 42 touchdowns. Cappelletti, who scored 155 points in 1964 (the third-highest season total in pro football history), was named Player of the Year that season. Cappelletti played in four AFL All-Star games. With 1,130 career points – he also scored 30 points in the NFL in 1970 – Cappelletti now ranks among the top 10 lifetime scorers.

Often it is obvious whether or not a team has gained first down yardage. But the suspense mounts when the "chain gang" has to come onto the field to measure if the ball (any part of it) extends beyond or touches the yard marker for a first down.

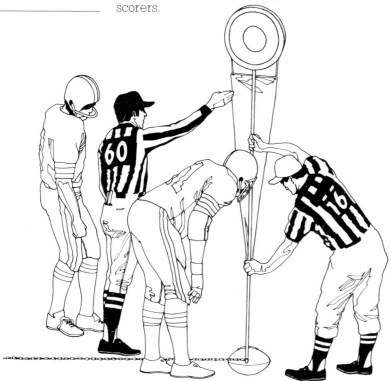

Card-Pitt

The Chicago Cardinals and Pittsburgh Steelers, beset with manpower shortages created by World War II, merged for the 1944 season. Phil Handler of the Cardinals and Walt Kiesling of the Steelers were the Card-Pitt co-coaches. The team lost all 10 games and was outscored 328-108. The Brooklyn Tigers also lost all their games that year. It is the only time since divisional play started that two teams have had winless seasons in the same year.

Carr, Joe

b. Columbus, Ohio, 22 October, 1880; d. 20 May 1939. Hall of Fame: 1963

Joe Carr, who developed the Columbus Panhandles pro football team in 1904, was elected president of the American Professional Football Association in 1921. A year later, the APFA changed its name to the National Football League, an organization that Carr served with distinction until his death.

Until Carr took over, pro football had operated in a haphazard, disorganized state. Copying many of the methods he had learned as a baseball executive, Carr quickly provided the stability and integrity pro football desperately needed. He established a standard player contract, ruled that no pro team could sign a college player until his eligibility was completed, and even canceled franchises when his edicts were ignored. Carr recognized the need for the NFL to locate in the nation's big cities and, in 1927, he was responsible for the reorganization of the NFL and its reduction to a manageable 12 teams. He also was instrumental in the birth of the New York Giants franchise in 1925.

The Catch

With the Dallas Cowboys leading 27-21 and time running out in the 1981 NFC championship game in San Francisco, the 49ers drove into Cowboys territory. On third down, with the ball on the Dallas 6-yard line, 49ers quarterback Joe Montana scrambled away from the Cowboys' rush and arched a high pass toward the back of the end zone. At the last instant, 49ers wide receiver Dwight Clark leaped high above the defenders to make a game-winning catch, and San Francisco won its first NFC title 28-27.

Center

1. The player who starts each scrimmage play by passing the ball backwards between his legs to the backfield player who is to receive it.
2. The act of passing the ball to start the play.

Chain Gang (or Crew)

At every NFL game, a six-man chain crew assists the game officials in yardage marking and serves as an information source to those viewing the game. Two crew members handle the 10-yard chains that measure first-down yardage. The down-indicator operator is assisted by another crew member. Other assignments include attending the drive-start indicator and the opposite-side first-down marker.

Chamberlin, Guy

b. Blue Springs, Nebraska, 16 January 1894; d. 4 April 1967. Hall of Fame: 1965

A legendary football hero at the University of Nebraska, the 6-2, 210-pound Guy Chamberlin became the premier end of the National Football League in the 1920s. An extremely durable two-way performer, Chamberlin was eagerly sought by many pro teams. He began his pro career with the pre-NFL Canton Bulldogs in 1919 but played with five teams, including a second term with the Bulldogs, in the first nine years of NFL play.

Chamberlin made a lasting mark on pro football as a coach. He was the player-coach of four NFL championship teams in a five-year period from 1922 to 1926. His title teams included the 1922-1923 Canton Bulldogs, the 1924 Cleveland Bulldogs, and the 1926 Frankford Yellow Jackets. Chamberlin concluded his career with the 1927 Chicago Cardinals. His six-year NFL coaching record was 58-16-6, a remarkable .780 winning percentage that surpasses the marks of all coaches with 50 or more pro wins.

Chicago Bears

The story of the Chicago Bears is largely the story of one man, George Halas, who founded the team and served it for 64 years until his death in 1983. The saga began in 1919, when Halas went to work for the A.E. Staley Starch Co. of Decatur, Illinois. The company had decided to sponsor a football team, and Halas was asked to organize it. A year later, the Decatur Staleys became a charter member of the American Professional Football Association, the direct forerunner to the National Football League.

In 1921, Halas took over the Staleys and moved the team to Chicago, where he renamed it the Bears the following season. Halas continued to play until 1929 and served the team for many more years in every way imaginable – as a general manager, business manager, ticket manager, publicity director, equipment man,

The National Football League's debt of gratitude to Joe Carr cannot be underestimated; his administrative skill and foresight created the basis of the League today.

trainer, and coach. Altogether, he coached the Bears for 40 years.

In 1925, the Bears signed Harold (Red) Grange, the most famous college football star of the decade, who proved to be a magnificent gate attraction. The Bears and Grange embarked on an extended coast-to-coast barnstorming tour, which did much to acquaint the fans of the nation with the quality of play in the National Football League.

The Chicago Staleys won the APFA championship in 1921. Halas's team didn't win the title again until 1932, when Bronko Nagurski's pass to Red Grange helped the Bears to a 9-0 victory over the Portsmouth Spartans in a game played indoors in Chicago Stadium. Ralph Jones was the Bears' head coach that year.

In 1933, the NFL split into divisions (later called conferences), with the two champions meeting in a season-ending showdown, and Halas returned as the Bears' coach. The Bears defeated the New York Giants in a 23-21 squeaker. Nagurski, the great fullback, again was a hero with two touchdown passes.

The Bears were particularly outstanding in the early 1940s, when they won five conference and four NFL championships in a seven-year period. The streak started in 1940 when the Bears showcased the revamped T-formation to perfection in an epic 73-0 victory over the Washington Redskins. The Monsters of the Midway, as the Bears were called, were loaded with a host of future Hall of Famers such as quarterback Sid Luckman, halfback George McAfee, and linemen Joe Stydahar, Dan Fortmann, and Clyde (Bulldog) Turner. The Bears

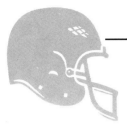

won the NFL championship again in 1941 and 1943, and ended their era of dominance with a 24-14 victory over the New York Giants for the 1946 title. Halas coached the team to the 1940, 1941, and 1946 NFL titles, while Hunk Anderson led Chicago to the 1943 championship, after Halas had joined the U.S. Navy.

For the next three decades, the Bears experienced leaner times. Perennially strong defensively with stars such as Doug Atkins, Bill George, and George Connor leading the way, they often were contenders but rarely were in the championship game. With long-time assistant Paddy Driscoll serving as head coach in 1956, the Bears won the Western Conference but lost to the New York Giants 47-7 in the title game. In 1963, the Bears won their final championship for Halas, who returned for his final tenure as head coach from 1958-1967. Using a new zone defense installed by assistant George Allen, the Bears became a superior defensive team, allowing only 144 points in 14 games. The offense was led by quarterback Bill Wade and tight end Mike Ditka as the Bears slipped past the Giants 14-10 in the title game.

Two of the most brilliant stars in pro football history, halfback Gale Sayers and linebacker Dick Butkus, joined the Bears in 1965 but could not bring Chicago a championship. The Bears finally made the playoffs as a wild-card entry in 1977, then lost to Dallas in the first round. In 1979, the Bears again were a wild-card team and again lost in the opening game of the playoffs, this time to Philadelphia. On January 20, 1982, the Bears entered a new era with the appointment of Ditka as head coach. It was one of the last major decisions Halas made – and one of his best. In 1984, his third season, Ditka led the Bears to their first divisional championship in 21 seasons. The next year, the Bears overwhelmed the entire NFL with a 15-1 regular-season mark and a 46-10 victory over New England in Super Bowl XX. Chicago won NFC Central titles again in 1986, 1987, and 1988 but failed to return to the Super Bowl.

The Bears' Super Bowl triumph was made possible by a rugged defense, fine quarterbacking by Jim McMahon, and the superb running of Walter Payton. In 13 seasons with the Bears, Payton became history's top rusher with 16,726 yards. He retired amid much league-wide adulation at the end of the 1987 season.

The Bears played in 38,000-seat Wrigley Field (originally named Cubs Park) for 50 years from 1921 until 1971, when they moved into 66,030-seat Soldier Field. As one of only two charter members of the National Football League still in operation, they can boast of more victories (545) and more Pro Football Hall of Fame members (25) than any other team.

Neal Anderson (35) looking for running room, does not want to be compared with his predecessor at Chicago, because Walter Payton was possibly the best ever. The Bears were supposed to be in transition in 1988, but they still won their division and played in the NFC championship game.

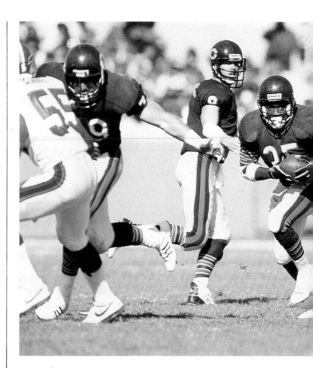

Members of the Hall of Fame:
(25) Doug Atkins, George Blanda, Dick Butkus, Guy Chamberlin, George Connor, Jimmy Conzelman, Mike Ditka, Paddy Driscoll, Dan Fortmann, Bill George, Red Grange, George Halas, Ed Healey, Bill Hewitt, Walt Kiesling, Bobby Layne, Sid Luckman, Roy (Link) Lyman, George McAfee, George Musso, Bronko Nagurski, Gale Sayers, Joe Stydahar, George Trafton, Clyde (Bulldog) Turner.

Championships Won:
Super Bowl: XX (1985)
NFL (pre-1970): 1921, 1932, 1933, 1940, 1941, 1943, 1946, 1963
NFL Western Conference: 1933, 1934, 1937, 1940, 1941, 1942, 1943, 1946, 1956, 1963
NFC: 1985
NFC Central Division: 1984, 1985, 1986, 1987, 1988

Overall Record:

Regular Season	533	331	42	.611
Postseason	12	11	0	.522
Total	545	342	42	.609

Christiansen, Jack

b. Sublette, Kansas, 20 December 1928;
d. 29 June 1986. Hall of Fame: 1970

The victim of a chance shooting accident as a high school senior, Jack Christiansen was certain he never would play football again. But after starring in college at Colorado A&M University, he joined the Detroit Lions in 1951 and became one of pro football's most formidable defensive safeties and a big-play return specialist. During a decade in which the Lions were one of the NFL's best teams, the 6-1, 185-

James Brooks (21) teamed with rookie Ickey Woods to form the most dangerous running combo in the NFL. The Bengals' 1988 AFC championship game against Buffalo marked the first time that both teams in this game had a losing record the previous season.

pound Christiansen was named all-pro six consecutive years. He won interception titles in 1953 and 1957, finishing his career with 46 interceptions for 717 yards and three touchdowns.

Christiansen also had 85 punt returns for 1,084 yards and eight touchdowns, an all-time record. The leader of "Chris's Crew," the outstanding Lions defensive secondary, Christiansen was a five-time Pro Bowl selection.

Christiansen was named head coach of the San Francisco 49ers in 1963 and held that post until the end of the 1967 season.

Chuck

A quick shove or push of an opponent who is in front of a defender. The tactic is used primarily against pass receivers.

Chucking

Chucking is a means of warding off an offensive opponent who is in front of a defender by jamming him with a quick extension of the arm or arms followed by the return of arm(s) to a flexed position.

Cincinnati Bengals

On September 27, 1967, a Cincinnati group headed by the former head coach of the Cleveland Browns, Paul Brown, was awarded an American Football League franchise. Brown called the team the Bengals, the name of the city's franchises in the second and third American Football Leagues (in 1937 and 1940).

In the annual AFL-NFL college draft in 1968, the Bengals selected Bob Johnson, an All-America center from Tennessee, in the first round. Because Riverfront Stadium, first approved by the Cincinnati City Council in 1966, was not yet completed, the 1968 Bengals played in Nippert Stadium on the University of Cincinnati campus. They won their first two league home games against Buffalo and Denver and wound up with a 3-11 record.

The next year, rookie quarterback Greg Cook won the AFL passing title, linebacker Bill Bergey was the AFL Rookie of the Year, and Brown earned AFL Coach of the Year honors. A brilliant cornerback, Ken Riley, also joined the team in 1969. In 1970, the first year of the merged 26-team NFL, the Bengals won the AFC Central Division with an 8-6 record. One of their key victories was a 14-10 upset of Brown's old team, the Cleveland Browns, before a crowd of 60,007 at Riverfront Stadium. In the Bengals' first playoff game, however, the Baltimore Colts won easily, 17-0.

In 1971, Cincinnati drafted quarterback Ken Anderson from little-known Augustana (Illinois) College. In the next 15 seasons, Anderson won four NFL passing titles. Two more prized rookies, running back Boobie Clark and wide receiver Isaac Curtis, joined the Bengals in 1973. That year they won their second AFC Central title but lost to Miami 34-16 in the first playoff game. The Bengals won a wild-card berth in 1975 but again lost in their first playoff game.

In 1976, Brown retired after 41 seasons of coaching and was replaced by Bill Johnson, his

long-time assistant. Homer Rice took over as head coach in 1978, then was replaced by Forrest Gregg in 1980. Gregg led the Bengals to their third division title in 1981, when they won the AFC championship over San Diego 27-7 in a game played in a wind-chill factor of 59 degrees below zero. In Super Bowl XVI, however, the San Francisco 49ers won 26-21. The Bengals reached postseason play with a 7-2 record in the strike-shortened 1982 season but failed to advance past the first playoff round.

Several outstanding young players, including offensive tackle Anthony Munoz and quarterback Boomer Esiason, have joined the Bengals in recent seasons. Those players, along with current head coach Sam Wyche, helped the Bengals return to the Super Bowl following the 1988 season. But Cincinnati was stopped by San Francisco again, this time 20-16.

Members of the Hall of Fame:
None (Paul Brown was elected before his career with the Bengals began)

Championships Won:
AFC: 1981, 1988
AFC Central Division: 1970, 1973, 1981, 1988

Overall Record:

AFL Regular Season	7	20	1	.268
NFL Regular Season	147	133	0	.525
NFL Postseason	4	6	0	.400
Total	158	159	1	.498

Clark, Earl (Dutch)

b. Fowler, Colorado, 11 October 1906;
d. 5 August 1978. Hall of Fame: 1963

The only All-America ever produced by Colorado College, Earl (Dutch) Clark was one of the most brilliant all-around athletes ever to play in the National Football League. Virtually blind in one eye, the quick-thinking Clark was an exceptional team leader. Because he called signals, he was termed a quarterback, winning all-pro honors six times in seven years. But he actually was a Single-Wing tailback who could pass, run, and catch passes, as well as play defense, superbly well.

Clark began his NFL career with a fine Portsmouth Spartans team in 1931. The Spartans played the Chicago Bears for the NFL title in 1932 but Clark had to miss the game because he had already returned to a coaching job at his alma mater. He sat out the 1933 season, then returned to the team when it moved to Detroit in 1934. In 1935, he was the principal architect of the Lions' first championship. The 6-0, 185-pound superstar was the Lions' player-coach in 1937 and 1938, his last two years. In seven seasons, he scored 369 points on 42 touchdowns, 72

conversions, and 15 field goals. He had one other distinction – he was the last player to regularly employ the dropkick for his field goal and extra point kicking.

From 1939 to 1942, Clark was head coach of the Cleveland Rams.

Cleveland Browns

Arthur (Mickey) McBride, who owned taxicab companies and various other businesses in the Cleveland area, was one of six prospective owners who met with Arch Ward in 1944 to make plans for the formation of the All-America Football Conference. The AAFC began play in 1946, and Cleveland was one of the charter members. McBride picked Paul Brown, a highly successful high school, college, and World War II military service coach, to lead his new team, which was named the Browns. Loaded with exceptional talent, Cleveland overwhelmed the Miami Seahawks 44-0 in the first AAFC game ever played on September 6, 1946. With future Hall of Fame members such as Otto Graham, Marion Motley, Lou Groza, Dante Lavelli, and Bill Willis leading the way, the Browns compiled a 47-4-3 regular-season record in four years. They won all four AAFC championships.

When the AAFC disbanded after the 1949 season, the Browns were accepted into the NFL, where they continued to be the dominant team in pro football. In a dramatic showdown, they defeated the defending NFL-champion Philadelphia Eagles 35-10 in the opening game of the 1950 season. Cleveland edged the Los Angeles Rams 30-28 for the 1950 NFL title, then played in championship games each of the next five years. The Browns won NFL titles again in 1954 and 1955. Cleveland experienced its first losing season in 1956, won a division title again in 1957, then did not make the playoffs again during the Paul Brown reign, which ended after the 1962 season. New owner Art Modell, who had purchased the team for $3,925,000 in 1961, replaced Brown with Blanton Collier, a long-time assistant to Brown.

In eight seasons with the club, Collier won an NFL championship (in 1964, with a 27-0 victory over Baltimore) and four Eastern Conference titles. Four coaches – Nick Skorich from 1971 to 1974, Forrest Gregg from 1975 to 1977, Sam Rutligiano from 1978 to 1984, and Marty Schottenheimer, who took over in mid-1984 and coached through the end of 1988 – have led the Browns since that time.

In 1973, Skorich's team finished with a 7-5 record, making it the twenty-seventh time in 28 years the Browns had a record better than .500. However, the team fell to 4-10 in 1974, and, for the next few years, experienced the poorest seasons, from a won-lost standpoint, in the franchise's history. The Browns didn't return to the playoffs until a young group of players known as "The Kardiac Kids" won the 1980 AFC Central title with an 11-5 record. Quarterback Brian Sipe was a hero in a season marked by come-from-behind victories. The Browns lost to Oakland 14-12 in the playoffs.

In their four full seasons under Schottenheimer, the Browns advanced to the playoffs each year. In 1985, they fell to Miami 24-21 in the first playoff round. In both 1986 and 1987, led by sensational, young quarterback Bernie Kosar, the Browns advanced to the AFC championship game against the Denver Broncos, losing each by narrow margins – 23-20 in overtime in 1986 and 38-33 in 1987. They lost the wild-card game to Houston in 1988.

Members of the Hall of Fame:

(14) Doug Atkins, Jim Brown, Paul Brown, Willie Davis, Len Ford, Frank Gatski, Otto Graham, Lou Groza, Dante Lavelli, Mike McCormack, Bobby Mitchell, Marion Motley, Paul Warfield, Bill Willis.

Championships Won:

AAFC: 1946, 1947, 1948, 1949
AAFC Western Division: 1946, 1947, 1948
NFL (pre-1970): 1950, 1954, 1955, 1964
NFL Eastern Conference: 1950, 1951, 1952, 1953, 1954, 1955, 1957, 1964, 1965, 1968, 1969
NFL Century Division: 1967, 1968, 1969
AFC Central Division: 1971, 1980, 1985, 1986, 1987

Overall Record:

AAFC Regular Season	47	4	3	.898
NFL Regular Season	326	203	9	.614
AAFC Playoffs	5	0	0	1.000
NFL Playoffs	9	17	0	.346
Total	387	224	12	.631

Clipping

An illegal block caused by throwing the body across the back of an opponent. Not called within three yards of the line of scrimmage (close line play). Clipping usually occurs downfield on punts, kickoffs, and interception returns.

Coach

The head coach is responsible for all aspects of the operation of a football team on the field. This includes determining the roster, the starting lineup, the order of substitution, the game plan, teaching, training camp, discipline, and media contact. Although the head coach remains responsible, he will delegate many duties to his staff of assistants. In 1988, NFL coaching staffs numbered between 10 and 14 men. A typical staff of assistants might include an offensive coordinator, a defensive coordinator, position coaches, and a strength and conditioning coach.

Coin Flip

The coin flip is a ritual that takes place before the start of each game. The captain (or captains) of each team meet at midfield with the officiating crew. The referee gives the visiting team the option of calling "heads" or "tails" just as he flips the coin into the air. The team that wins the toss has the option of kicking off or receiving the kickoff, or determining which goal it wishes to defend. After the winning team makes its decision, the losing team may exercise its option on the remaining choice. At the start of the third quarter, the team that lost the pregame coin toss has the first choice of options.

College All-Star Game

During the Century of Progress Exposition in Chicago in 1933, *Chicago Tribune* sports editor Arch Ward was assigned the task of lining up special sports events for the city. Ward approached the NFL about a game matching the pro champions against a team of just-graduated college all-stars. On August 31, 1934, the first College All-Star game was played before an amazing crowd of 79,432 in Chicago's Soldier Field. Intended to be a one-game affair, the College All-Star game instead became an annual late-summer attraction for the next 42 years (with the excepton of 1974, when no game was played). The 1934 game was a scoreless tie, the only one in the series. At the end (1976 was the last game), the pro champions held a 31-10-1 lead.

Commissioner

The chief administrative officer of the National Football League is known as the commissioner. Pete Rozelle, the present commissioner, has served in the position since 1960. He succeeded Bert Bell, who held the job from 1946 until his death in 1959. Elmer Layden, who served in the position from 1941 through the 1945 season, was the first person to carry the title of NFL commissioner. Before that, the NFL's chief administrative officer was called president. Jim Thorpe was the president of the American Professional Football Association in 1920. He was succeeded in 1921 by Joe Carr, who served as the NFL president until his death in 1939. Carl Storck was named acting president and stayed in the job until Layden's appointment two years later.

Completion

A forward pass caught by an eligible receiver.

Conference

When the All-America Football Conference and National Football League agreed to end their inter-league war in 1949, the "merged" league was split into two conferences (instead of divisions), the American Conference and the National Conference. After the 1952 season, the American Conference became the Eastern Conference and the National Conference became the Western Conference.

When the American and National Football Leagues completed their merger in 1970, the National Football League was divided into the American Football Conference and the National Football Conference, an alignment that remains in force today.

Connor, George

b. Chicago Illinois, 21 January 1925.
Hall of Fame: 1975

An All-America at both Holy Cross and Notre Dame, George Connor was the number one draft pick of the New York Giants in 1946. His rights were traded to the Bears, and for eight seasons from 1948 to 1955, he proved to be an extremely versatile two-way star. The 6-3, 240-pound Connor was an all-pro at three positions – offensive tackle, defensive tackle, and linebacker.

Connor made his biggest mark in pro football as a linebacker. He inherited the position when the Bears' coaching staff decided to shift the big, fast, and mobile lineman into a spot just behind the middle of the line where he would be able to stop running plays as well as short passes. Connor was particularly outstanding at reading "keys," the tips that movements of

Cleveland's defense hammers Stanley Wilson in the battle for the bragging rights of Ohio. After three seasons on top, the Browns gave way to Cincinnati in 1988, but Cleveland was hindered by serious injury problems in the backfield.

offensive players provide for the alert defender so that he can gain a split-second advantage in diagnosing where the play is going.

Conzelman, Jimmy

b. St. Louis, Missouri, 6 March 1898;
d. 31 July 1970. Hall of Fame: 1964

Without a doubt, Jimmy Conzelman was the most versatile individual ever elected to the Pro Football Hall of Fame. The 6-0, 180-pound graduate from Washington University of St. Louis began his pro career as a player with the 1920 Decatur Staleys. In the next seven seasons, he was a player-coach of four NFL teams – the Rock Island Independents, Milwaukee Badgers, Detroit Panthers, and Providence Steam Roller, which won the 1928 NFL championship. In his two years in Detroit in 1925-1926, he was also the team's owner.

After coaching Providence through the 1930 season, Conzelman decided he would try other fields. His endeavors included such varied pursuits as actor, singer, pianist, editor, publisher, and middle-weight boxing champion.

In 1940, Conzelman returned to the NFL as the Chicago Cardinals' coach. After a dismal 8-22-3 three-year record, he joined the St. Louis Browns baseball club until 1946, when he returned to the Cardinals. He led the team to the 1947 NFL championship, its first in 22 years, and to the 1948 Western Division title. He retired after the 1948 title game. His 15-year NFL coaching record was 92-69-17.

Cornerback

A defensive back who has the basic responsibility of covering one side of the secondary near the sideline. There are two cornerbacks, one for each side of the field.

Coryell, Don

b. Seattle, Washington, 17 October 1924.

In 1973, Don Coryell was named head coach of the St. Louis Cardinals, coming to the Cardinals after 12 highly successful seasons at San Diego State. In 14 NFL seasons with the St. Louis Cardinals (1973-77) and the San Diego Chargers (1978-1986), Coryell compiled a 114-89-1 record. He led the Cardinals to their only NFC Eastern Division championships in 1974 and 1975. In 1978, he became the Chargers' head coach, and as he had done in St. Louis, he turned a losing team into a winner. Powered by the "Air Coryell" offense, the Chargers won AFC Western Division championships in 1979, 1980, and 1981. Coryell played as a defensive back at the University of Washington.

Don Coryell with his pass master Dan Fouts (14) behind him. 'Air Coryell' was the most dangerous passing attack in the NFL for many years, but the Chargers' defense kept San Diego from championship contention.

Coverage

Pass defense. Also used to designate the type of pass defense employed (i.e., "double coverage").

Crackback

An eligible receiver who takes or moves into a position more than two yards outside the tackle may not crackback, that is, block an opponent below the waist if the receiver moves back toward the tackle's area.

Creekmur, Lou

b. Hopeland, New Jersey, 22 January 1927.

Lou Creekmur, a 6-4, 255-pound college star at William & Mary, joined the Detroit Lions in 1950 and quickly established himself as one of the most talented players on a team loaded with stars. Creekmur began his career as an offensive guard and won all-pro honors at that spot in 1951 and 1953. He then was shifted to offensive left tackle, where he was named all-pro four more times. Creekmur was selected to play in the first eight Pro Bowl games.

Crossing Pattern

Any path taken by a potential receiver who crosses from one side of the field to the other is a crossing pattern. On many plays, more than one receiver will run a crossing pattern.

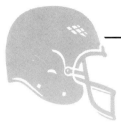

Csonka, Larry

b. Stow, Ohio, 25 December 1946.
Hall of Fame: 1987

In the early 1970s, when the Miami Dolphins dominated the NFL, 6-3, 235-pound Larry Csonka was the team's workhorse, rushing the most times for the most yards for five consecutive years. He also excelled as a punishing blocker. At his very best when the stakes were the highest, the former Syracuse All-America rushed for more than 1,000 yards each year from 1971 to 1973. He rambled for a game-high 112 yards in Super Bowl VII, then took Most Valuable Player honors in Super Bowl VIII with a record 145 rushing yards.

Csonka finished his career with 8,081 yards on 1,891 carries, tenth among the all-time leading rushers. Perhaps his most impressive statistic was his feat of fumbling only 21 times in 1,997 ball-handling opportunities – just one fumble every 95 carries.

Csonka was a number one draft pick of the Dolphins in 1968. He played with the team until 1975, when he defected to the Memphis Southmen of the rival World Football League. When that league folded, Csonka played with the New York Giants from 1976 to 1978. After the 1978 season with the Giants, he moved back to Miami for an excellent concluding season in 1979.

Larry Csonka was the main ball carrier for the Miami Dolphins when Don Shula's team went through the 1972 season with a 17-0 record. He scored two touchdowns in the Super Bowl VIII victory over Minnesota.

Cusack, Jack

b. Canton, Ohio, 17 November 1890;
d. 10 February 1973.

A recording clerk with the East Ohio Gas Company in Canton, Ohio, Jack Cusack also managed the Canton Bulldogs pro football team from 1912 to 1915. When told by his company that he could not continue on both jobs, he chose pro football. Later that year, he made history by signing the great American Indian athlete, Jim Thorpe, to a $250-a-game contract. The move paid off handsomely both on the field and at the gate. Pro football in Canton had been rocked by a gambling scandal in 1906 and Cusack is given much of the credit for restoring good management and integrity to the Bulldogs.

Cutback

A maneuver by a ball carrier reversing his direction against the flow of the play.

D ★★★★★★★★★★★★★★★★★★★★★★★★★★★★★★★★★

Dallas Cowboys

Two Dallas businessmen, Clint Murchison, Jr., and Bedford Wynne, were selected as owners-to-be of a new NFL franchise in the Texas city almost a year before the franchise actually was awarded in January, 1960. Tex Schramm, who had spent 10 years in the Los Angeles Rams' front office, was named general manager. Tom Landry, a former player and assistant coach with the New York Giants, was named the head coach. Those two still run the Cowboys today.

In the first three years of their existence, the Cowboys had to battle for attention against the Dallas Texans of the American Football League (that struggle ended in 1963 when the Texans moved to Kansas City). On the field, the 1960 Cowboys lost 11 games and tied one. But by

1961, the team's building program, under talent scout Gil Brandt, had begun to take shape. Brandt drafted Bob Lilly, an All-America defensive tackle from Texas Christian, to go along with two excellent stars, quarterback Don Meredith and fullback Don Perkins, whom the Cowboys had acquired in 1960.

The Cowboys broke even at 7-7 for the first time in 1965. The next year they started a string of 20 consecutive winning seasons that finally ended in 1986. They earned playoff berths 18 of those 20 years and won NFL championships in Super Bowls VI and XII. Dallas' first NFL Eastern Conference titles came in 1966 and 1967, but the Cowboys fell to eventual Super Bowl-champion Green Bay both years. Dallas reached the Eastern finals in 1968 and 1969, then won the National Football Conference title in 1970. Baltimore's last-second field goal beat the Cowboys in Super Bowl V in January, 1971.

With a dynamic quarterback, Roger Staubach, leading the way, the Cowboys enjoyed their best years with a cumulative 105-39 won-lost record in the 1970s. Staubach, who became a regular in 1971, led the team to six division titles from 1971 to 1979 and appearances in Super Bowls VI, X, XII and XIII. The Cowboys defeated the Miami Dolphins 24-3 in VI and the Denver Broncos 27-10 in XII, but fell victim to the Pittsburgh Steelers twice, 21-17 in X and 35-31 in XIII.

While Staubach was the leader, the Cowboys of the 1970s featured a well-balanced team with outstanding performers on both the offensive and defensive units. Halfback Calvin Hill became the first Cowboy to rush for more than 1,000 yards when he did so in 1972. A spectacu-

lar receiver, Drew Pearson, joined the team as a free agent in 1973. Heisman Trophy winner Tony Dorsett and wide receiver Tony Hill were drafted in 1977. Lilly retired after the 1974 season, but the Cowboys' defense remained in good hands with defensive end Ed (Too Tall) Jones, drafted in 1974, and defensive tackle Randy White, selected the next season.

In the 1980s, the rest of the NFL began to catch up to the Cowboys in both talent and victories, and Dallas has not been to the Super Bowl since Staubach retired. In their silver anniversary season in 1984, the Cowboys began a new era of ownership with a group headed by Dallas businessman H.R. (Bum) Bright. The new owners were presented with an NFC East championship in 1985 but the Cowboys experienced consecutive losing seasons in 1986 and 1987 for the first time in almost a quarter century, then suffered through a 3-13 season in 1988. In February 1989, new owner Jerry Jones sacked Tom Landry and hired Jimmy Johnson.

Members of the Hall of Fame:

(6) Herb Adderley, Lance Alworth, Mike Ditka, Forrest Gregg, Bob Lilly, Roger Staubach

Championships Won:

Super Bowl: VI (1971), XII (1977)
NFL Eastern Conference: 1966, 1967
NFL Capitol Division: 1967, 1968, 1969
NFC: 1970, 1971, 1975, 1977, 1978
NFC Eastern Division: 1970, 1971, 1973, 1976, 1977, 1978, 1979, 1981, 1985

Overall Record:

NFL Regular Season	250	162	6	.605
NFL Postseason	20	16	0	.556
Total	270	178	6	.601

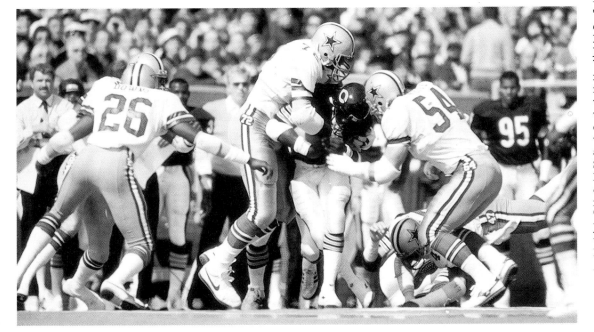

The Dallas Cowboys' defense stops Walter Payton. Ed (Too Tall) Jones (72) and Randy White (54) are the last remaining players from the glory days when the Cowboys went through 20 consecutive seasons with a winning record and appeared in five Super Bowls. In February 1989, new owner, Jerry Jones replaced head coach Tom Landry with Jimmy Johnson, from the University of Miami.

The two most common NFL defenses take their names from the numbers of linemen and linebackers present in each alignment.

The 4-3 defense features four defensive linemen (two ends and two tackles) and three linebackers (a middle linebacker and two outside linebackers).

The 3-4 defense features three defensive linemen (a nose tackle in the middle, flanked by two defensive ends) and four linebackers (two outside and two inside).

Dallas Texans

In January, 1952, a new NFL franchise was awarded to a group from Dallas. Long a hotbed of high school and college football, Texas seemed to be an ideal spot for pro football, but the venture ended in disaster. The Texans averaged less than 15,000 spectators in the first four home games and the owners turned the club back to the NFL in midseason. For the last five games of the year, the commissioner's office operated the Texans as a road team, using Hershey, Pennsylvania, as a home base. At the end of the season, the franchise was canceled. It was the last time an NFL team failed.

Davis, Willie

b. Lisbon, Louisiana, 24 July 1934.
Hall of Fame 1981.

Willie Davis, a graduate of Grambling, was a fifteenth-round draft pick of the Cleveland Browns in 1956. Army service prevented him from reporting to the Browns for two years. He played briefly at several different positions in Cleveland in 1958 and 1959 before being traded to Green Bay in 1960. There he develop-

ed into one of pro football's finest defensive ends.

The 6-3, 245-pound Davis had the attributes Packers head coach Vince Lombardi considered essential for a defensive end – speed, agility, and size – which he combined with the intangibles – dedication, intelligence, and leadership – to become a Green Bay fixture. Davis was an all-pro selection five times in six years from 1962 to 1967. He played in five NFL championship games and Super Bowls I and II. Davis retired in 1969.

Dawson, Len

b. Alliance, Ohio, 20 June 1935.
Hall of Fame: 1987

Len Dawson, a star college quarterback at Purdue, was picked by the Pittsburgh Steelers ahead of the fabled Jim Brown in the first round of the 1957 NFL draft. Yet in his first five seasons of pro football with the Steelers in 1957-1959 and the Cleveland Browns in 1960 and 1961, Dawson threw a total of only 45 passes. When he asked for and received his release from the Browns, Dawson signed with the Dallas Texans of the American Football League.

The calm, poised 6-0, 190-pound signal-caller was an instant hit in the AFL. He led the Texans to their first AFL title and won Player of the Year honors in 1962. The Texans moved to Kansas City in 1963, but Dawson remained as the team's field leader for 13 more years until his retirement after the 1975 season. Dawson won four AFL passing titles, led his team to three championships – more than any other AFL team – and to Super Bowls I and IV.

Dawson's ultimate achievement came in Super Bowl IV when he was the game's Most Valuable Player. He completed 12 of 17 passes for 142 yards and a game-clinching 46-yard scoring pass. His outstanding performance came after a trying week during which he was accused of having been associated with a gambler – a charge that was completely refuted. In 19 pro seasons, Dawson completed 2,136 of 3,731 passes for 28,711 yards and 239 touchdowns.

Dead Ball

When the ball no longer can be advanced, it is whistled dead by the officials. Penalties committed after a whistle are called "dead-ball fouls."

Defense

1. The team without the ball.
2. The tactics of that team.

Defensive Backs

The men who play in the defensive secondary, behind the defensive line and the linebackers; the cornerbacks and safeties.

Delay of Game

A five-yard penalty assessed to the offense when it fails to put the ball in play before the expiration of the 45-second clock, or to any player who impedes the progress of the game.

Dempsey, Tom

b. Milwaukee, Wisconsin, 12 January 1947.

Tom Dempsey made his mark in NFL history in 1970 when he kicked an all-time record 63-yard field goal to enable the New Orleans Saints to defeat the Detroit Lions 19-17 on the game's final play. Making the epic kick more intriguing was the fact that Dempsey was born with a stub of a right hand and half a right foot. Dempsey, a 6-1, 260-pounder, kicked with a specially designed shoe. He wound up his 11-year career with the Saints, Philadelphia Eagles, Los Angeles Rams, Houston Oilers, and Buffalo Bills with 729 points scored on 252 extra points and 159 field goals.

Denver Broncos

The Denver Broncos, with long-time baseball executive Bob Howsam as their principal owner, were one of six charter members of the American Football League, which was formally organized on August 14, 1959. Frank Filchock

Above: Tom Dempsey shows what can be done in spite of physical handicaps (he was born with half a right foot). His 63-yard kick in 1970 is the only instance of a field goal on which the kicking team snapped the ball in its own half of the field.

was named the team's first coach, with Dean Griffing the general manager. The Broncos' first draft pick was Roger LeClerc, a center from Trinity College in Connecticut, who signed with the Chicago Bears. Except for wide receiver Lionel Taylor and safety Goose Gonsoulin, the Broncos had few quality players and the losses, both on the field and at the box office, piled up.

In a desperate effort to find a winning combination, the Broncos tried several head coaches – Filchock, Jack Faulkner, Mac Speedie, Ray Malavasi, and Lou Saban – before John Ralston led them to a 7-5-2 season, their first year above .500, in 1973. A former Denver assistant, Red Miller, took over in 1977 and led the Broncos to their first AFC title and a trip to Super Bowl XII, where they lost to Dallas, 27-10. Quarterback Craig Morton was the AFC Player of the Year.

Since 1975, Denver has had only one losing season, that coming in the strike-shortened 1982 season. In the last five years, with Dan Reeves

Left: Len Dawson showed a lot more class in the week leading up to Super Bowl IV than the people who were trying to smear his reputation. His performance against Minnesota earned him MVP honors.

as head coach, the Broncos have won three AFC West championships and two AFC titles (1986 and 1987). Even though they lost by big margins to the New York Giants in Super Bowl XXI (39-20) and the Washington Redskins in Super Bowl XXII (42-10), the Broncos still rank as one of the NFL's most successful teams in the 19 years since the merged NFL began play in 1970.

The Denver quarterback since 1983 has been John Elway, a tremendous threat both as a passer and a runner, who was acquired in a trade with the Baltimore Colts on draft day.

In the early years, attendance was so poor that a majority bloc of owners who had acquired the Broncos from Howsam in 1961 banded together to sell the team after the 1964 season. When the sale to Atlanta interests fell through, the majority owners sold out to Gerry and Allan Phipps, who already owned 42 percent of the Broncos and had remained firm in their resolve to keep the team in Denver. In a spontaneous outburst of enthusiasm, fans swelled the season-ticket sales from under 8,000 in 1964 to more than 22,000 in 1965. The future of pro football in Denver was assured.

Today the Broncos play in 76,274-seat Mile High Stadium, an expanded version of Bears Stadium (34,657), which housed the original Denver AFL team. The Broncos have been sold

out for every non-strike home game – 137 consecutive games at the start of the 1988 season – for the past 18 years. Approximately 75,000 season tickets are sold annually, and there are 61,000 names on the waiting list.

At the height of the team's popularity in 1981, the Phipps brothers sold the Broncos to Edgar F. Kaiser, Jr. Three years later, Kaiser sold the team to Pat Bowlen, the present owner.

Members of the Hall of Fame:
(1) Willie Brown

Championships Won:
AFC: 1977, 1986, 1987
AFC Western Division: 1977, 1978, 1984, 1986, 1987

Overall Record:

AFL Regular Season	39	97	4	.293
NFL Regular Season	157	117	6	.571
NFL Postseason	6	7	0	.462
Total	202	221	10	.478

Detroit Lions

The Portsmouth, Ohio, Spartans, an independent team, entered the National Football League in 1930. In the faster company of the NFL, they proved to be quite competitive under head coach George (Potsy) Clark. After a respectable 5-6-3 season in 1930, they welcomed an amazing collection of outstanding rookies in 1931, including backs Earl (Dutch) Clark and Glenn Presnell, and linemen George Christiansen and Grover (Ox) Emerson.

Portsmouth won 11 of 14 games in 1931, finishing a game behind defending champion Green Bay. With the addition of rookie halfback LeRoy (Ace) Gutowsky, the Spartans were even better in 1932. With a 6-1-4 record, they tied the Chicago Bears (6-1-6) for first place. Because tie games did not count in the standings, the two teams hastily scheduled an indoor game in Chicago Stadium. The Bears won 9-0. Although the team's triple-threat back, Dutch Clark, did not play, the Spartans finished second in the newly formed Western Division in 1933.

Before the 1934 season, George Richards, a radio station owner, purchased the Spartans for $15,000, plus $6,500 to pay off the team's debts. He moved his club to Detroit and staged a fan contest to determine the team name, Lions, then lined up the 25,000-seat University of Detroit Stadium as a home field. With a game against the Bears on Thanksgiving Day, the tradition of Thanksgiving football in Detroit began.

Still coached by Potsy Clark, the Lions won the NFL Western Conference with a 7-3-2 record in 1935, then went on to overpower the New York Giants 26-7 for their first league championship. Historically, it was a significant

Dan Reeves has led Denver to two Super Bowls – XXI and XXII. In 1985 the Broncos had an 11-5 record, the best ever for a team missing the playoffs; Cleveland, despite an 8-8 record, made the playoffs as Central Division Champion.

accomplishment because it marked the only time in the NFL's first 13 years of championship playoffs that the Bears, Packers, Giants, or Redskins did not win the championship. In 1936, the Lions featured a powerful ground game that netted 2,885 yards, a record that stood for 37 years.

In 1940, Richards sold the Lions to Fred Mandel, a Chicago department store magnate, for $225,000. Although the team acquired stars such as Byron (Whizzer) White and Bill Dudley, Detroit football fell on hard times during the World War II years. In 1948, a discouraged Mandel sold the team for $185,000 to a syndicate of Detroit businessmen headed by Edwin Anderson.

The Lions' fortunes shot upward beginning in 1951 when Buddy Parker was named head coach. Parker lined up a host of exceptional players, including quarterback Bobby Layne, halfback Doak Walker, tackles Thurman McGraw and Lou Creekmur, and three exceptional defensive backs – Jack Christiansen, Yale Lary, and Jim David. In 1953, linebacker Joe Schmidt joined the talented team. Detroit won three successive Western Conference championships, capturing NFL titles in 1952 and 1953. In the championship showdowns, the Lions beat the Browns 17-7 in 1952 and 17-16 in 1953, but fell to Cleveland 56-10 in 1954. Parker resigned just before the first preseason game in 1957 – he was replaced by George Wilson – but the Lions, with quarterback Tobin Rote and running back John Henry Johnson providing the firepower, marched to a fourth conference title in six years. In the title game, they overwhelmed the Browns 59-14.

In the 31 years since their last NFL title, the Lions have had winning records only 10 times. They finished second to the Green Bay Packers with an 11-3 record in 1962 and parlayed a 10-4 mark in 1970 into a wild-card playoff berth. They lost to the Dallas Cowboys 5-0 in the first playoff round. Detroit qualified for the playoffs in the strike-shortened 1982 season, but lost in the first playoff round. A 9-7 finish in 1983 earned the Lions the NFC Central Division title, their first championship of any kind in 26 years. However, they lost 24-23 to the San Francisco 49ers in the playoffs.

William Clay Ford spent $6 million to gain full control of the Lions in 1964. He immediately appointed Russ Thomas as general manager. Thomas still serves in that role today. The best Detroit players in the Ford-Thomas era have been defensive back Lem Barney, defensive tackle Doug English, and running back Billy Sims. The Lions, who doubled their potential attendance by moving to Briggs Stadium in 1938, found a new home 37 years later in sub-

Art Donovan's defensive play was a major reason behind the emergence of the Baltimore Colts in the late 1950s, less than 10 years after the original franchise collapsed.

urban Pontiac, Michigan, when the 80,638-seat Pontiac Silverdome was opened.

Members of the Hall of Fame:

(12) Jack Christiansen, Earl (Dutch) Clark, Bill Dudley, John Henry Johnson, Dick (Night Train) Lane, Yale Lary, Bobby Layne, Ollie Matson, Hugh McElhenny, Joe Schmidt, Doak Walker, Alex Wojciechowicz.

Championships Won:

NFL (pre-1970): 1935, 1952, 1953, 1957
NFL Western Conference: 1935, 1952, 1953, 1954, 1957
NFC Central Division: 1983

Overall Record:

NFL Regular Season	362	375	32	.492
NFL Postseason	6	4	0	.600
Total	368	379	32	.493

Dewveall, Willard

b. Springtown, Texas, 29 April 1936.

Willard Dewveall, a 6-4, 230-pound offensive end at Southern Methodist University, played in the Canadian Football League for a year in 1958 before joining the Chicago Bears in 1959. Two seasons later, he became the first NFL player to jump to the AFL when he played out his option with the Bears and joined the Houston Oilers in 1961. Dewveall retired after the 1964 season with 161 career receptions for 2,661 yards and 22 touchdowns.

Dickerson, Eric

b. Sealy, Texas, 2 September 1960.

Eric Dickerson, a 6-3, 218-pound All-America

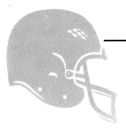

running back from Southern Methodist University, was the second player selected in the 1983 NFL draft. As a Los Angeles Rams rookie, he rushed for 1,808 yards, an all-time record for a rookie. In his second season in 1984, he rushed for 2,105 yards to surpass the single-season record O.J. Simpson established in 1973. He led the NFL in rushing again in 1986 when he carried for 1,821 yards.

In 1987, Dickerson became involved in a contractual dispute with the Rams, who sent him to the Indianapolis Colts in a complicated three-team transaction that involved six draft choices and three players, in addition to Dickerson. In nine games with Indianapolis, he rushed for 1,011 yards and won the AFC rushing championship. In 1988, he led the NFL with 1,659 rushing yards. Still active, Dickerson, was named all-pro five times in his first six seasons, and played in five Pro Bowls. After only six seasons, he ranked among the top 10 all-time rushing leaders with 9,915 yards and 75 touchdowns. Dickerson now holds the single season rushing records for the Colts and the Rams.

Ditka, Mike

b. Carnegie, Pennsylvania, 18 October 1939.
Hall of Fame: 1988

The Chicago Bears drafted 6-3, 225-pound Mike Ditka in the first round of the 1961 NFL draft and quickly targeted the University of Pittsburgh All-America for the relatively new position of tight end. Almost immediately, the rugged and talented rookie added a new dimension to the job. Besides being a devastating blocker, which was expected of a tight end, Ditka began to catch passes in big numbers, something no other tight end had done.

Ditka caught 56 passes for 1,076 yards in 1961. He was named Rookie of the Year and all-pro and was picked for the first of his five Pro

Bowls. Ditka was all-pro again in 1962, 1963, and 1964. When the Bears won their first championship in 17 years in 1963, he played a major role with clutch receiving and crushing blocking. In the rugged title showdown with New York, Ditka's 12-yard reception in heavy traffic put the ball on the Giants' one-yard line to set up the winning touchdown. In 1964, he caught 75 passes, a record for tight ends that stood until the advent of the 16-game season. In his 12-year career, he recorded 427 receptions for 5,812 yards and 43 touchdowns.

After six seasons in Chicago, Ditka was traded to the Philadelphia Eagles in 1967 and then moved on to Dallas in 1969. He played four more seasons with the Cowboys, retiring after 1972. He immediately turned to coaching and spent the next nine years as a Cowboys assistant. In 1982, Ditka returned to Chicago as the Bears' head coach. The Bears' victory in Super Bowl XX, the team's first championship since 1963, when Ditka was a star player, has been the highlight of his coaching career to date. Ditka became the first tight end to be elected to the Pro Football Hall of Fame.

Division

For the first 13 years of its history (1920 to 1932), the National Football League awarded the annual championship to the team with the best record. In 1933, the NFL divided itself into the Eastern Division and the Western Division, with the two yearly winners playing for the NFL championship. In 1950, the term "division" was dropped in favor of the term "conference." From 1967 to 1969, four-team Capitol and Century divisions were created within the Eastern Conference, and Coastal and Central

Below: The Detroit Lions' defense makes absolutely certain that George Rogers is not going far. The Lions have struggled in recent seasons, but new head coach Wayne Fontes is hoping that the team from the Silverdome has turned the corner.

Below right: Mike Ditka is all alone as he makes a catch against the Los Angeles Rams in the Coliseum. As a receiving tight end he had no peers; as a coach he has taken the Bears back to the top of the NFL.

divisions within the NFL Western Conference.

Today, the AFC and NFC each consist of 14 teams that play in three divisions – Eastern, Central, and Western.

Domed Stadiums

Although pro football games were played indoors in New York's Madison Square Garden in 1902 and in Chicago Stadium in 1932, it was not on a regular basis until the Houston Oilers moved into the Astrodome in 1968. In addition to the Oilers, the New Orleans Saints (Louisiana Superdome), Detroit Lions (Pontiac Silverdome), Seattle Seahawks (Kingdome), Minnesota Vikings (Hubert H. Humphrey Metrodome), and Indianapolis Colts (Hoosier Dome) now play all their home games in domed stadiums. AstroTurf, a synthetic grass developed after attempts to grow natural grass in the Astrodome failed, now serves as the playing surface in all six stadiums.

Donovan, Art

b. Bronx, New York, 5 June 1925.
Hall of Fame: 1968

Art Donovan, a son of the famous boxing referee of the same name, was a 25-year-old rookie when he first joined the Baltimore Colts in 1950. Donovan, who served in the US Marines during World War II, spent his first three seasons of pro football with three teams, each in its last year of operation – the Colts in 1950, the New York Yankees in 1951, and the Dallas Texans in 1952. The three teams had a cumulative 3-31-2 won-lost record.

In 1953, the 6-3, 265-pound Boston College graduate found himself with a new Baltimore Colts team, and he found a new lease on his pro football life. An expert at pass rushing and equally adept at rushing defense, Donovan became a key element in the Colts' climb toward their championship years of 1958 and 1959. He was all-pro four straight years from 1954 to 1957 and also played in five consecutive Pro Bowls. Donovan's 12-season NFL career ended after 1961. Donovan became the first Colt elected to the Pro Football Hall of Fame.

Doomsday Defense

When the Dallas Cowboys won their first NFL Eastern Conference championship in 1966, Gary Cartwright, a Dallas Morning News sports writer, coined the term "Doomsday Defense." Popular until Dallas won Super Bowl VI, the name fell out of use for a time and then resurfaced as Doomsday II when the Cowboys won Super Bowl XII.

Tony Dorsett, in his still-unfamiliar Denver uniform, breaks into the open. Only Walter Payton has carried the ball for more career yards than the former Dallas Cowboys standout.

Dorsett, Tony

b. Rochester, Pennsylvania, 7 April 1954.

Tony Dorsett, the 1976 Heisman Trophy winner and an All-America at the University of Pittsburgh, was the Dallas Cowboys' first-round pick in the 1977 NFL draft. The 5-11, 185-pound running back rushed for 1,007 yards and was a consensus choice as Rookie of the Year. Dorsett rushed for more than 1,000 yards eight of his first nine NFL seasons, enjoying his finest season in 1981 when he rushed for 1,646 yards and added 325 yards on 32 receptions. In January, 1983, against Minnesota, he ran 99 yards for a touchdown, an NFL record that can be tied but never broken. Dorsett has played in four Pro Bowls.

He was traded to the Denver Broncos in 1988. His 11-year totals with the Cowboys included 12,036 yards rushing, 3,432 yards on 382 pass receptions, and 86 touchdowns. In the fourth game of the 1988 season, he moved past Jim Brown to become the NFL's second leading rusher.

Double Coverage

Two defensive players covering one receiver.

Double-Teaming

Two offensive blockers working against one defender.

Down

1. A play from scrimmage; the offense gets four downs numbered in sequence, first to fourth, to gain 10 yards and make another first down.
2. When a ball carrier is tackled or his forward progress is stopped, he is considered *down* and the play ends.
3. On a punt, the kicking team may touch the ball and *down* it at the spot it is touched, ending the play. On a kickoff, the receiving team may *down* the ball in the end zone for a touchback by indicating the kick will not be returned. The ball is then brought out to the 20-yard line.

Draft

In the mid-1930s, Bert Bell, the owner of the Philadelphia Eagles, sensed there was a need for more balance of talent among the NFL teams. He proposed an annual selection of graduating college seniors with the teams picking in the inverse order of their finish the previous year. Bell's proposal was accepted, and, in 1936, the NFL conducted its first draft. Philadelphia had the first pick and selected Jay Berwanger, an All-America halfback from the University of Chicago. Berwanger, however, opted not to play pro football.

Draw

A delayed, fake-pass play. The quarterback drops back as if to pass, drawing in the defensive linemen. He then hands the ball to a back who runs through the gap left by the charging defenders.

Driscoll, John (Paddy)

b. Evanston, Illinois, 11 January 1896;
d. 29 June 1968. Hall of Fame: 1965

John (Paddy) Driscoll, a 5-11, 160-pound quarterback from Northwestern University, began his pro career with the 1919 Hammond Pros. A year later, he found himself in the new American Professional Football Association with the Chicago Cardinals, with whom he played for six years, three of them (1920-22) as player/

After terrorizing the Chicago Bears whilst playing (and coaching) the cross-town Cardinals, John (Paddy) Driscoll was the man George Halas named to replace himself as coach of the Bears. Under Driscoll, they won the 1956 Western Conference.

coach. He had a 17-8-4 record in that time.

Not big, even by 1920 standards, Driscoll was a true triple-threat on offense and a brilliant field general who excelled as a punter and a dropkicker. For years, his 50-yard dropkick field goal in 1925 was the NFL record. Driscoll specialized in making life miserable for the cross-town rival Bears. When Red Grange made his debut with the Bears in 1925, Driscoll neutralized Grange by punting the ball away from him. In 1926, Driscoll was traded to the Bears, with whom he finished his playing career after the 1929 season. A close friend of George Halas, Driscoll spent a two seasons as coach of the Bears when Halas stepped down in 1956.

The Drive

The Cleveland Browns held a 20-13 lead when the Denver Broncos took the ball at their own 2-yard line with 5:43 remaining in the 1986 AFC championship game at Cleveland Stadium. After three plays that gained just 10 yards, Denver's quarterback, John Elway, took personal charge. He scrambled for 11 yards and passed to Steve Sewell for a 22-yard gain to the Denver 48. Another strike, this one to Steve Watson, put the Broncos on the Cleveland 40 with 1:59 to play. On third-and-18, Elway hit Mark Jackson for a 22-yard gain.

The Browns intensified their pass rush, but a screen pass to Steve Sewell gained 14; another scramble by Elway put the ball on the 5-yard line with 39 seconds to play. On third down, Elway threw a perfect strike to Jackson in the end zone. Rich Karlis kicked the extra point for the tie. On Denver's first possession in overtime, Elway orchestrated a march that set up Karlis, whose 33-yard field goal sent the Broncos to Super Bowl XXI.

Drop

1. The movement of the quarterback after the snap as he retreats into the backfield to set up the pass.
2. The movement of a linebacker as he retreats into pass coverage.

Dropkick

An alternative to the placekick on extra points and field goals. The kicker lets the ball drop to the ground in a controlled manner and kicks it at the precise moment it touches the ground. Once a popular kicking method, the dropkick fell out of use when rule changes made the ball less round.

Dudley, Bill

b. Bluefield, Virginia, 24 December 1921.
Hall of Fame: 1966

Bill Dudley was nicknamed "Bullet," although he was small and slow, with unorthodox passing and kicking motions. But on the football field, he was extremely versatile and efficient. The first All-America in the history of the University of Virginia, the 5-10, 176-pound Dudley was the number one draft choice of the Pittsburgh Steelers in 1942. He was not only named all-pro as a rookie, he won the rushing crown as well. Dudley served in the US Army for the next 2½ years but, in his first full post-war season in 1946, he became the third and last winner of an unusual "triple crown", with individual statistical championships in rushing, punt returns, and interceptions. He was again an all-pro pick. Dudley was traded to Detroit in 1947. He played three seasons with the Lions and three more with the Washington Redskins in 1950, 1951, and 1953. In nine NFL seasons, Dudley amassed a respectable 3,057 yards rushing, but he also had significant figures as a receiver, punt, kickoff returner, passer, punter, and intercepter. He scored 484 points on 44 touchdowns, 121 extra points, and 33 field goals.

Number-One Draft Choices, 1936-1988

Season	Team	Player, Position	College
1988	Atlanta	Aundray Bruce, LB	Auburn
1987	Tampa Bay	Vinny Testaverde, QB	Miami (Fla.)
1986	Tampa Bay	Bo Jackson, RB	Auburn
1985	Buffalo	Bruce Smith, DE	Virginia Tech
1984	New England	Irving Fryar, WR	Nebraska
1983	Baltimore	John Elway, QB	Stanford
1982	New England	Kenneth Sims, DT	Texas
1981	New Orleans	George Rogers, RB	South Carolina
1980	Detroit	Billy Sims, RB	Oklahoma
1979	Buffalo	Tom Cousineau, LB	Ohio State
1978	Houston	Earl Campbell, RB	Texas
1977	Tampa Bay	Ricky Bell, RB	USC
1976	Tampa Bay	Lee Roy Selmon, DE	Oklahoma
1975	Atlanta	Steve Bartkowski, QB	California
1974	Dallas	Ed Jones, DE	Tennessee State
1973	Houston	John Matuszak, DE	Tampa
1972	Buffalo	Walt Patulski, DE	Notre Dame
1971	New England	Jim Plunkett, QB	Stanford
1970	Pittsburgh	Terry Bradshaw, QB	Louisiana Tech
1969	Buffalo (AFL)	O.J. Simpson, RB	USC
1968	Minnesota	Ron Yary, T	USC
1967	Baltimore	Bubba Smith, DT	Michigan State
1966	Atlanta	Tommy Nobis, LB	Texas
	Miami (AFL)	Jim Grabowski, RB	Illinois
1965	N.Y. Giants	Tucker Frederickson, RB	Auburn
	Houston (AFL)	Lawrence Elkins, E	Baylor
1964	San Francisco	Dave Parks, E	Texas Tech
	Boston (AFL)	Jack Concannon, QB	Boston College
1963	Los Angeles	Terry Baker, QB	Oregon State
	Kansas City (AFL)	Buck Buchanan, DT	Grambling
1962	Washington	Ernie Davis, RB	Syracuse
	Oakland (AFL)	Roman Gabriel, QB	No. Carolina St.
1961	Minnesota	Tommy Mason, RB	Tulane
	Buffalo (AFL)	Ken Rice, G	Auburn
1960	Los Angeles	Billy Cannon, RB	LSU
1959	Green Bay	Randy Duncan, QB	Iowa
1958*	Chi. Cardinals	King Hill, QB	Rice
1957*	Green Bay	Paul Hornung, HB	Notre Dame
1956*	Pittsburgh	Gary Glick, DB	Colorado A&M
1955*	Baltimore	George Shaw, QB	Oregon
1954*	Cleveland	Bobby Garrett, QB	Stanford
1953*	San Francisco	Harry Babcock, E	Georgia
1952*	Los Angeles	Billy Wade, QB	Vanderbilt
1951*	N.Y. Giants	Kyle Rote, HB	SMU
1950*	Detroit	Leon Hart, E	Notre Dame
1949*	Philadelphia	Chuck Bednarik, C	Pennsylvania
1948*	Washington	Harry Gilmer, QB	Alabama
1947*	Chicago Bears	Bob Fenimore, HB	Oklahoma A&M
1946	Boston	Frank Dancewicz, QB	Notre Dame
1945	Chi. Cardinals	Charley Trippi, HB	Georgia
1944	Boston	Angelo Bertelli, QB	Notre Dame
1943	Detroit	Frank Sinkwich, HB	Georgia
1942	Pittsburgh	Bill Dudley, HB	Virginia
1941	Chicago Bears	Tom Harmon, HB	Michigan
1940	Chi. Cardinals	George Cafego, HB	Tennessee
1939	Chi. Cardinals	Ki Aldrich, C	Texas Christian
1938	Cleveland	Corbett Davis, FB	Indiana
1937	Philadelphia	Sam Francis, FB	Nebraska
1936	Philadelphia	Jay Berwanger, HB	Chicago

* From 1947 through 1958, the first selection in the draft was a Bonus pick, awarded in a random draw. The winner forfeited its last-round draft choice and was eliminated from future draws. The system was abolished after 1958, by which time all clubs had received a bonus choice.

Duluth Eskimos

With the departure of the fabled Red Grange to a rival football league in 1926, the National Football League desperately needed a name player to take his place. Ernie Nevers, a Stanford All-America halfback and the star of the 1925 Rose Bowl loss to Notre Dame, filled the role. What was astounding was that one of the league's most financially beleaguered franchises, the Duluth Eskimos, set out to sign Nevers.

The owners of the Eskimos, Ole Haugsrud and Dewey Scanlon, had purchased the Duluth franchise just a few months earlier for $1. The NFL agreed to help pay the bill when Haugsrud landed Nevers for $15,000 and a 25 percent share of the gate. Even the Duluth players cooperated by agreeing to accept $50 a game if they lost, $60 if they tied, and $75 if they won.

The 1926 Duluth team played the season opener at home and then went on the road for an ambitious 29-game schedule that took them 17,000 miles from the Atlantic to the Pacific over a 111-day period. The team was outfitted with handsome white mackinaws with an igloo on the backs along with the inscription: "Ernie Nevers Eskimos." Playing with only a 13-man squad – Haugsrud and Scanlon sometimes would suit up and work out to lessen the embarrassment – the Eskimos finished with a 6-5-3 record in NFL play and 19-7-3 for the entire tour.

The Eskimos operated again in 1927 but with much less fanfare (the intra-league war lasted just one year), posting a dismal 1-8 playing record. The team was sold after the season.

E ★

Eagle Defense

The Eagle defense was instituted by Earle (Greasy) Neale, head coach of the Philadelphia Eagles, in the 1940s. In the alignment, the five defensive linemen set up opposite the center, just outside the two guards and just outside the two ends. Two linebackers then lined up in front of the holes between the tackles and ends. This defense was particularly effective in stopping the run.

Edwards, Glen (Turk)

b. Mold, Washington, 28 September 1907; d. 12 January 1973. Hall of Fame: 1969

Glen (Turk) Edwards, 6-2 and 260 pounds, was one of the biggest pro football players during his career, which lasted from 1932 until 1940 with one team that had several names – the Boston Braves, Boston Redskins, and Washington Redskins. The former Washington State All-America, who signed with the Braves for $150 a game, typified overwhelming strength and power as the anchor of his team's offensive and defensive lines. A true "iron man," Edwards played all but 10 minutes in one 12-game season while the club was still in Boston. He won official all-pro honors his first two seasons in 1932 and 1933, and again in 1936 and 1937. During the Edwards era, the Redskins won three divisional championships and the 1937 NFL title.

In spite of his playing excellence, Edwards may be best remembered for the bizarre way his career ended, when he was injured at a coin-tossing ceremony at the start of the 1940 season. Before a game with the New York Giants, Edwards went to mid-field to meet Giants captain Mel Hein, who happened to be his best friend. After the coin was flipped, Edwards wheeled to return to the bench, but his spikes caught in the turf and his oft-injured knee gave way for a final time.

Glen (Turk) Edwards' strength and power were vital to the Boston/Washington Braves/Redskins franchise. His career ended with a most bizarre injury.

Eller, Carl

b. Winston-Salem, North Carolina, 25 February 1942.

Carl Eller, a consensus All-America at the University of Minnesota, was picked by both the Minnesota Vikings of the NFL and the Buffalo Bills of the AFL in the 1964 pro football draft. Eller opted for the more familiar environment in Minnesota. For 15 years, he was the left end on the "Purple People Eaters" defensive line that helped make the Vikings one of the NFL's dominant teams. Extremely quick for his size, the 6-6, 247-pound Eller was equally adept at defending the run and the pass.

Eller recorded 44 sacks in one three-season streak from 1975 to 1977. He recovered 23 opponents' fumbles in his career. Eller was all-pro from 1968 to 1973 and then again in 1975, and he played in six Pro Bowls. In 1979, he closed his career with Seattle.

Elway, John

b. Port Angeles, Washington, 18 June 1960.

Few rookies have been more widely coveted than John Elway, the two-time All-America quarterback at Stanford University, who was drafted by the Baltimore Colts as the first player selected in 1983. The multi-talented Elway was also drafted by the New York Yankees baseball team. The Colts then traded the 6-3, 210-pound Elway to the Denver Broncos for two players and a number-one draft pick. In his first six seasons, he completed 1,442 passes for 18,144 yards and 102 touchdowns. Blessed with great scrambling ability, he also rushed for 1,431 yards and eight touchdowns.

Elway led the Broncos to AFC Western Division championships in 1984, 1986, and 1987, and to AFC titles in 1986 and 1987. His 15-play, 98-yard drive that enabled the Broncos to tie the Cleveland Browns and eventually win the 1986 AFC championship game in overtime is considered one of the classic performances of all time. In 1987, Elway was a consensus all-pro and the NFL Player of the Year. He played in the Pro Bowl following the 1986 and 1987 seasons.

Encroachment

A penalty called when a player in the neutral zone makes contact with an opponent before the ball is snapped.

End

1. Originally the ends on the offensive line positioned themselves immediately outside

Defensive coaches don't know whether to leave John Elway in the pocket to find a receiver, or flush him out and then watch him run 20 yards downfield for a first down.

the two tackles. With the advent of spread offenses, the tight end continued to line up next to the right tackle but the other end lined up 10 or more yards outside the left tackle and was known as the split end.

2. The two outside players on the defensive line.

End Around

A variation of a reverse play in which the tight end or a wide receiver becomes the ball carrier on a sweep.

End Line

The line at the back of the end zone.

End Zone

The area, 10 yards deep, bounded by the goal line, end line, and both sidelines.

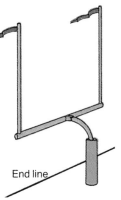

End line

All goal posts, which are inset from the end line, used in the NFL are the same size and type, and are bright yellow in color.

Weeb Ewbank was the successful coach in two of the most famous games in football history, leading Baltimore to its 1958 NFL championship game victory over the New York Giants, and then masterminding the Jets' defeat of Baltimore in Super Bowl III.

Ewbank, Weeb

b. Richmond, Indiana, 6 May 1907.
Hall of Fame: 1978

Weeb Ewbank, a product of the "cradle of coaches," the University of Miami of Ohio, has the unique distinction of being the only head coach to win championships in both the American and National Football Leagues. His Baltimore Colts won NFL titles in 1958 and 1959; a decade later, his 1968 New York Jets followed up their AFL championship with a stunning upset of Ewbank's old team, the Colts, in Super Bowl III.

Most historians agree that Baltimore's 23-17 overtime victory over the New York Giants in the 1958 NFL championship game and the Jets' 16-7 triumph in Super Bowl III played dominant

roles in transforming pro football into an enormously popular sport. The 1958 game has been popularly termed "the greatest game ever played." The Jets' incredible triumph in January, 1969, assured the competitive viability of the Super Bowl series.

Ewbank coached the Colts for nine years (1954-1962) and the Jets for 11 seasons (1963-1973). In both Baltimore and New York, Ewbank took over a struggling young team and had to spend several years of building before producing a champion. As a result, his cumulative 20-year coaching record – 130-129-7 – does not reflect the impact he made on pro football.

Expansion Franchises

The National Football League welcomed many new franchises during its first 40 years but it embarked on a calculated expansion program for the first time in 1960. The NFL owners agreed to admit the Dallas Cowboys that year and the Minnesota Vikings in 1961.

Later in the decade, the Atlanta Falcons (1966) and the New Orleans Saints (1967) joined the NFL, and the Miami Dolphins (1966) and Cincinnati Bengals (1968) entered the American Football League. After the 1970 merger that turned the 16-team NFL into a 26-team league, the NFL expanded one more time. Both the Seattle Seahawks and Tampa Bay Buccaneers began play in 1976.

Extra Point

The one-point play allowed a team after it scores a touchdown; it may be attempted by a run, pass, dropkick or (almost always) a place-kick. Also called the "point after touchdown" (PAT) or "conversion."

F

Face Mask

1. The protective cage or bar on the front of a football helmet.
2. A penalty: five yards for grasping the face mask of an opponent, 15 yards for twisting, turning, or pulling an opponent by the mask.

Fair Catch

An unhindered catch by the receiver of a punt or kickoff. To signal a fair catch, the player raises one arm over his head while the kick is in flight. Once he makes the signal, the player

cannot run with the ball or be touched. A penalty is assessed if either occurs.

False Start

A penalty called when an interior offensive lineman moves after assuming a three-point stance.

Fears, Tom

b. Los Angeles, California, 3 December 1923.
Hall of Fame: 1970

When Tom Fears joined the Los Angeles Rams

in 1948 after an outstanding college career at the University of Santa Clara and UCLA, he was ticketed to be a defensive specialist. However, Rams head coach Clark Shaughnessy correctly realized that Fears' running and catching abilities should be utilized on offense. The 6-2, 215-pound Fears responded with NFL pass receiving championships his first three seasons with 51 catches in 1948, 77 in 1949, and 84 in 1950. In nine NFL seasons, he caught 400 passes for 5,397 yards and 38 touchdowns.

Fears became an integral part of the revolutionary three-receiver formation that Shaughnessy introduced in 1949. The new attack plan called for Fears to line up 10 yards to the outside of the right tackle. The Rams had two outstanding passers (Bob Waterfield and Norm Van Brocklin) and the result was a point outburst with Fears as one of the ring-leaders. A clutch performer, he enjoyed many big days – three touchdown catches in the 1950 Western Division playoff game against the Chicago Bears; the winning score on a 73-yard reception in the 1951 championship victory over the Cleveland Browns; and an 18-reception day against Green Bay in 1950. The latter single-game record performance still stands. Fears retired after the 1956 season. He became the first coach of the New Orleans Saints in 1967, but was dismissed during the 1970 season.

Fearsome Foursome

During the 1960s, when the Los Angeles Rams were among the NFL's leading defensive teams each year, they were led by a rugged defensive line known as the "Fearsome Foursome." The unit, which played together from 1963 to 1967, consisted of ends David (Deacon) Jones and Lamar Lundy, and tackles Merlin Olsen and Roosevelt Grier. The foursome, which averaged 6-5½ and 271 pounds, was noted for its outstanding pass rushing, but it was also effective against running plays. When Grier was injured in 1967, he was replaced by another 295-pounder, Roger Brown.

Feathers, Beattie

b. Bristol, Virginia, 20 August 1909.

In his rookie season in 1934, Beattie Feathers, a 5-11, 188-pound halfback from the University of Tennessee, became the first NFL player to rush for more than 1,000 yards, totaling 1,004 yards on 101 carries. His average gain of 9.94 yards per carry stands today as an all-time NFL record. Feathers scored a career-high nine touchdowns, eight of them by rushing, that year. Injuries took their toll even before his record-making season was over. He missed the last two games of the regular season and the NFL championship game against the New York Giants.

Feathers stayed with the Bears through the 1937 season and then played for the Brooklyn Dodgers (1938-39) and the Green Bay Packers (1940). He gained a total of 976 yards in his final six seasons.

The Los Angeles Rams' defense was one of the most feared in the NFL in the early 1960s. The 'Fearsome Foursome' defensive line of (from left) Lamar Lundy, Roosevelt Grier, Merlin Olsen and David 'Deacon' Jones weighed nearly half a ton.

Field

The field is 100 yards from goal line to goal line and 53 yards and 1 foot wide. The end zones are 10 yards deep. Yard lines, parallel to the goal lines, appear on the field of play at intervals of five yards. The hashmarks, which are shorter lines, are spaced one yard apart the length of the field and are 23 yards, 21 inches from each sideline. There are white arrows (adjacent to the yard-line numerals) every 10 yards (except the 50) pointing toward the nearest goal line.

A six-foot wide white border rims the field. Six feet outside that border is a dashed yellow restraining line encompassing the entire field except the coaching areas between the 32-yard lines, where the yellow line is solid. The four intersections of goal lines and sidelines are marked by pylons mounted on flexible shafts. Two pylons are placed at each end line.

Field Goal

A scoring placekick or dropkick worth three points that may be attempted from anywhere on the field. The ball must go between the goal post's uprights and over the crossbar. The measurement of a kick's length is from the kicking point (7-8 yards behind the line of scrim-

mage) to the goal posts, so if the ball is snapped on the 20-yard line: 20 + 8 + 10 = 38-yard field goal.

Field Position

The spot on the playing field, usually measured by yard line, where a team has possession of the ball.

First-and-10

At the start of each ball possession, the offensive team is allowed four plays in which to gain 10 yards. The term "first-and-10" describes the first play of the series. If the team does gain 10 yards in four downs or less, another "first down" or "first-and-10" is awarded.

First Championship Game Broadcast

The Chicago Bears' 73-0 victory over the Washington Redskins in the 1940 NFL championship game was broadcast to 120 stations of the Mutual Broadcasting System. It was the first NFL championship game to be networked.

First Indoor Football Game

Playing football in brightly lit, air-conditioned

The Field

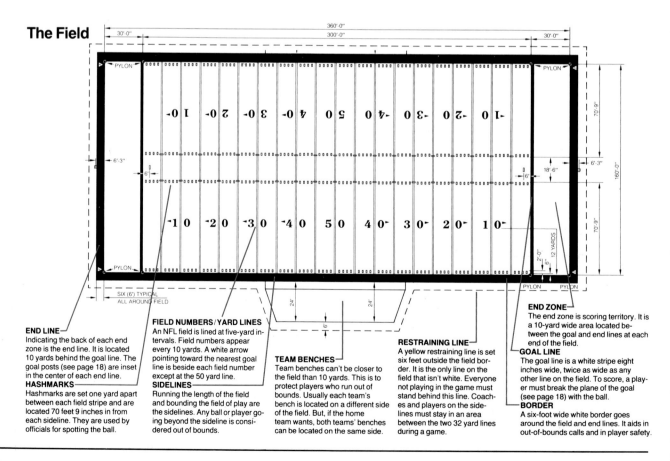

END LINE
Indicating the back of each end zone is the end line. It is located 10 yards behind the goal line. The goal posts (see page 18) are inset in the center of each end line.

HASHMARKS
Hashmarks are set one yard apart between each field stripe and are located 70 feet 9 inches in from each sideline. They are used by officials for spotting the ball.

FIELD NUMBERS/YARD LINES
An NFL field is lined at five-yard intervals. Field numbers appear every 10 yards. A white arrow pointing toward the nearest goal line is beside each field number except at the 50 yard line.

SIDELINES
Running the length of the field and bounding the field of play are the sidelines. Any ball or player going beyond the sideline is considered out of bounds.

TEAM BENCHES
Team benches can't be closer to the field than 10 yards. This is to protect players who run out of bounds. Usually each team's bench is located on a different side of the field. But, if the home team wants, both teams' benches can be located on the same side.

RESTRAINING LINE
A yellow restraining line is set six feet outside the field border. It is the only line on the field that isn't white. Everyone not playing in the game must stand behind this line. Coaches and players on the sidelines must stay in an area between the two 32 yard lines during a game.

END ZONE
The end zone is scoring territory. It is a 10-yard wide area located between the goal and end lines at each end of the field.

GOAL LINE
The goal line is a white stripe eight inches wide, twice as wide as any other line on the field. To score, a player must break the plane of the goal (see page 18) with the ball.

BORDER
A six-foot wide white border goes around the field and end lines. It aids in out-of-bounds calls and in player safety.

indoor arenas is assumed to be a product of the modern age. In truth, the first indoor football games were played in New York's Madison Square Garden almost nine decades ago. Manager Tom O'Rourke was seeking a premier attraction to fill his arena during the 1902-1903 New Year's holiday and he hit upon the idea of a football "world series." Five teams from New York, New Jersey, and Pennsylvania participated in the tournament, which was won by the Syracuse, New York, Athletic Club.

To play the games, the wooden flooring of the arena was removed and replaced by an earthen surface that proved to be too sticky for adequate maneuvering. The goal lines were 70 yards apart and the playing surface was barely 35 yards wide. With the arena seats inching close to the sidelines, the playing field proved to be a physical hazard to the players.

First Interleague Playoff

New York Giants owner Tim Mara bore the financial brunt of history's first interleague war. As the 1926 season neared its end and it was obvious that the rival American Football League was going out of business, Mara wanted one more crack at his hated and costly rival. He challenged Pyle's Yankees to a game. Pyle first agreed, then backed down.

Mara then turned to the AFL champion Philadelphia Quakers, who agreed to play in the Polo Grounds on December 12, 1926. The Quakers won seven of nine AFL games, while the Giants had an 8-4-1 record and a seventh-place finish in the NFL. Nevertheless, the game was no contest. The Quakers managed only one first down and the Giants won 31-0. Snow obliterated the yard markers and only 5,000 people were in the stands.

Nevertheless, the first AFL accomplished in one otherwise unsuccessful year what other NFL challengers could not achieve for the next 40 years – an interleague playoff.

First National Radio Broadcast

The first national radio coverage of a National Football League game was the Columbia Broadcasting System's broadcast of the 1934 Thanksgiving Day game in which the Chicago Bears defeated the hometown Detroit Lions 19-16.

First Night Game

The Philadelphia Athletics football team, coached by the famous baseball manager, Connie Mack, was involved in the first night football game in 1902. An Athletics game against the Kanaweola Athletic Club in Elmira, New York, was scheduled to begin after dark. Lights were placed at ground level, bordering the field. The lights hampered the game because they shone directly into the player's eyes.

The first NFL game played at night was staged in Kinsley Park in Providence, Rhode Island, on November 6, 1929. Two rows of large floodlights lit the field, and the football was painted white for better visibility. The Chicago Cardinals defeated the Providence Steam Roller 16-0.

First Player Deal

The first recorded player deal in the American Professional Football Association occurred on December 5, 1920, when the Akron Pros sold the contract of tackle Bob Nash to the Buffalo All-Americans for $300 and five percent of the gate receipts from that day's game between the two teams.

The First Seven Pros

For several years in the late 1880s, it was standard practice for club and town football teams to offer generous expense allowances – well in excess of actual expenses – to star amateur players before most crucial games. Thus, it is possible that there were actual pro players before November 12, 1892, the established pro football birthdate. It is known the Pittsburgh Athletic Club had at least one player, and probably more, under contract for the 1893 season, but the identity of the player(s) is not known. Listed below are the first seven players *known* to have been openly paid to play football.

1. WILLIAM (PUDGE) HEFFELFINGER, Allegheny Athletic Association, Pittsburgh, $500 for one game on November 12, 1892.
2. BEN (SPORT) DONNELLY, Allegheny Athletic Association, $250 for one game on November 19, 1892.
3-4-5. PETER WRIGHT, JIM VAN CLEVE, OLLIE RAFFERTY, Allegheny Athletic Association, each received $50 per game (under contract) for the entire 1893 season.
6. LAWSON FISCUS, Greensburg (Pennsylvania) Athletic Association, $20 per game and expenses for the entire 1894 season.
7. JOHN BRALLIER, Latrobe (Pennsylvania) YMCA, $10 and expenses for one game on September 3, 1895.

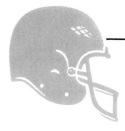

First Televised NFL Game

On October 22, 1939, the National Football League experienced a preliminary taste of television coverage. The Brooklyn Dodgers-Philadelphia Eagles game in Ebbets Field was locally televised by the National Broadcasting Company. At the time, there were approximately 1,000 television sets in New York.

Flag

The yellow cloth an official drops to indicate a foul has been committed that will result in a penalty against the offending team.

Right: Ray Flaherty's Redskins teams won four division titles and two league championships in just seven seasons. But in the 1940 NFL championship game, his team lost 73-0 to the Chicago Bears in the most famous blowout in history.

Centre: Charles Follis, seated 2nd row, extreme right, became the first black professional football player when he signed to play for the Shelby, Ohio, Athletic Club in 1904. The halfback's career lasted just five seasons.

Flaherty, Ray

b. Spokane, Washington, 1 September 1904.
Hall of Fame: 1976

Ray Flaherty was an outstanding end at Gonzaga University and with the New York Giants in the NFL but he made his mark in pro football as a highly successful coach, compiling an 80-37-5 record in seven seasons with the Boston/Washington Redskins in the National Football League (1936-1942), and the New York Yankees (1946-1948) and Chicago Hornets (1949) in the All-America Football Conference.

His Redskins teams won Eastern Division titles in 1936, 1937, 1940, and 1942, and overall NFL championships in 1937 and 1942. His first two Yankees teams won AAFC divisional crowns. Flaherty's 1940 Redskins endured the worst beating in pro football history, a 73-0 rout by the Chicago Bears. Two years later, Flaherty evened the score with a 14-6 victory over the

previously undefeated Bears in the 1942 NFL championship game, his last with the Redskins.

Flanker

The wide receiver on the tight end's side of the field; officially a member of the backfield who must set up one yard behind the line of scrimmage.

Flare Pass

A short pass to a running back, usually in the flat.

Flat

The area on either side of the line of scrimmage between the offensive line and the sidelines.

Flea-Flicker

A term originally devised to describe a passing gadget play on which a receiver, immediately after catching a pass, laterals the ball to a trailing teammate. It now is used to identify a number of other gadget plays.

Flooding the Zone

To send more pass receivers than there are defenders into an area of the field.

Fly Pattern

A long pass pattern on which a wide receiver runs downfield at full speed. Also called a "go" pattern.

Flying Wedge

An antiquated blocking formation used in the early days of football in which 10 players would form a V-shape cordon around the ball carrier, link arms, and fend off tacklers. In response to public outcry over the physical dangers of football, a rules committee banned the formation in 1906.

Follis, Charles

b. Cloverdale, Virginia, 3 February 1879;
d. 5 April 1910.

Charles Follis, a halfback from Wooster, Ohio, played football with the Shelby, Ohio, Athletic Club from 1902 to 1906, and documented evidence shows that he signed a contract to play for pay in 1904. He was the first black player in pro football.

Force

The defensive responsibility of a safety or cornerback to turn a running play toward the middle of the field.

Ford, Len

b. Washington, DC, 18 February 1926;
d. 14 March 1972. Hall of Fame: 1976

Len Ford, who played college football at Morgan State College and the University of Michigan, joined the Los Angeles Dons of the All-America Football Conference in 1948 as an

Foreman, Chuck

b. Frederick, Maryland, 26 October 1950.

Chuck Foreman, a 6-2, 207-pound power runner from the University of Miami (Florida), was selected in the first round of the 1973 NFL draft by the Minnesota Vikings. He was a Rookie-of-the-Year choice in 1973 and made the AFC-NFC Pro Bowl in his first five seasons. In 1975, he led the NFL with 73 receptions, and he had 1,000-yard rushing seasons in 1975, 1976, and 1977. In his eight-year career, Foreman rushed for 5,950 yards, caught 350 passes for 3,156 yards, and scored 76 touchdowns.

As a rookie, Chuck Foreman was a vital part of head coach Bud Grant's successful Minnesota Vikings team of 1973. He averaged more than 1,100 combined rushing and receiving yards in his eight years with the Vikings and played in three Super Bowls.

offensive end. In two seasons, the 6-5, 260-pound Ford caught 67 passes for 1,175 yards and eight touchdowns.

When the AAFC folded after the 1949 season, Ford was acquired by the Cleveland Browns, who had moved from the AAFC to the NFL. Head coach Paul Brown shifted Ford to defensive end, where he developed into such a devastating pass rusher that the Browns changed their defensive alignment to take advantage of his talents. By using linebackers behind two ends and two tackles, Cleveland created the first 4-3 defense. Ford overcame a serious nose and face injury to star in the 1950 NFL championship game. From 1951 to 1955, he was a virtually unanimous all-pro choice. He also played in four Pro Bowls. He stayed with Cleveland until 1957, then finished his career with the 1958 Green Bay Packers.

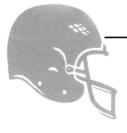

Formation

The alignment of offensive or defensive players on a play.

Fortmann, Dan

b. Pearl River, New York, 11 April 1916.
Hall of Fame: 1965

Dan Fortmann, a guard from Colgate University, was a ninth-round pick of the Chicago Bears in the first-ever NFL draft in 1936. Without the benefit of modern-day scouting methods, Bears' head coach George Halas supposedly picked Fortmann simply because he liked the sound of his name. At 6-0 and 207 pounds, Fortmann was too small for pro football line play, but the Phi Beta Kappa scholar was determined to prove Halas had made a good choice.

The youngest starter in the NFL in 1936, Fortmann was soon excelling as a little man in a big man's game. On offense, he called signals and was an excellent blocker. On defense, he was a genius at diagnosing enemy plays and making hard-hitting tackles. The Bears were one of pro football's dominant teams during Fortmann's eight-year career, which ended after the 1943 season. He was all-pro from 1938 to 1943.

Forty-five Second Clock

In 1988, the NFL voted to utilize a 45-second clock to replace the 30-second clock, which had been in use since 1976, to note the official time between the *ready-for-play signal* and the snap of the ball on the succeeding play. For a normal sequence of plays, the 45-second clock, which is visible to both teams, is started at the time the ball is *signaled dead* from the last play. After certain administrative stoppages and game delays, the clock is still started at 30 seconds.

Forward Progress

The furthest point of a ball carrier's advancement; a critical factor in the spotting of the ball by the officials after a play, particularly prior to a measurement for a first down.

Four-Three

A defensive formation featuring four linemen and three linebackers.

Fouts, Dan

b. San Francisco, California, 10 June 1951.
Dan Fouts, a 6-3, 210-pound quarterback from the University of Oregon, was a third-round

Dan Fortmann was only 19 when the Chicago Bears made him their ninth pick of the first college draft in 1936. He retired in 1943, at the age of 27, but in each of his final six seasons he was an all-pro selection.

choice of the San Diego Chargers in the 1973 draft. Fouts played with the Chargers for 15 seasons and amassed awesome passing records that have been surpassed in NFL history only by Fran Tarkenton. He retired in 1988. His career totals include 3,297 completions for 43,040 yards, 254 touchdowns, and an excellent 80.2 passing rating. He also rushed for 476 yards and 13 touchdowns.

Fouts holds eight NFL records. Included are 51 300-yard and six 400-yard passing games. In 1979, 1980, and 1981, when he led the Chargers to AFC Western Division championships, Fouts passed for more than 4,000 yards each year. He had a career-high 4,802 yards and 33 touchdowns in 1981. In the first playoff game that season, Fouts passed for 433 yards in leading the Chargers to an overtime victory over the Miami Dolphins.

Frankford Yellow Jackets

Frankford, Pennsylvania, a suburb of Philadelphia, was granted an NFL franchise in 1924. The team was called the Yellow Jackets and was one of the NFL's most successful teams during its eight-season tenure that ended when the club folded midway through the 1931 season. The Yellow Jackets won the 1926 NFL championship with a 14-1-1 record. Because of a Philadelphia law preventing spectator sports on Sunday, the Yellow Jackets played home games on Saturday and away games on Sunday.

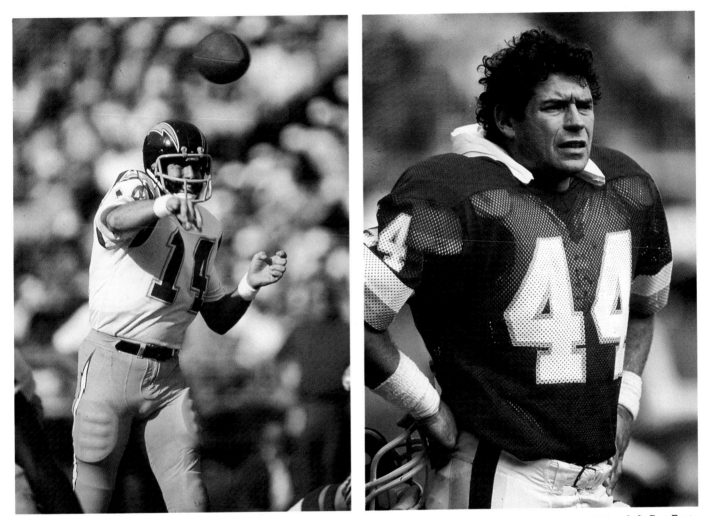

Free Agent

A player who can be signed by any club.

Free Kick

1. A kickoff.
2. A kick that puts the ball in play following a safety (or, infrequently, another kick). It can be a placekick, dropkick, or punt.
3. A kick after a fair catch.

Free Safety

A position in the defensive secondary. The free safety is not responsible for any specific offensive player but he follows the play and responds to its direction.

Friedman, Benny

b. Cleveland, Ohio, 18 March 1905;
d. 23 November 1982.
Benny Friedman, a 5-11, 175-pound quarterback, was considered by many to be the first authentic forward passing threat in the NFL. He also was an outstanding field leader. The former University of Michigan All-America began his pro career with the 1926 Kansas City Cowboys, then moved to the Cleveland Bulldogs in 1927. He went to the Detroit Wolverines in 1928 and to the New York Giants in 1929. After three seasons in New York, he became a part-owner of, as well as player with, the Brooklyn Dodgers in 1932. His career as an active player ended in 1934. Like all players of his time, Friedman played both offense and defense.

Fullback

The large offensive back stationed behind the quarterback who often is called upon to block or to carry the ball when a short gain is needed for a first down or touchdown.

Fumble

A loss of possession of the football by the ball carrier, punter, or kick holder. Anyone can recover a fumble.

Above left: Dan Fouts launches another raid by Air Coryell. With a receiving corps that included Charlie Joiner, Wes Chandler, and Kellen Winslow, the opposing defense was forced to play as if every down was a third-and-long situation.

Above: As the archetypal fullback, 240-pound John Riggins was almost unstoppable, especially with Washington's 'Hogs' on the offensive line. When he lined up in short yardage situations behind Joe Theismann, everybody knew what was going to happen, but few defenses could stop him.

The perfect gang tackle. Green Bay's Kenneth Davis is met by Brian Bosworth (55) of Seattle and a few of his friends, and this play is about to end abruptly.

G ★★★★★★★★★★★★★★★★★★★★

Gadget Play

A trick play.

Game Plan

The strategy and list of plays drawn up by the coaching staff before a game.

Gang Tackle

To stop a ball carrier with more than one – and often more than two – defenders.

Gap

1. The space between two offensive linemen.
2. A defense with a man in every gap.

Gatski, Frank

b. Farmington, West Virginia, 13 March 1922.
Hall of Fame: 1985

Frank Gatski was one of pro football's premier centers during his 12-year career that began with the 1946 Cleveland Browns of the All-America Football Conference. Gatski stayed with the Browns after they moved to the National Football League in 1950 and through the 1956 season. He retired after spending the 1957 season with the Detroit Lions.

Frank Gifford was versatile. He gained almost 10,000 combined yards – rushing, receiving, and returning kicks and interceptions – scoring 78 touchdowns. He also passed for 823 yards and 14 touchdowns, and kicked two field goals and 10 extra points.

The 6-3, 240-pound Gatski anchored the Browns' offensive line for 11 seasons without missing a single practice or game. An all-pro for four consecutive years in the early 1950s, Gatski played on 11 divisional or league championship teams in 12 seasons. The Browns won four AAFC titles and three more in the NFL. In the final game of his career, the 1957 NFL championship game, Gatski earned his eighth championship ring when the Lions whipped his old team, the Browns, 59-14. Gatski played college football at Marshall College and Auburn University.

Gehrke, Fred

b. Salt Lake City, Utah, 24 April 1918.

Fred Gehrke, a 5-11, 190-pound University of Utah graduate, began his NFL career as a halfback with the Cleveland Rams in 1940. He did not play again until 1945, and his post-war career lasted only six seasons. While Gehrke was a talented two-way player, he made his most lasting mark in pro football with his paint brush. In 1947, Rams coach Bob Snyder complained about the team's drab uniforms, and Gehrke, who worked as a technical illustrator between football seasons, responded by painting golden rams' horns on the team's dark blue helmets. The new helmets were an instant hit and all pro football clubs soon were developing more colorful uniforms.

George, Bill

b. Waynesburg, Pennsylvania, 27 October 1930; d. 30 September 1982. Hall of Fame: 1974

During the 1950s and early 1960s, when the Chicago Bears were one of pro football's most feared defensive teams, Bill George not only had to learn assistant coach Clark Shaughnessy's complicated system, but, as captain, he had to make it work on the field. The 6-2, 230-pound Wake Forest graduate carried out his job to near perfection.

George began his NFL career in 1952 as a middle guard in a five-man line. Two years later, a mid-game adjustment to combat the short passing attack of the Philadelphia Eagles resulted in George becoming a middle linebacker. A two-time all-pro choice as a middle guard, George then became an all-league middle linebacker six times in the next seven seasons. He was also selected for eight straight Pro Bowls. He played with the Bears for 14 seasons, then moved to the Los Angeles Rams for a final season in 1966. George died in an automobile accident in 1982.

Gibbs, Joe

b. Mocksville, North Carolina, 25 November 1940.

After 17 seasons as an assistant coach with four colleges and the St. Louis Cardinals, Tampa Bay Buccaneers, and San Diego Chargers of the NFL, Joe Gibbs was named the head coach of the Washington Redskins in 1981. After an 8-8 season in 1981, Gibbs launched the Redskins on a surge that produced four NFC East-ern Division championships, five playoff appearances, and two Super Bowl victories in a six-year period. In 1982, his second season, Gibbs led the Redskins to a 27-17 victory over the Miami Dolphins in Super Bowl XVII. He was named the NFL Coach of the Year, an honor he repeated in 1983 when the Redskins reached the Super Bowl before losing to the Los Angeles Raiders 38-9. In 1987, Washington defeated Minnesota 17-10 in the NFC championship game and then scored a record 35 points in the second quarter to defeat the Denver Broncos 42-10 in Super Bowl XXII.

Gibbs has led the Redskins to an 81-39-0 regular season record in his first eight years. His postseason record is even better, with 11 wins in 14 games. The Redskins' 7-9 record in 1988 was Gibbs' first losing season as head coach.

Gifford, Frank

b. Santa Monica, California, 16 August 1930. Hall of Fame: 1977

Frank Gifford's 12-year NFL tenure can be divided into two distinct parts, the first nine years from 1952 to 1960 when he was a do-everything running back for the New York Giants, and a final three seasons from 1962 to 1964 when he excelled as a wide receiver. The change in jobs came about because of a serious injury he suffered in 1960, when he was felled by a vicious but clean tackle by Philadelphia Eagles linebacker Chuck Bednarik. Gifford had to sit out the entire 1961 season.

The 6-1, 195-pound Gifford joined the 1952 Giants as a first-round draft choice after an All-America collegiate career at the University of Southern California. Extremely versatile, he was pressed into two-way service in 1953, a task that proved too much in the era of one-way specialists. Gifford developed into a major star only after new assistant coach Vince Lombardi claimed him exclusively for the offensive unit in 1954.

Gifford was named all-pro four times and won NFL Player-of-the-Year honors in 1956. He played in seven Pro Bowls, the first as a defensive back, the next five as an offensive halfback, and the seventh as a flanker. His career chart shows 3,609 yards rushing and 5,434 yards on 367 receptions. He also passed for 14 touchdowns and saw duty as a punt-return and kickoff-return specialist. He scored 484 points on 78 touchdowns, two field goals, and 10 conversions.

Gifford has since become part of the commentary team on the highly popular Monday Night Football telecasts, and spent a year anchoring the football coverage on British television.

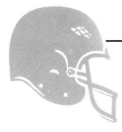

Gillman, Sid

b. Minneapolis, Minnesota, 26 October 1911.
Hall of Fame: 1983

Sid Gillman was the first coach to win divisional titles in both the American and National Football Leagues. His 1955 Los Angeles Rams won the NFL Western Conference title, and his 1960 Los Angeles Chargers won the AFL Western Conference title. After the Chargers moved to San Diego in 1961, Gillman continued to produce high-scoring teams that won four more divisional titles and the 1963 AFL championship. Gillman became widely recognized as a leading authority on passing theories and tactics.

As general manager-head coach of the Chargers, Gillman used his organizational skills both on and off the field to give both the Chargers and the AFL respect.

The Ohio State University graduate stayed with the Chargers until illness forced him to retire in 1969. He returned to the Chargers in 1971, but resigned in late season. His final head-coaching assignment came with the 1973-1974 Houston Oilers, and he was named the AFC Coach of the Year in 1974. His 18-year pro record was 123-104-7.

Sid Gillman's record as a coach in both the NFL and the early years of the AFL justifiably earned him a place in the Hall of Fame. Since his election in 1983, no other coaches have been so honored.

Goal Line

The line that marks the start of the end zone. A player scores a touchdown when the ball is above or over the goal line.

Goal Post

A Y-shaped, 40-foot, bright gold post positioned at each end line. A field goal or extra point kick must travel between the uprights (vertical posts) and over the horizontal crossbar, which is 18 feet, 6 inches in length and 10 feet above the ground.

Gogolak, Pete

b. Budapest, Hungary, 18 April 1941.

A twelfth-round draft choice of the Buffalo Bills of the American Football League in 1964, kicker Pete Gogolak from Cornell University became pro football's first soccer-style placekicker. After two excellent seasons in Buffalo, he played out his option and signed with the New York Giants of the rival NFL. Gogolak played nine more seasons with the Giants and wound up his 11-year pro career in 1974 with 863 points on 173 field goals and 344 extra points.

Gradishar, Randy

b. Warren, Ohio, 3 March 1952.

A first-round draft choice of the Denver Broncos in 1974, middle linebacker Randy Gradishar became the heart of one of the most outstanding defensive units in the NFL. The 6-2, 231-pound Ohio State graduate was named all-pro five straight years from 1977 to 1981. Gradishar played in Super Bowl XII and in seven Pro Bowls. He intercepted 20 passes and recovered 13 opponents' fumbles in his 10-year career.

Graham, Otto

b. Waukegan, Illinois, 6 December 1921.
Hall of Fame: 1965

Otto Graham was a tailback at Northwestern University and with the Chapel Hill, North Carolina, Pre-Flight team. But when head coach Paul Brown signed Graham for his new Cleveland Browns team in the All-America Football Conference, he envisioned him as the perfect quarterback for his T-formation attack. The 6-1, 195-pound Graham quickly learned the mechanics of the "T."

Graham led the Browns to either a divisional title or the AAFC or National Football League championship in each of the 10 years he played from 1946 through 1955. Led by Graham's passing and field leadership, the Browns won all four AAFC titles (1946-49), and NFL championships in 1950, 1954, and 1955. It is a record no other quarterback has ever matched.

Graham's finest title-game performance came in Cleveland's 56-10 lacing of the Detroit Lions in 1954. He threw three touchdown passes and

ran for three more scores. In his final game against the Los Angeles Rams in the 1955 NFL championship game, Graham ran for two touchdowns and passed for two others in a 38-14 victory. He was named all-pro nine times in 10 seasons. Graham's career passing record included 1,464 completions in 2,626 attempts for 23,584 yards, 174 touchdowns, and an 86.8 passing rating. In 1966, Graham was appointed coach of the Washington Redskins, a post he held for three seasons.

Grange, Harold (Red)

b. Forksville, Pennsylvania, 13 June 1903.
Hall of Fame: 1963

Nicknamed the "Galloping Ghost" because of his exceptional performances as a three-time All-America halfback at the University of Illinois, Harold (Red) Grange joined the Chicago Bears on Thanksgiving Day, 1925, just 10 days after his final college game. When he signed Grange, Bears owner-coach George Halas envisioned that Grange's popularity would draw attention not only to the Chicago team but to NFL football as a whole. Halas' hopes were realized when 36,000 filled Chicago's Wrigley Field to see Grange's debut. Sensing that a rare opportunity was at hand, Grange's agent, C.C. (Cash and Carry) Pyle, along with Halas, quickly lined up an 18-game coast-to-coast barnstorming tour. More than 400,000 fans saw the 6-0, 185-pound Grange in action with crowds of more than 70,000 in New York's Polo Grounds and 75,000 in the Los Angeles Coliseum highlighting the tour.

Pyle and Halas could not agree on terms for the 1926 season, so Pyle formed the rival American Football League, with Grange being assigned to the league's flagship team, the New York Yankees. The AFL folded after one year but the Yankees and Grange were accepted into the NFL in 1927. Because of a serious knee injury suffered in the 1927 season, Grange did not play in 1928, but he returned to his original team, the Bears, in 1929. He continued to play for the Bears through the 1934 season.

By Grange's own admission, he was "just an ordinary ball-carrier" after his injury. However, he did develop into an above-average defensive back who made a game-saving tackle to preserve the Bears' 23-21 victory over the New York Giants in the NFL's first official championship game in 1933. Grange enjoyed only moderate on-the-field success as a pro, yet he remains a key figure in pro football history.

Grant, Bud

b. Superior, Wisconsin, 20 May 1927.
Bud Grant was the Minnesota Vikings' head coach from 1967 to 1983 and then again in 1985.

Above: Red Grange was used as a pawn in the first interleague war, after his agent, C.C. Pyle, had a disagreement with George Halas. He had been the main attraction on Halas's barnstorming country-wide exhibition with the Bears in 1925.

Above left: Bud Grant looks concerned. The only title to elude the Vikings coach was the Super Bowl. He and Don Shula are the only coaches to lose four times, but Shula won on two occasions.

In 18 years, his teams compiled a .620 winning percentage (158-96-5) in regular-season play. His 168 coaching victories, including 10 in the postseason, place him eighth among all pro football coaches. In 1968, he launched the Vikings on a string of championships rarely equaled in sports. The Vikings won the NFL/NFC Central Division championship 11 times in 13 seasons from 1968 to 1980. Minnesota won the 1969 NFL championship, and NFC championships in 1973, 1974, and 1976. The Vikings played in four Super Bowls, losing all of them.

Grant was a three-sport star at the University of Minnesota. He first turned pro as a Minneapolis Lakers basketball player in 1949. In 1951, Grant signed with the NFL's Philadelphia Eagles, with whom he played for two years. Grant played four more seasons with Winnipeg of the Canadian Football League and coached the team for 10 seasons.

Greatest Game Ever Played

The 1958 NFL championship game, played before a sellout crowd of 64,185 in New York's Yankee Stadium and a large national television audience, was the first overtime playoff game in NFL history. The New York Giants trailed the Baltimore Colts 14-3 at halftime but Charlie Conerly's 15-yard touchdown pass to Frank Gifford on the first play of the fourth quarter put New York ahead 17-14. With 1:56 remaining, the Colts started a last-ditch drive from their own 14. Their 25-year-old quarterback, Johnny Unitas, passed seven consecutive times. He completed four, three of them to Raymond Berry, who caught a championship game-record 12 passes. With seven seconds remaining, Steve Myrha kicked a 20-yard field goal that sent the game into overtime.

In overtime, the Colts got the ball on their own 20. With textbook-perfect play selection, Unitas directed the Colts to a first down at the Giants' 8-yard line. On second-and-goal from the 7-yard line, he stunned the crowd by passing to tight end Jim Mutscheller at the 1-yard line. On third down, fullback Alan Ameche slashed off right tackle for the touchdown that gave the Colts a 23-17 victory after 8:15 of overtime.

The headline on the game story in *Sports Illustrated* called it "The Best Football Game Ever Played."

Green Bay Packers

The Green Bay Packers were big winners in two years of independent play before they joined the American Professional Football Association (the direct forerunner to the National Football League) in 1921. Today, the Packers exist as the third-oldest team in pro football, a sort of sports "dinosaur" as a small-city franchise in the big-city world of modern-day professional athletics. The 67-year history of the Green Bay team has been punctuated with both exhilarating success and the abyss of defeat.

If it hadn't been for Earl (Curly) Lambeau, the Packers' tenure in the NFL might have been limited to their initial 1921 season. In 1919, Lambeau, along with Earl Calhoun, talked his employer at the Indian Packing Company into providing $500 for equipment for a football team, plus use of the company athletic field for practice. With these tie-ins, the name Packers was a natural. After winning 19 of their first 22 games in 1919 and 1920, the Packers joined the APFA in 1921. After the season, however, owner John Clair was ordered to surrender the Green Bay franchise for using players who still were enrolled in college. At that point, Lambeau, who had served the team as tailback, head coach, general manager, publicity man, and ticket salesman, solicited help from other Green Bay businessmen to raise the cash to save the team. After Lambeau agreed to obey all league rules, he was awarded the franchise.

Under player-coach Lambeau, the Packers had a winning record every season in the 1920s, but they did not win their first championship until 1929. They won again in 1930 and 1931 to become the first NFL team to win three successive titles. Only one other club – the Packers themselves in 1965, 1966, and 1967 – has repeated the feat. The first Green Bay title team was powered by such all-time greats as halfback Johnny (Blood) McNally, tackle Cal Hubbard, and guard Mike Michalske.

Rifle-armed Arnie Herber joined the team in 1930, and fullback Clarke Hinkle came along two years later. Had ties counted as a half-win, half-loss as they do today, the 1932 Packers (10-3-1) would have won a fourth straight title.

In 1935, the team acquired another landmark player, end Don Hutson, who teamed with Herber and, later, Cecil Isbell to completely change the offensive face of pro football. A pioneer in developing the forward pass into an integral part of a pro offense, Lambeau made full use of Hutson's abilities. The Packers defeated the Boston Redskins 21-6 for the 1936 NFL championship. They won again in 1939 with a 27-0 victory over the New York Giants that avenged a 23-17 loss in the 1938 finale. Green Bay won its sixth and last championship under Lambeau by beating the Giants 14-7 in 1944. The Packers slipped badly in 1948 and 1949, and Lambeau resigned. He left Green Bay with a 212-106-21 record, having produced winning teams in 26 of his first 27 seasons.

The next decade was the lowest in the franchise's history. In the 1950s, four head coaches – Gene Ronzani, Hugh Devore, Lisle Blackbourn, and Scooter McLean – tried in vain to produce a winner. Finally, in 1959, Vince Lombardi, an assistant coach from the New York Giants, was hired. Lombardi promised he could produce results in five years, but he did better than that. In 1959, he guided the Packers to their first winning season in 12 years. The next year, Green Bay won the Western Conference title but lost the NFL championship game to Philadelphia.

In the next seven years, the Packers won conference and NFL championships in 1961, 1962, 1965, 1966, and 1967. They capped the last two seasons with victories in Super Bowls I and II. Green Bay heroes were commonplace. Quarterback Bart Starr led the offense with quality efforts from fullback Jim Taylor, halfback Paul Hornung, tackle Forrest Gregg, and center Jim Ringo. On defense, end Willie Davis, linebacker Ray Nitschke, cornerback Herb Adderley, and safety Willie Wood were perennial all-pros.

Before the 1968 season, Lombardi retired as the coach. He retained his general manager duties for one more year. Lombardi's nine-year record was 98-30-4. Football in Green Bay has not been the same since he left. The Packers' one moment of glory in the post-Lombardi era came in 1972 when they won the NFC Central Division title but lost to Washington in the first playoff game. In the 1980s, they have had one winning record and four .500 seasons. Four head coaches – including two former Packers playing stars, Starr and Gregg – have tried and failed to revive the winning tradition. In 1988, Lindy Infante became the team's fifth coach in 20 years.

Since 1955, the Packers have split their home games between Green Bay and Milwaukee. They play in Green Bay at 56,194-seat Lambeau Field and at 55,958-seat County Stadium in Milwaukee.

Members of the Hall of Fame:

(20) Herb Adderley, Tony Canadeo, Willie Davis, Forrest Gregg, Arnie Herber, Clarke Hinkle, Paul Hornung, Cal Hubbard, Don Hutson, Walt Kiesling, Earl (Curly) Lambeau, Vince Lombardi, Johnny (Blood) McNally, Mike Michalske, Ray Nitschke, Jim Ringo, Bart Starr, Jim Taylor, Emlen Tunnell, Willie Wood.

Championships Won:

Super Bowl: I (1966), II (1967)
NFL (pre-1970): 1929, 1930, 1931, 1936, 1939, 1944, 1961, 1962, 1965, 1966, 1967

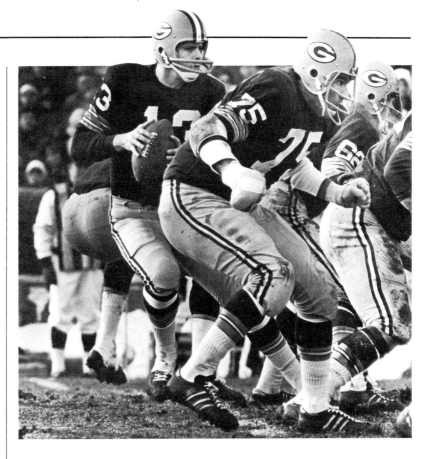

Western Conference: 1936, 1938, 1939, 1944, 1960, 1961, 1962, 1965, 1966, 1967
NFC Central Division: 1972

Overall Record:

NFL Regular Season	456	380	36	.544
NFL Postseason	13	5	0	.722
Total	469	385	36	.547

Forrest Gregg (75) was part of the Packers' dynasty of the 1960s, but as a coach he was unable to turn the Green Bay franchise around. He returned to coach his alma mater, S.M.U., after the college's two year suspension from football by the National Collegiate Athletic Association.

Gregg, Forrest

b. Birthright, Texas, 18 October 1933.
Hall of Fame: 1977

Although he wanted to play on the defensive line, Forrest Gregg was assigned to play offensive tackle by head coach Lisle Blackbourn when he joined the Green Bay Packers in 1956. Gregg knew he was too small to play that position, but he went right to work to build up his physical strength and to learn the methods he might use to finesse his much larger opponents into submission.

Gregg was in the military service in 1957 but he returned to the Packers in 1958 and played 13 standout seasons. He played a final year in 1971 with the Dallas Cowboys. The 6-4, 250-pound Southern Methodist University graduate was named all-pro eight consecutive years from 1960 through 1967, as Green Bay won five NFL championships. He also played in nine straight Pro Bowls. Injury-induced crises forced Gregg

to play guard in 1961 and again in 1965 but he made the switch with no loss of effectiveness. Gregg played in a then-record 188 straight games from 1958 until 1971.

Gregg spent 11 seasons coaching three teams – the Cleveland Browns, Cincinnati Bengals, and Green Bay Packers – compiling a 77-87-1 record. In January 1982, he led Cincinnati to Super Bowl XVI, where they were narrowly defeated by San Francisco.

Griese, Bob

b. Evansville, Indiana, 3 February 1945.

A two-time All-America at Purdue, Bob Griese was the Miami Dolphins' number-one draft choice in their second year in 1967. For 14 seasons until 1980, the 6-1, 190-pound quarterback was the poised leader of a classic ball-control offense that produced AFC championships in 1971, 1972, and 1973, and victories in Super Bowls VII and VIII. Honors came frequently for the bespectacled Griese. He was the NFL Player of the Year in 1971 and all-pro or all-AFC in 1971, 1973, and 1977. He played in two AFL All-Star games and six AFC-NFC Pro Bowls. The AFC passing leader in 1971 and the NFL passing champion in 1977, Griese had a career record of 1,926 pass completions for 25,092 yards and 192 touchdowns. His career passer rating was 77.3.

Groza, Lou

b. Martin's Ferry, Ohio, 25 January 1924.
Hall of Fame: 1974

Lou Groza played 21 seasons from 1946 until 1967 (he didn't play in 1960) with the Cleveland

Joe Greene is looking pensive. The Hall of Fame lineman need not worry because that is exactly what the opposition's offense is probably doing, trying to work out a plan to open Pittsburgh's steel curtain.

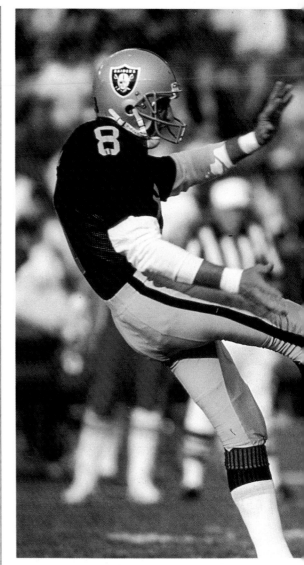

Browns and is best remembered as "The Toe," the first true kicking specialist in pro football. However, the 6-3, 250-pound Groza was also an excellent offensive tackle who was named all-pro six of the first eight years Cleveland was in the National Football League. In 1954, he was named Player of the Year. He played in nine Pro Bowls, six of them as a starting tackle.

Groza was a regular in the offensive line until a back injury forced him to miss the entire 1960 season. He returned in 1961 at the age of 37 and played seven more years solely as a kicker. In 21 seasons – the longest tenure of any player up to that time – the former Ohio State University player scored 1,608 points and for years ranked as the all-time leading scorer. He produced numerous Cleveland victories with his clutch kicking, but his most famous field goal came with time running out to give the Browns a 30-28 victory in the 1950 NFL championship game against the Los Angeles Rams.

Guyon, Joe

b. White Earth Indian Reservation, Mahnomen, Minnesota, 26 November 1892;
d. 27 November 1971. Hall of Fame: 1966

Joe Guyon, born O-Gee-Chidah, is one of only two American Indians to be elected to the Pro Football Hall of Fame (Jim Thorpe is the other). The versatile 6-1, 180-pounder used his athletic skills to gain a college education, something not ordinarily available to Indians in those years. He played on two national championship colle-

Below: The Packers' defense pushes back Matt Suhey of Chicago. For most the 1980s, it has been other NFL teams that have been doing the pushing on Green Bay; the Packers have not won a division title since 1972.

Guard

An offensive lineman who plays directly beside the center. There are two guards on each offensive line.

Guy, Ray

b. Swainsboro, Georgia, 22 December 1949.

In 1973, Ray Guy became the first punter drafted in the first round by an NFL team. He was selected by the Oakland Raiders, for whom he played the next 13 seasons. The 6-3, 205-pounder from the University of Southern Mississippi averaged 42.6 yards on his 959 career punts. He led the NFL in punting in 1974, 1975, and 1977. A seven-time Pro Bowl selection, Guy played in 191 consecutive regular-season games, plus 22 postseason games.

giate teams, Carlisle Indian School in 1912 and Georgia Tech in 1917. A halfback at Carlisle, Guyon was an All-America tackle at Georgia Tech.

His pro career as a triple-threat halfback began with the pre-NFL Canton Bulldogs in 1919. He played for six different teams, in all – the Bulldogs, Cleveland Indians, Oorang Indians, Rock Island Independents, Kansas City Cowboys, and New York Giants – in the NFL's first eight seasons. Because he played with Thorpe on four of those teams, Guyon did not get the attention he deserved until he joined the New York Giants in 1927. Playing before the media and fans of the nation's largest city, Guyon led the Giants to the 1927 NFL title. His touchdown pass in a 13-7 victory over the Chicago Bears was a key play in his team's drive to the championship.

Above left: Early in Super Bowl XVIII, the Los Angeles Raiders are punting at midfield. The snap goes 10 feet in the air. Ray Guy leaps, catches the ball single-handed, and punts it through the Redskins' end zone. Such athletic ability is one of the reasons he became the first punter ever drafted in the first round.

Hail Mary

In a 1975 NFC divisional playoff game, the favored Minnesota Vikings, playing at home, were leading Dallas 14-10 with 32 seconds to play. The Cowboys had the ball at the 50-yard-line. From the shotgun formation, Cowboys quarterback Roger Staubach threw a long pass toward wide receiver Drew Pearson, who streaked down the right sideline. As Minnesota cornerback Nate Wright adjusted to the flight of the pass, which was a little short, he slipped and fell. Pearson caught the ball on the 5-yard line and stepped in for the winning touchdown. Staubach, discussing the play after the game, said, "It was just a Hail Mary pass . . . a very, very lucky play."

Halas, George

b. Chicago, Illinois, 2 February 1895; d. 31 October 1983. Hall of Fame: 1963

One of the founders of the National Football League, the "Mr. Everything" of pro football, George Halas was in the NFL for 64 years – from 1920 until his death.

The University of Illinois graduate founded the Decatur Staleys in 1919 and brought his team into the American Professional Football Association (the direct forerunner of the NFL) at the first organizational meeting in Canton in 1920. At one time or another, particularly in the early years, Halas filled the roles of owner, general manager, player (he was an end), promoter, and ticket manager for the Bears, while being an influential policy maker at league level.

But it was as a coach that he excelled. He served four 10-year terms as the Bears' coach – 40 years in all – and led his teams to 325 victories, far more than any other coach (his total record was 325-151-31). His Bears teams won six NFL titles, the first coming in 1921 after his Decatur Staleys moved to Chicago and the last in 1963. Halas was a player-coach from 1920 to 1929. He "fired" himself as coach when he retired as a player, but, three years later, in 1933, he hired himself back because the Bears were in financial difficulty and "I came cheap." His

second tenure was terminated by a Navy call in 1942, and he aborted a third term in 1955 to give his old friend, Paddy Driscoll, a chance to run the team. He finally called it quits for good in 1968, when he was 73. As a coach, Halas was a true innovator, the first to hold daily practice sessions, to utilize films of opponents' games for study, to schedule a barnstorming tour, and to have his team's games broadcast on radio. Along with Ralph Jones, his coach from 1930 to 1932, and consultant Clark Shaughnessy, Halas perfected the T-formation attack with the man in motion. In the 1940 NFL championship game, his T-powered Bears annihilated the Washington Redskins, 73-0, in the NFL's most one-sided defeat ever. It was the crowning achievement of a career filled with outstanding successes.

Half

A 30-minute period; two make up a game.

Halfback

A player in the offensive backfield who usually lines up behind and to one side of the quarterback. He generally is the fastest member of the backfield and often is the most-used ball carrier.

Halftime

The intermission (usually 15 minutes) between the first and second halves of a game. During halftime, teams leave the field, rest, and prepare second half strategy.

Ham, Jack

b. Johnstown, Pennsylvania, 23 December 1948. Hall of Fame: 1988

Jack Ham, an All-America linebacker from Penn State, joined the Pittsburgh Steelers as a number two draft pick in 1971. With three interceptions in the last preseason game against the New York Giants, the 6-1, 225-pound Ham won the starting left linebacker job as a rookie and was never anything but a starter in a 12-year tenure that ended after the 1982 season. With speed, intelligence, and an exceptional ability to diagnose plays, Ham gained a reputation as a big-play defender. In his career, he had 25½ sacks, recovered 21 fumbles, and made 32 interceptions.

Ham was an all-pro or all-AFC pick seven consecutive years from 1973 to 1979. He also was named to eight straight Pro Bowls. He played in Super Bowls IX, X, and XIII but sat out XIV because of injuries. In his first year of eligibility, Ham became the second Steeler from the dynasty years to be elected to the Hall of Fame.

Hanburger, Chris

b. Hampton, Virginia, 13 August 1941.

Chris Hanburger was selected by the Washington Redskins on the eighteenth round of the 1964 draft. He excelled as an outside linebacker and defensive signal-caller with the Redskins for 14 seasons until 1978. The University of North Carolina graduate was a nine-time Pro Bowl selection and was named all-pro in 1972, 1973, and 1976. The 6-2, 218-pound Virginian played 135 consecutive games starting in 1967 and continuing until he was sidelined by appendicitis in 1977. He intercepted 19 passes and recovered 14 opponents' fumbles in his career.

Handoff

Giving the ball, hand to hand, to another player. Usually occurs between the quarterback and a running back.

Hannah, John

b. Canton, Georgia, 4 April 1951.

John Hannah, a 6-3, 265-pound guard, was the New England Patriots' first-round selection in the 1973 NFL draft. During the next 13 seasons, the two-time consensus All-America from the University of Alabama was a nine-time Pro Bowl selection. Hannah concluded his career in 1985, when he won all-pro honors for the fourth time and played a major role in the Patriots' drive to their first AFC championship.

Harder, Merlin (Pat)

b. Milwaukee, Wisconsin, 6 May 1922.

Merlin (Pat) Harder, an All-America fullback at the University of Wisconsin, served two years in the U.S. Marines before beginning his pro football career with the Chicago Cardinals in 1946. He played with the Cardinals through the 1950 season, then was traded to the Detroit Lions, with whom he played through the 1953 season. Harder, an all-pro choice in 1947, 1948, and 1949, also played in the first two Pro Bowls. The 5-11, 205-pounder was an excellent ball carrier, a reliable pass receiver, and a sure-footed placekicker. He led the NFL in scoring in 1947, 1948, and 1949. In his career, he scored 531 points on 38 touchdowns, 198 extra points, and 35 field goals. He also rushed for 3,016 yards and caught 92 passes for 864 yards in his career.

Harris, Franco

b. Fort Dix, New Jersey, 7 March 1950.

Franco Harris, a 6-2, 225-pound running back from Penn State, was the first-round draft pick of the Pittsburgh Steelers in 1972. He played with the Steelers for 12 seasons before finishing his career with the Seattle Seahawks in 1984. In 1972, Harris had the first of his eight 1,000 rushing seasons and was the only rookie to be selected for the Pro Bowl. In a 1972 AFC playoff game, he was involved in one of history's most famous plays, the so-called "Immaculate Reception" of a deflected forward pass that gave Pittsburgh a 13-7 win over Oakland with five seconds left. Harris was a three-time all-AFC pick and a Pro Bowl choice nine straight years from 1972 to 1980.

Harris holds the Super Bowl record for the most career yards rushing (354) and the most

As halfbacks go, few are as elusive as Eric Dickerson. He wears nearly every form of protection allowed by the NFL, believing that if it can be used to protect a player, he should wear it.

touchdowns (4). His 400 rushes for 1,556 yards and 16 touchdowns all are NFL postseason records. In 13 years, he rushed 2,949 times for 12,120 yards and 91 touchdowns. He also had 307 receptions for 2,287 yards and scored 600 points on 100 touchdowns. He now ranks fourth among lifetime rushing leaders.

Above: Jack Ham, patrolling the field from his outside linebacker position, was another powerful reason the Pittsburgh Steelers were such a dominant team in the 1970s.

Hashmarks

The lines one yard apart on the field that are used for spotting the ball. The marks are located 70 feet, 9 inches from each sideline.

Hay, Ralph

b. Canton, Ohio, 12 January 1891;
d. 29 July 1944.

Ralph Hay was the owner-manager of the Canton Bulldogs at the time the American Professional Football Association held its organizational meeting at his behest on September 17, 1920. He operated a Hupmobile automobile dealership, and the meeting was held in his showroom. There were not enough chairs in the room and some of those present, including George Halas of the Decatur Staleys, had to sit on the running boards and fenders of the automobiles.

Hayes, Bob

b. Jacksonville, Florida, 20 December 1942.

Bob Hayes was billed as the "World's Fastest Human" when he joined the Dallas Cowboys in 1965. Mixing football with track at Florida A&M, Hayes set world records in both the 100-yard and 100-meter dashes and won two gold medals in the 1964 Olympics. The 5-11, 185-pound speedster was an immediate hit with the Cowboys with 46 pass receptions for 1,003 yards and a sensational 21.8-yard average per catch in his rookie season. In 1968, he led the NFL in punt returns. Hayes played with the Cowboys for 10 years before moving to San Francisco for a final season in 1975. In 11 seasons, he had 371 pass receptions for 7,414 yards, a 20.0-yard average, and 71 touchdowns.

Haynes, Abner

b. Denton, Texas, 19 September 1937.

Abner Haynes, a 6-1, 198-pound halfback from North Texas State University, was the AFL's first Player of the Year in 1960 as a rookie with the Dallas Texans. That season, he led the AFL in rushing, punt returns, and combined net yards. He rushed for 1,049 yards in 1962 and scored two touchdowns in the Texans' 20-17 overtime win over Houston in the AFL championship game. Haynes was a three-time All-AFL selection and played in three of the first four AFL All-Star games. He was traded to the Denver Broncos in 1965 and finished his career with Miami and the New York Jets in 1967. In eight years, Haynes accumulated 4,630 yards rushing, 3,535 yards on receptions, 875 yards on punt returns, and 3,025 yards on kickoff returns.

Healey, Ed

b. Indian Orchard, Massachusetts, 28 December 1894; d. 9 December 1978. Hall of Fame: 1964.

Ed Healey had enjoyed only average success as an end at Dartmouth College and was loading meat into railroad cars in Omaha, Nebraska, when he heard of a new professional league being formed. He took an overnight train to Rock Island, Illinois, to try out with the Independents. He did well enough against the Chicago Tigers to be offered $100 a game to join the team on a permanent basis.

Healey always did particularly well against George Halas, the player-coach of the Chicago Bears. So late in the 1922 season, Halas decided to buy the 6-3, 220-pound tackle. He offered the Independents $100, the exact amount the Rock Island team owed the Bears in back gate receipts and the deal was closed. Healey was an unofficial all-pro pick five times before his retirement after the 1927 season.

Heffelfinger, William (Pudge)

b. Minneapolis, Minnesota, 20 December 1867; d. 2 April 1953.

William (Pudge) Heffelfinger is the first person known to have been paid cash for playing football. He received $500 for playing for the Allegheny Athletic Association against the Pittsburgh Athletic Club on November 12, 1892. While $500 would have been unusually high pay for a guard even several decades later, Heffelfinger did score the game's only touchdown when he forced a fumble, picked up the ball, and ran 35 yards for a touchdown, which was four points in those days. Heffelfinger had been an All-America star at Yale in 1889, 1890, and 1891, and the most revered gridiron hero in the nation after graduation. When he was recruited by the AAA, he was on leave of absence from a railroad job in Omaha, Nebraska, and playing with the excellent Chicago Athletic Association team that attracted its players with "double expense money," a more-or-less standard practice in the early 1890s. Heffelfinger, who never admitted he ever had been paid to play football, was first offered $250 to play for the Pittsburgh Athletic Club against the AAA but declined on the grounds that he couldn't risk his amateur standing. But apparently, for $500, his amateur standing wasn't that important.

Heidi Game

On November 17, 1968, the New York Jets and Oakland Raiders were locked in a tense game in Oakland. The Jets led 32-29 with 1:05 to play

when NBC television cut away from the game to begin the movie, *Heidi.* The network's switchboards lit up with angry protests when the Raiders rallied for two late touchdowns to win 43-32 in what later was called the "Heidi Game."

Hein, Mel

b. Redding, California, 22 August 1909. Hall of Fame: 1963

Mel Hein led Washington State to the Rose Bowl in 1930, and during his college career was an outstanding player at three positions – tackle, guard, and center. Yet, he had to write three NFL teams to offer his services. He first accepted a $135-a-game offer from the Providence Steam Roller but wired the Providence postmaster to intercept the contract when the New York Giants upped the ante to $150 a game. To make the 25-man squad and earn a $200 advance he had received from the Giants, the 6-2, 225-pound Hein had to beat out two veteran performers.

That was the last time in Hein's pro career he had to worry about a paycheck. For the next 15 years, he was a fixture at center for the Giants. Hein was a 60-minute star – a center on offense and a linebacker on defense – who called time

Pat Harder was an offensive threat both as a rusher and receiver. He also was an accurate kicker, and led the NFL in scoring for three consecutive seasons, 1947-1949, earning all-pro honors each year.

Opposite bottom: John Hannah was possibly the best offensive lineman of the last two decades. He played his final game for the Patriots, his only team, in Super Bowl XX, when Chicago's 46 defense destroyed New England 46-10.

out just once for hasty repairs to a broken nose in 1941. Hein was named the official all-pro center eight straight years from 1933 to 1940. In 1938, he was selected as the league's Most Valuable Player, a rare honor for a center.

Helmet

The protective piece of equipment that is worn on each player's head.

Hendricks, Ted

b. Guatemala City, Guatemala, 1 November 1947.

Ted Hendricks, a 6-7, 235-pound All-America linebacker from the University of Miami (Florida), was a second-round pick of the Baltimore Colts in the 1969 NFL draft. In his 15-year pro football career, he played five years with the Colts, one season (1974) with the Green Bay Packers, and the last nine years (1975-1983) with the Oakland/Los Angeles Raiders. Hendricks played in eight Pro Bowls, plus seven AFC championship games and four Super Bowls. In his career, he intercepted 26 passes. His four recoveries of opponents' fumbles in postseason games tie the all-time record.

Hennigan, Charley

b. Bienville, Louisville, 19 March 1935.

Charley Hennigan, a 1958 graduate of Northwestern Louisiana State College, was teaching biology when he wrote the Houston Oilers for a tryout and went on to make their new AFL team in 1960. The 6-1, 193-pound flanker quickly developed into one of pro football's premier pass receivers. In 1964, he had 101 receptions, a record surpassed only by Washington's Art Monk in 1984. A four-time All-AFL star, Hennigan played in the first five AFL All-Star games. He retired in 1966, after catching 410 passes for 6,183 yards and 51 touchdowns in his seven-year career.

Henry, Wilbur (Pete)

*b. Mansfield, Ohio, 31 October 1897;
d. 7 February 1952. Hall of Fame: 1963*

At 6-0, 250 pounds, seemingly both short and pudgy, Wilbur (Pete) Henry did not look like a football player. But the Washington and Jefferson College graduate was an uncompromising competitor as a two-way tackle and a superior punter, placekicker, and dropkicker. For many years, his name was in the NFL record book for his exceptional kicking achievements – a 50-yard dropkick field goal in 1922 and a 94-yard punt the next year.

Wilbur (Pete) (or Fats) Henry's signing with the Canton Bulldogs was the biggest item of news in Ohio that day and the formation of the APFA (the NFL's forerunner) was relegated to a minor page.

The news of Henry's signing with the Canton Bulldogs on September 17, 1920, drew banner headlines in the *Canton Repository* while the formation of the American Professional Football Association (soon to be called the NFL) that same day in Canton was relegated to the third sports page. "Fats," as he was also known, played 60 minutes every game in the Bulldogs' 1922 and 1923 championship seasons. His 40-yard field goal that tied Akron 3-3 preserved Canton's undefeated 1922 season. Henry played with the Bulldogs from 1920 to 1923, and in 1925 and 1926. He finished his career with the 1927 New York Giants and the 1927 and 1928 Pottsville Maroons.

Herber, Arnie

*b. Green Bay, Wisconsin, 2 April 1910;
d. 14 October 1969. Hall of Fame: 1966*

A native of Green Bay, Arnie Herber was working in the Packers' clubhouse when coach Curly Lambeau decided to give the 20-year-old a tryout. Herber, who had played briefly at the University of Wisconsin and Regis College in Denver, was signed to a $75-a-game contract. The 6-1, 200-pounder threw a touchdown pass to give Green Bay a 7-0 victory in his first game as a rookie in 1930, and throughout his 11 years in Green Bay, the Packers were perpetual contenders, winning four NFL titles. Herber was also a fine runner and punter.

Herber won NFL passing championships three of the first five years such records were kept. In 1935, he joined with a heralded new end, Don Hutson, to form pro football's first lethal pass-catch team. Herber-to-Hutson passes provided major headaches for NFL defenders until the quarterback retired after the 1940 season. He returned to action in 1944 with the manpower-short New York Giants and then retired for good after the 1945 season. He passed for 8,033 yards and 79 touchdowns in his career.

Hewitt, Bill

b. Bay City, Michigan, 8 October 1909;
d. 14 January 1947. Hall of Fame: 1971

Bill Hewitt was only an average football player at the University of Michigan, but he became an outstanding NFL end with the Chicago Bears from 1932 to 1936 and the Philadelphia Eagles from 1937 to 1939. He also played a final 1943 season with the wartime-merged Eagles-Steelers team. The 5-11, 191-pound Hewitt was an "iron-man" performer, a skilled receiver on offense, and a sure tackler on defense.

Hewitt was the first player to be named to the official all-NFL honor roll with two different teams. He was all-pro with the Bears in 1933, 1934, and 1936, and with the Eagles in 1937. Innovative and clever, he was always thinking of ways to outsmart the opposition. One of his special plays called for a jump pass from fullback Bronko Nagurski to Hewitt, who would, in turn, lateral to another end, Bill Karr, racing toward the goal line. It was this play that gave the Bears a 23-21 victory in the first NFL championship game in 1933. Three years after he retired, Hewitt died in an automobile accident.

Hickerson, Gene

b. Trenton, Tennessee, 15 February 1936.

Gene Hickerson's pro football career began with the 1958 Cleveland Browns and continued for 15 seasons until 1973. Except for the entire 1961 season, which he missed with a broken leg, the 6-3, 260-pound guard from the University of Mississippi did not sit out a single game in his career. Hickerson was named all-pro in 1967, 1968, 1969, and 1970. He played in six consecutive Pro Bowls from 1965 to 1970.

Highest-Scoring Game

On November 27, 1966, the New York Giants scored 41 points against the Washington Redskins . . . and lost by 31 points! The 113 points scored by both teams in Washington's 72-41 victory are the most in an NFL game.

Hinkle, Clarke

b. Toronto, Ohio, 10 April 1912;
d. 9 November 1988. Hall of Fame: 1964

Best known for his head-to-head duels with Bronko Nagurski, the Chicago Bears' battering ram fullback, Clarke Hinkle played 10 seasons with the Green Bay Packers from 1932 to 1941. The 5-11, 201-pound fullback from Bucknell University was a pile-driving runner and a savage blocker. He was an excellent receiver, and also was the Packers' punter and placekicker. He was even more effective as a linebacker on the defensive unit.

Hinkle was signed for $125 a game after Green Bay head coach Curly Lambeau watched him play in the 1932 East-West Shrine game in San Francisco. He was named all-pro four times in 10 years. Nagurski was his biggest rival on the field but also one of his staunchest admirers. When Hinkle was elected to the Hall of Fame, Nagurski was presenter at the induction ceremonies.

Far left: Gene Hickerson's career was one of the longest in the NFL. The offensive lineman (66) did not miss a single game from 1958-1960 and 1962-1973.

Left: Clarke Hinkle is best known for success in dealing with Bronko Nagurski. Their battles were a major feature of games between Green Bay and Chicago, especially as both were two-way players in the fullback-linebacker mold.

Paul Hornung dives into the end zone. He is the only player to have rushed for more than 50 touchdowns and successfully kicked more than 50 field goals. In 1960, he scored 15 touchdowns, 15 field goals and 41 conversions, for 176 points.

Hirsch, Elroy (Crazylegs)

b. Wausau, Wisconsin, 17 June 1923.
Hall of Fame: 1968

Elroy (Crazylegs) Hirsch spent three years as a halfback with the Chicago Rockets of the All-America Football Conference from 1946 to 1948. A series of injuries culminating with a fractured skull in 1948 almost ended his career, but the determined Hirsch moved to the Los Angeles Rams in 1949. In 1950, he was shifted to end by new Rams' head coach Joe Stydahar. One year later, Hirsch enjoyed a great season while leading the Rams to the NFL championship.

The 6-2, 190-pounder scored a record-tying 17 touchdowns on pass receptions in 1951 but it was the distance of his scoring strikes that awed opponents and teammates alike. Tops was a 91-yard catch and run against the Chicago Bears but Hirsch also had scoring receptions of 34, 44, 47, 53, 70, 72, 76, 79, and 81 yards that season. An All-America at both the Universities of Wisconsin and Michigan, Hirsch caught 387 passes in his pro career that ended after the 1957 season. His receptions accounted for 7,029 yards and 60 touchdowns. He also recorded 15 interceptions during his days as a two-way player early in his career.

Holder

One player, the holder, is allowed to prop the ball upright with his finger to aid the place-kicker on field goals, extra points, and, during windy games, kickoffs.

Holding

A penalty called for illegal grabbing or grasping of another player.

Hole

1. The space opened by blockers for a runner.
2. A numbered space in the offensive line.

Hornung, Paul

b. Louisville, Kentucky, 23 December 1935.
Hall of Fame: 1986

A Heisman Trophy-winning quarterback at Notre Dame in 1956, Paul Hornung was the bonus draft pick of the Green Bay Packers in 1957. The 6-2, 220-pound Hornung split his playing time between halfback and quarterback until 1959, when first-year head coach Vince Lombardi installed him at left halfback. Outstanding as a runner, receiver, and place-kicker, he led the NFL in scoring three consecutive years beginning in 1959, with his top season coming in 1960, when he scored a record 176 points. In nine NFL seasons, he scored 760 points, rushing for 3,711 yards and catching 130 passes for 1,480 more. He even threw five touchdown passes.

In both 1960 and 1961, when the Packers began their string of championship seasons, "The Golden Boy" was named the NFL's Most Valuable Player. In the 1961 NFL championship game, Hornung got a Christmas leave from the Army, then scored a playoff-record 19 points in

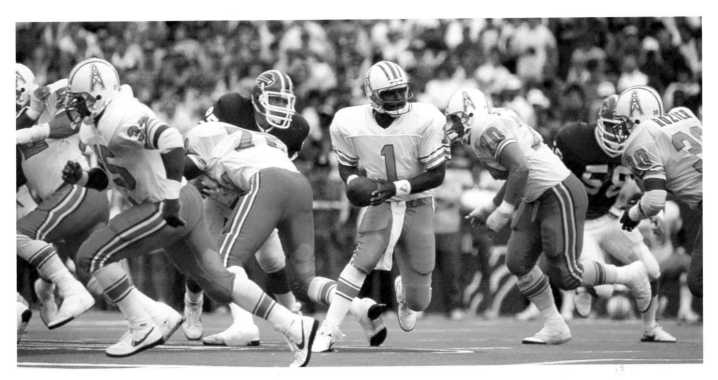

Green Bay's 37-0 victory over the New York Giants. Although he scored five touchdowns against the Baltimore Colts in 1965, Hornung never really regained his old-time form when he returned to action after a one-year suspension for gambling in 1963. He retired after the 1966 season. Hornung abd Chuck Bednarik are the only two bonus first round picks to be elected to the pro Football Hall of Fame.

Houston, Ken

b. Lufkin, Texas, 12 November 1944.
Hall of Fame: 1986

Ken Houston had an outstanding 14-year career as a safety, beginning with the Houston Oilers in 1967 and concluding with the Washington Redskins in 1980. After six seasons with the Oilers, he was sent to the Redskins in exchange for five players, three of whom became instant regulars for the Oilers. He was either all-pro or all-AFC/ NFC eight of nine years from 1971 through 1979. He was selected for two AFL All-Star games and 10 Pro Bowls. Only Rams defensive tackle Merlin Olsen has been named to more Pro Bowls.

Blessed with excellent speed and quickness, the 6-3, 198-pound Prairie View A&M graduate was a punishing tackler. And although Houston never won a league interception title, he did make 49 interceptions in 14 years. They were returned for 898 yards and nine touchdowns, the latter an all-time record. In his first year of eligibility, Houston was elected to the Hall of Fame.

Houston Oilers

When the American Football League was formally organized on August 14, 1959, K.S. (Bud) Adams, Jr., of Houston was awarded one of six charter franchises. He called his team the Oilers; named Billy Cannon, the All-America from Louisiana State, as his first draft choice; and leased Jeppesen Stadium, a high school facility, increasing its capacity from 22,000 to 36,000. George Blanda, a former Chicago Bears quarterback, was lured out of retirement, and the Oilers were ready to play.

They started fast, defeating the Los Angeles Chargers 24-16 in the 1960 AFL Championship Game, and repeating in 1961 with a 10-3 victory over the Chargers, who had moved to San Diego. With 36 touchdown passes in 1961, Blanda was the AFL's Most Valuable Player, and the Oilers became the first pro team to score more than 500 points in a single season. Houston's 11-3 regular-season record in 1962 still stands as the best in the franchise's history. But the Oilers lost 20-17 to the Dallas Texans in a classic six-quarter, two-overtime championship game. In spite of the team's success, three different head coaches – Lou Rymkus, Wally Lemm, and Frank (Pop) Ivy – served Houston in the first three seasons. In 1964, wide receiver Charley Hennigan set an all-time record with 101 receptions.

Blanda was traded to the Oakland Raiders in 1967, but Lemm returned for a second term as head coach. In 1967, the Oilers combined the powerful running of Hoyle Granger and a sur-

Houston Oilers quarterback Warren Moon takes the snap. The Oilers were a wild-card team in both 1987 and 1988, winning their first game, but then losing in the divisional playoff round each year.

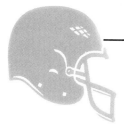

prisingly strong defense led by rookie linebacker George Webster to win their fourth divisional championship. Ken Houston, destined to become one of the best strong safeties of his time, also joined the Oilers in 1967. In the AFL championship game, however, the Oakland Raiders prevailed 40-7. Houston moved into 70,000-seat Rice Stadium in 1965, but three years later made a permanent shift to the 50,594-seat Astrodome.

The early 1970s were not good years for the Oilers. After consecutive 1-13 seasons, former Chargers head coach Sid Gillman led Houston to a 7-7 record in 1974 and was named the AFC Coach of the Year. The Oilers made further progress under O.A. (Bum) Phillips, who replaced Gillman the next year. They finished second to the Pittsburgh Steelers in the AFC Central Division three consecutive years (1978, 1979, and 1980), winning wild-card playoff spots each year. They lost to Pittsburgh in two AFC championship games – 34-5 in 1978, and 27-13 in 1979. In 1980, the Oilers lost to Oakland 27-7 in the first-round playoff game. Houston was powered by the running of Earl Campbell and the passing of Dan Pastorini and Ken Stabler. Three days after the 1980 playoff loss, however, Phillips was fired.

Houston suffered through six consecutive losing seasons from 1981 through 1986 but finished second in its division in 1987 with a 9-6 record under head coach Jerry Glanville. The Oilers defeated Seattle 23-20 in a wild-card playoff game but fell to the eventual AFC-champion Denver Broncos 34-10 in the second round. The Oilers earned another wild-card berth in 1988 with a 10-6 record, and defeated Cleveland in the playoffs before losing to Buffalo.

Members of the Hall of Fame:
(4) George Blanda, Sid Gillman, Ken Houston, John Henry Johnson

Championships Won:
AFL: 1960, 1961
AFL Eastern Division: 1960, 1961, 1962, 1967

Overall Record:
AFL Regular Season	70	66	4	.514
AFL Postseason	2	3	0	.400
NFL Regular Season	113	165	2	.407
NFL Postseason	6	5	0	.545
Total	191	239	6	.445

Howley, Chuck

b. Wheeling, West Virginia, 28 June 1936.
Chuck Howley's pro football career began in 1958, when he was the first-round draft pick of the Chicago Bears. After missing the entire 1960 season with an injury, the 6-2, 225-pound outside linebacker was traded to the Dallas

Cowboys in 1961. With the Cowboys, the West Virginia University graduate became a key man in Dallas's "Doomsday Defense" for 13 seasons. Howley was named all-pro in the five seasons from 1966 through 1970. He was named the Most Valuable Player in Super Bowl V, the only player from a losing team to be selected. In his career, Howley intercepted 25 passes, which he returned for 399 yards and two touchdowns.

Hubbard, Robert (Cal)

b. Keytesville, Missouri, 31 October 1900;
d. 17 October 1977. Hall of Fame: 1963
A 6-5, 250-pounder, Robert (Cal) Hubbard played nine seasons in the NFL. As a linebacker on defense, Hubbard used his height to become proficient at blocking passes just as they were thrown. After playing at both Centenary College and Geneva College, Hubbard joined the 1927 New York Giants as a $150-a-game rookie. He was an overnight sensation, using his speed to plug holes other linemen could not reach. Traded to the Green Bay Packers in 1929 after playing end with the Giants, Hubbard became a five-time all-pro tackle with the Packers. He played in Green Bay through the 1935 season.

Hubbard retired after the 1936 season with the New York Giants and Pittsburgh Steelers, then turned to baseball umpiring, a career for which he had been preparing. Hubbard is the only man to be elected to both the Pro Football and Baseball Halls of Fame.

Huddle

A brief, separated gathering by the offense and the defense for calling the next play between downs.

Sam Huff's expression epitomizes the heart and soul of life in the trenches. The New York and Washington defensive star intercepted 30 passes, the second-best figure for a Hall of Fame linebacker.

Huff, Sam

b. Morgantown, West Virginia, 4 October 1934.
Hall of Fame: 1982

Sam Huff began his career as the New York Giants' middle linebacker in 1956. The Giants were a winning team in the nation's largest city, and Huff soon became one of the most publicized of all pro players, the symbol of the new glamour era for defensive football. The University of West Virginia All-America was named all-pro four times, picked as the NFL's top linebacker in 1959, and selected for five Pro Bowls, four of them in his eight seasons with the Giants. The 6-1, 230-pound Huff was best known for his personal duels with great running backs such as Jim Brown and Jim Taylor, but he was also adept at pass defense as his 30 career pass interceptions indicate. When Huff first joined the Giants, the team's coaches were having a difficult time finding the correct position for him. Then Ray Beck, the regular middle linebacker, was injured. Huff got a chance to fill in, and he never had to worry about a regular football job again. In 1964, he was traded to the Washington Redskins, with whom he played until 1967. He returned after a year's retirement for a final season in 1969.

Hunt, Lamar

b. El Dorado, Arkansas, 2 August 1932.
Hall of Fame: 1972

Continually frustrated in his attempts to buy an NFL franchise, Lamar Hunt, a 26-year-old Southern Methodist University graduate, decided to form his own football league. He first approached K.S. (Bud) Adams, Jr., of Houston, who had also been trying to obtain an NFL team. Several others joined in and, on 14 August 1959, the American Football League (the fourth league to have that name) was born. In September 1960, the AFL began play, and six years later, on 8 June 1966, the AFL-NFL merger ended sports history's longest and most costly inter-league war.

Hunt's AFL team was the Dallas Texans, and, although they did well in their intra-city rivalry with the NFL's Cowboys, Hunt moved the team to Kansas City in 1963. During the AFL's 10-year lifetime, the Texans/Chiefs had the best won-lost record (87-48-5) of any AFL team. They won three league championships, played in the first Super Bowl, and in the last game ever played by an AFL team, they upset the Minnesota Vikings 23-7 in Super Bowl IV.

Hunt's election to the Hall of Fame came in recognition of his bold move in challenging the established NFL that forever changed, for the better, the entire pro football world.

Hutson, Don

b. Pine Bluff, Arkansas, 31 January 1913.
Hall of Fame: 1963

Don Hutson, who played with the Green Bay Packers from 1935 to 1945, was pro football's first game-breaking pass receiver. The All-America from the University of Alabama scored on an 83-yard pass on his very first scrimmage play as a rookie. When he retired after 11 superb seasons, he led all receivers with 488 catches (the number two career receiver at the time had just 190 receptions).

The mere presence of the 6-1, 180-pound speedster changed the defensive concept of pro football. With two excellent quarterbacks (Arnie Herber and Cecil Isbell) to throw to him, Hutson could out-maneuver and outrace virtually every NFL defender. Such measures as double-teaming and even triple-teaming were hastily introduced. Making Hutson's achievements even more remarkable was the fact that he also played safety on defense. In his final five seasons, he intercepted 24 passes, including one he returned 85 yards for a touchdown. Hutson also served as the Packers' kicking specialist, scoring almost 200 points by kicking and winding up his career with 823 points. He scored 105 touchdowns and his 99 scoring receptions is still an NFL record.

In these days of specialization, two-sport players are almost unheard of, so Cal Hubbard's election to both the Pro Football and the Major League Baseball Hall of Fame is a feat unlikely to be repeated.

Bart Starr dives in to score the decisive touchdown as Green Bay defeats Dallas 21-17 on frozen Lambeau Field to win the 1967 NFL championship in what has become known as the Ice Bowl. The Packers have not won an NFL championship since.

I-Formation

The backfield formation featuring two running backs in line directly behind the quarterback.

Ice Bowl

The temperature at Lambeau Field in Green Bay was 13 degrees below zero, and the wind was swirling at 15 miles-per-hour when the Packers and Dallas Cowboys lined up for the NFL championship game on December 31, 1967. With 4:50 left, Dallas led 17-14 when the Packers got the ball for the last time. Twelve plays later, with time running out, they opted to go for the win instead of a game-tying field goal. Quarterback Bart Starr's one-yard touchdown sneak behind guard Jerry Kramer's block with 13 seconds remaining gave Green Bay a 21-17 victory and its third consecutive NFL championship. The game came to be called the "Ice Bowl."

Immaculate Reception

The Pittsburgh Steelers, the AFC Central Division champions, faced the Oakland Raiders in the playoff game in 1972. Oakland scored with 1:13 left to take a 7-6 lead. With fourth and 10 and only 22 seconds to play, Steelers quarterback Terry Bradshaw threw a desperation pass far down field. The pass was intended for John (Frenchy) Fuqua but bounced off the hands of Oakland safety Jack Tatum to Pittsburgh's Franco Harris, who caught it off his shoe tops and raced 60 yards to give the Steelers a 13-7

victory. Because of the circumstances of the play, Harris' stunning catch has become known as "The Immaculate Reception."

Incomplete Pass

A pass neither caught nor intercepted.

Indianapolis Colts

A team named the Baltimore Colts played in the All-America Football Conference from 1947 to 1949 and in the National Football League in 1950. That franchise was disbanded after the 1950 season. In December, 1952, NFL Commissioner Bert Bell agreed to grant a new franchise to Baltimore if the city's fans would buy 15,000 season tickets, and a suitable owner could be found. The fans bought 15,000 season tickets in just one month, and Carroll Rosenbloom, a Baltimore businessman, was handpicked by Bell as the owner. The new Colts received the assets, including the players, of the recently disbanded Dallas franchise. Included were two future Hall of Fame defensive linemen, Art Donovan and Gino Marchetti, and halfback Buddy Young. Despite a 3-9 record, home crowds averaged more than 28,000 in 1953, the Colts' first year.

Rosenbloom hired Weeb Ewbank in 1954, and the new head coach told Rosenbloom he would produce a champion within five years. Ewbank acquired end Raymond Berry in 1955, and defensive tackle Gene (Big Daddy) Lipscomb, halfback Lenny Moore, and quarterback Johnny Unitas in 1956. Unitas, who joined

the Colts as a free agent, teamed with Berry to form one of the most productive pass-receiving duos ever. In 1958, the Colts won their first Western Conference title with a 9-3 record, then slipped past the New York Giants 23-17 in overtime in the NFL championship game. Baltimore repeated in 1959 with another 9-3 record and a 31-16 championship game victory over the Giants.

The Colts had .500 records in the early 1960s. In 1963, Don Shula was hired to replace Ewbank. During his seven-year tenure, Shula led Baltimore to Western Conference championships in 1964 and 1968 and a 75-26-4 cumulative record. Unitas continued to excel, and his job was made easier by the blocks of veteran guard-tackle Jim Parker. The 1968 Colts won the NFL championship with a 34-0 victory over Cleveland but were upset by Ewbank's New York Jets 16-7 in Super Bowl III. After the 1969 season, Shula left the Colts to accept a job with the Miami Dolphins. Early in 1970, Baltimore was transferred to the American Football

Conference along with Cleveland and Pittsburgh in the newly merged NFL.

With new head coach Don McCafferty in charge, the 1970 Colts won the first AFC championship with a 27-17 victory over the Oakland Raiders. In Super Bowl V, they edged the Dallas Cowboys 16-13 on a 32-yard field goal by rookie Jim O'Brien with five seconds left. The next year, they lost to Miami in the AFC championship game. In 1972, Rosenbloom was involved in an unusual franchise trade in which he ended up with the Los Angeles Rams, and a new owner, Robert Irsay, took over in Baltimore. In 1973, an era ended when Unitas was traded to San Diego and a new quarterback, Bert Jones, was drafted. In 1975, 1976, and 1977, under head coach Ted Marchibroda, the Colts won the AFC Eastern Division championship, but lost in the first playoff game each year. They didn't have another winning season for the next six seasons.

In March, 1984, Irsay transferred the Colts to Indianapolis to play in the new 61,000-seat Hoo-

The Indianapolis Colts' offensive line, led by Ben Utt (64) gives rookie quarterback Chris Chandler protection as he looks for an open receiver. Chandler was the first quarterback taken in the 1988 draft – in the third round.

sier Dome. Two weeks after season tickets were put on sale, the club had received 143,000 orders. In 1984, 1985, and 1986, the team fared no better on the field in Indianapolis than it had in Baltimore in its final year. But in 1987, the Colts marched to a 9-6 record under head coach Ron Meyer and won the AFC Eastern Division championship, their first in 10 years. They lost to the Cleveland Browns 38-21 in a divisional playoff game In 1988, Eric Dickerson

led the NFL in rushing with 1,659 yards, but the Colts only mastered a 9-7 record and missed the playoffs.

Members of the Hall of Fame:

(10) Raymond Berry, George Blanda, Art Donovan, Weeb Ewbank, Gino Marchetti, Lenny Moore, Jim Parker, Joe Parker, Y.A. Tittle, Johnny Unitas.

Championships Won:

Super Bowl: V (1970)
NFL (pre-1970): 1958, 1959, 1968
NFL Western Conference: 1958, 1959, 1964, 1968
AFC: 1970
AFC Eastern Division: 1970, 1975, 1976, 1977, 1987

Overall Record:

NFL Regular Season	252	243	7	.509
NFL Postseason	8	8	0	.500
Total	260	251	7	.509

Ineligible Receiver

The center, guards, and tackles are not allowed to catch a forward pass, with the following exception: A tackle may become an eligible receiver if he notifies the referee prior to the snap. A receiver loses his eligibility if he steps out of bounds before making a reception.

Inside

The area between the two offensive tackles where running plays can be directed.

Bottom: International football has been staged by the NFL in preseason play for many years, and the number of games is growing as worldwide interest expands.

Instant Replay

For the third year in 1988, the NFL continued its policy of utilizing limited instant replay during all of its games. The replay official, who usually is a former NFL on-field official, is positioned above the playing field in a press box booth. With the help of two monitors showing the television network's feed and two high-speed VCRs, he corrects obvious errors if there is indisputable visual evidence. The system concentrates only on plays of possession or touching (e.g. fumbles, receptions, interceptions, muffs) and most plays involving out-of-bounds.

Intentional Grounding

A penalty called when the quarterback purposely throws the ball away to avoid being tackled for a loss.

Interception

A change of possession that occurs when a defensive player catches a pass intended for an offensive player.

Interference

A penalty called when either an offensive or defensive player illegally interferes with an opponent's opportunity to catch a pass.

International Games

In 1985, the NFL owners voted to begin a series of overseas pre-season games in 1986, with one game to be played in England/Europe and/or one game in Japan each year. However, NFL and AFL teams, acting on their own, played 13 pre-season games on international soil from 1950 to 1983. Since the NFL owners' resolution, the American Bowl in London was created; games were played in Sweden and Canada.

International Games Involving NFL, AFL Teams

Date	Teams, Score	City, Stadium	Attendance
8-12-50	New York Giants 27 Ottawa Rough Riders 6	Ottawa, Canada Landsdowne Park	15,000
8-11-51	New York Giants 38 Ottawa Rough Riders 6	Ottawa, Canada Landsdowne Park	10,000
8-5-59	Chicago Cardinals 55 Toronto Argonauts 26	Toronto, Canada Exhibition Stadium	27,770
8-6-60	Pittsburgh Steelers 43 Toronto Argonauts 7	Toronto, Canada Exhibition Stadium	23,170
8-15-60	Chicago Bears 16 New York Giants 7	Toronto, Canada Varsity Stadium	5,401
8-2-61	St. Louis Cardinals 36 Toronto Argonauts 7	Toronto, Canada Exhibition Stadium	24,376
8-5-61	Chicago Bears 34 Montreal Alouettes 16	Montreal, Canada McGill Stadium	N/A
8-8-61	Hamilton Tiger-Cats 38 Buffalo Bills (AFL) 21	Hamilton, Canada Ivor Wynne Stadium	12,000
8-25-69	Detroit Lions 22 Boston Patriots (AFL) 9	Montreal, Canada Jarry Stadium	8,212
9-11-69	Pittsburgh Steelers 17 New York Giants 13	Montreal, Canada Jarry Stadium	N/A
8-16-76	St. Louis Cardinals 20 San Diego Chargers 10	Tokyo, Japan Korakuen Stadium	38,000
8-5-78	New Orleans Saints 14 Philadelphia Eagles 7	Mexico City, Mexico City of Sports Stadium	30,000
8-6-83	Minnesota Vikings 28 St. Louis Cardinals 10	London, England Wembley Stadium	32,847
8-3-86	*Chicago Bears 17 Dallas Cowboys 6	London, England Wembley Stadium	82,699
8-9-87	*Los Angeles Rams 28 Denver Broncos 27	London, England Wembley Stadium	72,786
7-31-88	*Miami Dolphins 27 San Francisco 49ers 21	London, England Wembley Stadium	70,500
8-14-88	Minnesota Vikings 28 Chicago Bears 21	Gothenberg, Sweden Ullevi Stadium	33,150
8-18-88	New York Jets 11 Cleveland Browns 7	Montreal, Canada Olympic Stadium	39,112

* American Bowl

Johnson, John Henry

b. Waterproof, Louisiana, 24 November 1929.
Hall of Fame: 1987

John Henry Johnson was a 6-2, 215-pound fullback who was an outstanding runner and a superior blocker. He first gained fame as a rookie with the San Francisco 49ers' "Million Dollar Backfield" in 1954. Teamed with three other future Pro Football Hall of Fame members – Joe Perry, Hugh McElhenny, and Y.A. Tittle – Johnson finished second in the NFL with 681 yards rushing. In 1957, Johnson was traded to the Detroit Lions; in 1960, he went to the Pittsburgh Steelers.

Johnson enjoyed his finest years with the Steelers, the team that originally had drafted him in 1953 after he finished his college career at St. Mary's and Arizona State University. With 1,141 yards in 1962 and 1,048 yards in 1964, he

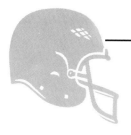

became the first Steeler to rush for more than 1,000 yards in a season. Johnson played with the Steelers until 1965, and finished his career with the Houston Oilers in 1966. In 13 seasons, he rushed for 6,803 yards and 48 touchdowns. He also caught 186 passes for 1,478 yards and seven touchdowns.

Joiner, Charlie

b. Many, Louisiana, 14 October 1947.

Charlie Joiner's career began when he was a fourth-round draft choice of the Houston Oilers in 1969. Halfway through the 1972 season, the Oilers traded the 5-11, 180-pound Grambling graduate to the Cincinnati Bengals, with whom he played until 1976, when he was traded to the San Diego Chargers. With the pass-minded Chargers, he became an outstanding receiver, continuing the tradition in Southern California which began with Lance Alworth. He never had fewer than 33 receptions in any of his 11 seasons with the Chargers. Joiner concluded his 18-year career after the 1986 season. His 750 receptions and 12,146 receiving yards both were NFL records that have since been broken by Seattle's Steve Largent. Joiner also scored 65 touchdowns.

Right: Sonny Jurgensen was a winner amongst losers; neither Philadelphia nor Washington were particularly successful while Jurgensen was with them, but his statistics were consistently near the top of the NFL rankings.

Below: Bubby Brister of Pittsburgh is about to have his perspective of life altered as Ed (Too Tall) Jones bears down on him. At 6-9, Jones once was told that he was *too tall* to be a football player.

Jones, David (Deacon)

b. Eatonville, Florida, 9 December 1938.
Hall of Fame: 1980

David (Deacon) Jones played in college at South Carolina State and Mississippi Vocational and was a fourteenth-round draft pick of the Los Angeles Rams in 1961. It wasn't long, however, before the 6-5 defensive end was grabbing the headlines with his defensive play and his flamboyant personality. He started by creating his own nickname, Deacon, because he reasoned no one would remember a player named David Jones. He then invented the term "sack" for tackling a quarterback because it fit better in a newspaper headline.

The 250-pound Jones backed up his many words with outstanding accomplishments on the field. For 10 seasons, he teamed with Merlin Olsen to give the Rams a solid all-pro left side for their famous "Fearsome Foursome" defensive front. Jones, was a consensus all-pro six consecutive years from 1965 through 1970. He played in eight Pro Bowls and twice was named the NFL Defensive Player of the Year.

After 11 years with the Rams, Jones was traded to the San Diego Chargers, with whom he played in 1972 and 1973. He finished his career with the 1974 Washington Redskins. Jones was elected to the Hall of Fame in his first year of eligibility.

Jones, Ed (Too Tall)

b. Kingston, Jamaica, 23 February 1951.

Ed (Too Tall) Jones, an All-America defensive end from Tennessee State University, was drafted in the first round by the Dallas Cowboys in 1974. The 6-9, 273-pound Jones played 72 consecutive games for the Cowboys until he retired in 1979 to take up professional boxing. After a year away from the NFL – he won all six of his fights – Jones returned to the Cowboys in 1980. He immediately started a new string of consecutive games that reached 120 at the start of the 1988 season. Jones was named all-pro in 1981 and 1982 and was picked for three Pro Bowls.

Jurgensen, Sonny

b. Wilmington, North Carolina, 23 August 1934.
Hall of Fame: 1983

Christened with the name Christian Adolph Jurgensen III, Jurgensen knew he had to be good to last in the football world. For 18 NFL seasons, the first seven with the Philadelphia Eagles starting in 1957, and the last 11 with the Washington Redskins, he was a sensational quarterback. Even in his final season in 1974, when he was 40 years old, the Duke University graduate led the NFC in passing.

Jurgensen's election to the Hall of Fame is classic proof that a player can win such an honor on his own merits rather than the success of his teams. In 18 seasons, the 6-0, 203-pound Jurgensen played on only eight teams that had better than .500 records. Jurgensen completed 2,433 passes for 32,224 yards and 255 touchdowns in his long career. He led the NFL in passing in 1967 and 1969 and was voted to the Pro Bowl three times. He also rushed for 493 yards and 15 touchdowns.

San Diego wide receiver Charlie Joiner (18) dives to make a catch in the end zone during a game against Cincinnati. The Chargers retired his number 18 jersey when he retired in 1986.

★ ★

Kansas City Chiefs

Unsuccessful in his attempts to acquire a National Football League team in 1959, Lamar Hunt founded the American Football League, the fourth league to bear that name. Not long after Hunt's Dallas Texans went into business, the NFL established a rival team in the Texas city.

Hunt signed his share of talented players, many of them from Texas, and also named Hank Stram as head coach. The 1960 Texans played in the Cotton Bowl, attracting 51,000 for a final preseason game and averaging an AFL-

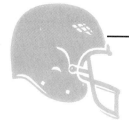

high 24,000 for regular-season home games. In 1962, Stram invited Len Dawson, who had played little in five NFL seasons, to join the Texans. Dawson led the Texans to the Western Division championship and was named the AFL's Most Valuable Player. Dallas then defeated Houston 20-17 in two overtime periods for the 1962 AFL championship.

The Texans had done well in their head-to-head battle with the NFL Cowboys, but Hunt decided to move his team to Kansas City in 1963, where it was renamed the Chiefs. The Kansas City mayor promised to enlarge the city's Municipal Stadium to 40,000 and guaranteed Hunt three times as many season-ticket sales as the Texans had in Dallas.

The Chiefs struggled their first three years in Kansas City, attendance was disappointing, and there was even some concern about the future of pro football there. However, in 1966, the Chiefs defeated Buffalo 31-7 to win the AFL championship and earn a shot at the Green Bay Packers in the first Super Bowl. The Chiefs trailed only 14-10 at halftime but eventually lost 35-10.

Three years later, Kansas City finished second in the AFL Western Division but upset the Super Bowl III champions, the New York Jets, and the Oakland Raiders in the playoffs to win the final AFL championship. In the last game ever played by an AFL team, the Chiefs stunned the Minnesota Vikings 23-7 in Super Bowl IV to even the AFL-NFL rivalry in the Super Bowl series at two games each.

Hunt's team finished the 1960s as the AFL's most successful club. The Texans/Chiefs were the only AFL team to win three championships and their 87-48-5 record was the best in the league. Seven Chiefs – more than from any other team – were named to the all-time AFL team. They were tight end Fred Arbanas, tackle Jim Tyrer, guard Ed Budde, defensive end Jerry Mays, linebacker Bobby Bell, safety Johnny Robinson, and punter Jerrel Wilson. Although Dawson did not make the team, he won four AFL passing championships in his eight years in the AFL.

In 1971, the second year after the merger, the Chiefs won the AFC Western Division championship but lost a 27-24 double-overtime game to the Miami Dolphins in a first-round playoff game. In 1972, the team moved into new Arrowhead Stadium, with a seating capacity of 78,097. But their fortunes on the field began to deteriorate.

Stram, who had coached the Texans/Chiefs throughout their first 15 seasons, was dismissed after the 1974 season, and Dawson retired a year later. Since Stram's departure, five different men have served as head coaches, but

the Chiefs have finished above .500 only in 1981 and 1986. John Mackovic led the Chiefs to their first playoff appearance in 15 years in 1986, but they lost to the New York Jets 35-15 in the first playoff round. Mackovic was let go shortly after the season and was replaced by Frank Gansz. Gansz was fired in January 1989 after compiling a 8-22-1 record over two seasons, and Marty Schottenheimer replaced him.

Members of the Hall of Fame:
(4) Bobby Bell, Len Dawson, Lamar Hunt, Willie Lanier.

Championships Won:
Super Bowl: IV (1969)
AFL: 1962, 1966, 1969
AFL Western Division: 1962, 1966, 1968 (tie)
AFC Western Division: 1971

Overall Record:

AFL Regular Season	87	48	5	.639
AFL Postseason	5	2	0	.714
NFL Regular Season	118	156	6	.432
NFL Postseason	0	2	0	.000
Total	210	208	11	.502

Kelly, Leroy

b. Philadelphia, Pennsylvania, 20 May 1942.

Leroy Kelly, a 6-0, 205-pound running back from Morgan State, understudied the great Jim Brown in 1964 and 1965, Kelly's first two seasons with the Cleveland Browns. After Brown retired in 1966, Kelly exploded with three straight 1,000-yard rushing seasons. He won consecutive NFL rushing championships with 1,205 yards in 1967 and 1,239 yards in 1968. Kelly also won the NFL scoring championship with 120 points in 1968.

Kelly still ranks among the lifetime leaders in several categories. He is the fourteenth-leading rusher with 7,274 yards, and is tied for tenth with 90 touchdowns. Kelly, who retired after the 1973 season, played in five Pro Bowl games from 1966 to 1970.

Kemp, Jack

b. Los Angeles, California, 13 July 1935.

If it hadn't been for the AFL, Jack Kemp's pro football career might have ended after one season. The 6-foot, 205-pound quarterback from Occidental College played with the 1957 Pittsburgh Steelers, then languished on the taxi squads of two NFL teams the next two years. In 1960, Kemp was signed by the Los Angeles Chargers as a free agent and won the AFL passing championship in his first season. Two years later, he suffered a hand injury, and the Chargers tried to slip him through waivers to the reserve list. But Buffalo alertly claimed him for the $100 waiver price. Kemp led the Bills to

AFL championships in 1964 and 1965. He completed his career in 1969 as one of only 19 men who played all 10 seasons in the AFL. In 10 pro seasons, he passed for 21,218 yards and 114 touchdowns and ran for 40 touchdowns.

Kemp now serves as a member of President George Bush's Cabinet.

Key

An alignment or movement that can tell a defensive player where the ball is going or what blocks to expect.

Kickoff

The running kick of the football, which usually is placed on a tee, that starts play in each quarter, and after each touchdown or field goal. Unless a penalty has been assessed, the kickoff is from the kicking team's 35-yard line. Any player can carry the ball from a kickoff, but the kicking team must let it travel 10 yards downfield first.

Kickoff Return

The running action by the player who receives the kickoff.

Kiesling, Walt

b. St Paul, Minnesota, 27 March 1903;
d. 2 March 1962. Hall of Fame: 1966

At the time of his retirement in 1956, Walt Kiesling had served in the National Football League for 34 years, longer than any other person except George Halas. His election to the Hall of Fame came in recognition of his lengthy service as a player and coach. Kiesling played as a 6-2, 245-pound guard for 13 seasons for six different teams – the Duluth Eskimos, Pottsville Maroons, Chicago Cardinals, Chicago Bears, Green Bay Packers, and Pittsburgh Pirates – from 1926 through 1938.

The St. Thomas (Minnesota) College graduate was a player-coach in 1937 and 1938, then became a full-time head coach and assistant coach for the 23 years that preceded his death. Kiesling had three different head coaching tenures with the Pittsburgh Pirates/Steelers, the last concluding in 1956. His best season was in 1942, when he led the Steelers to a 7-4 second-place finish. His career head coaching record was 25-39-4. Kiesling was co-coach in the two wartime seasons when Pittsburgh merged with the Philadelphia Eagles (coached by Earl (Greasy) Neale) and the Chicago Cardinals (coached by Phil Handler).

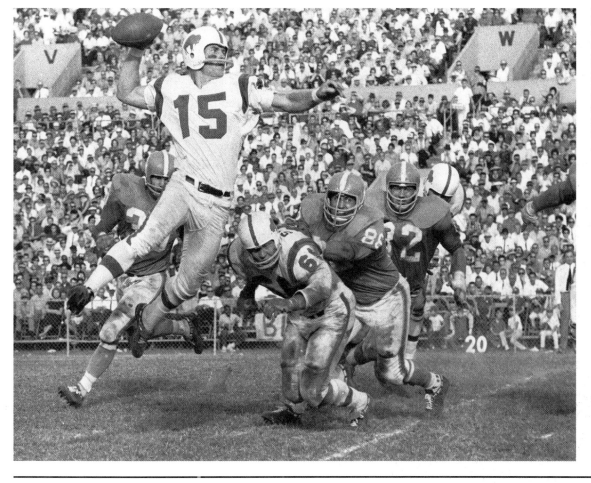

Buffalo's Jack Kemp goes airborne looking downfield for a receiver in a game at Houston. With his son, Jeff, they form the only father-and-son combination who both played quarterback in the NFL.

Frank (Bruiser) Kinard's brilliant play for the Dodgers and Yankees earned him all-league honors in both the NFL and AAFC. He was the only player from the senior league to go on to gain such recognition in the latter.

Kinard, Frank (Bruiser)

b. Pelahatchie, Mississippi, 23 October 1914; d. 7 September 1985. Hall of Fame: 1971

The Brooklyn Dodgers missed divisional titles by only one game in both 1940 and 1941. One of the principal reasons for the team's success was the dynamic line play of Frank (Bruiser) Kinard, a 6-1, 210-pound tackle, a key blocker on offense and a smothering tackler on defense. Kinard joined the Dodgers in 1938 as a second-round draft pick from the University of Mississippi, where he had been a two-time All-America.

Kinard was named all-pro in five of his seven seasons with the Dodgers. When he moved to the All-America Football Conference after a year in the Navy in 1945, he was the mainstay of the New York Yankees, winning all-AAFC honors in 1946. Kinard was the only one of more than 100 NFL players who moved to the AAFC to win all-league honors in both the NFL and AAFC. He retired after the 1947 season.

Knox, Chuck

b. Sewickley, Pennsylvania, 27 April 1932.

Chuck Knox's head coaching career in pro football began with the Los Angeles Rams in 1973 and continues today with the Seattle Seahawks. He coached the Rams from 1973 to 1977, the Buffalo Bills from 1978 to 1982, and the Seahawks beginning in 1983. His cumulative won-lost record, counting playoffs, for his first 16 years as an NFL coach was 155-100-1. Knox's

Christian Okoye (35) takes a handoff from Bill Kenney (9) and looks for running room. The Nigerian running back is one of new head coach Marty Schottenheimer's main offensive weapons in Kansas City.

Rams teams won NFC Western Division championships every year from 1973 to 1977. His overall .737 winning percentage on a 57-20-1 record is the best in Rams' history. In Buffalo, he led the 1980 Bills to an 11-5 record and the AFC Eastern Division championship, their first in 14 years. During his six five years in Seattle, the Seahawks were a wild-card playoff team in 1983, 1984, and 1987, and won their first-ever divisional title in 1988. He was named NFL Coach of the Year in 1973, 1980, and 1984. Knox played football at Juniata College.

Kramer, Jerry

b. Jordan, Montana, 23 January 1938.

Jerry Kramer was a fourth-round draft pick of the Green Bay Packers in 1958. Except for two seasons when he was injured Kramer was the Packers' regular right guard for 11 seasons until his retirement in 1968. The 6-3, 245-pound Idaho University graduate also scored 177 points in three seasons as the Packers' kicking specialist. Kramer was named all-pro five times and played in five NFL championship games and Super Bowls I and II.

Kramer is best remembered for one key play in the noted 1967 "Ice Bowl," when his block of Cowboys' defender Jethro Pugh enabled Bart Starr to score the winning touchdown.

Krause, Paul

b. Flint, Michigan, 19 February 1942.

Paul Krause, a 6-3, 205-pound safety from the

University of Iowa, began his NFL career with the Washington Redskins in 1964. He played with the Redskins four seasons, then was traded in 1968 to the Minnesota Vikings, with whom he played until 1979. Krause ended his career as the all-time NFL leader with 81 pass interceptions, which he returned for 1,185 yards and three touchdowns. He led the league in interceptions with 12 in 1964, his rookie season, and with 10 in 1975. Krause played in eight Pro Bowl games.

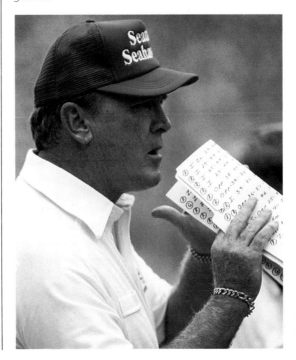

Seattle's Chuck Knox has won division titles with all three of his NFL teams (Los Angeles Rams and Buffalo Bills were the others), but although his teams have progressed to conference championship games, he has yet to coach a team to the Super Bowl.

L

★ ★

Lambeau, Earl (Curly)

b. Green Bay, Wisconsin, 9 April 1898;
d. 1 June 1965. Hall of Fame: 1963

Earl (Curly) Lambeau founded the Green Bay Packers in 1919, and soon became the team's coach and leading player. In 1921, the Packers joined the American Professional Football Association only to lose their franchise when they used college players performing under assumed names. Lambeau quickly promised to obey all the rules, used $50 of his own money to buy the franchise, and raised $2,500 so he could put a team on the field for the 1922 season. Lambeau played as a halfback during the 1920s, but continued to coach the team until 1949. More than any other man, he is respon-

sible for the existence today of the Packers' unique small-town franchise in the big-city world of professional sports.

Lambeau, who played one year at Notre Dame, was the first pass-minded coach in the NFL. His teams were like their leader – impatient and explosive. He always made sure the Packers were fortified with an outstanding passer. Green Bay was the first NFL team to win three consecutive titles (1929, 1930, and 1931). Later in the 1930s and 1940s, the Packers won four divisional titles and NFL championships in 1936, 1939, and 1944. The Packers' fortunes faded in the late 1940s, and Lambeau began to lose his one-man control of the team. He resigned early in 1950. Two-year coaching terms with the Chicago Cardinals in 1950 and

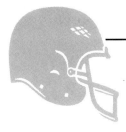

1951 and the Washington Redskins in 1952 and 1953 were unsuccessful.

It was obvious to all that Lambeau had left his heart in Green Bay, where he was born and died. He compiled a 229-134-22 coaching record over 33 years.

Earl (Curly) Lambeau is almost singularly responsible for Green Bay's place in professional football. It remains the only small-town team in major professional sport in the USA. Lambeau spent more than 30 years with the Packers as owner, coach, and player.

Lambert, Jack

b. Mantua, Ohio, 8 July 1952.

A three-year starter at middle linebacker at Kent State University, 6-4, 220-pound Jack Lambert was the Pittsburgh Steelers' second-round draft pick in 1974. In his 11-year NFL career, he was an all-pro choice seven times and was selected as the NFL Defensive Player of the Year in 1976 and 1979. Lambert played in nine straight Pro Bowls from 1976 to 1984, and intercepted 28 passes in his career.

Landry, Tom

b. Mission, Texas, 11 September 1924.

In 1960, Tom Landry was named the head coach of the Dallas Cowboys. The 1988 season was Landry's twenty-ninth as the only coach in the Cowboys' history. In 1966, the Cowboys won their first NFL Eastern Division championship with a 10-3-1 record, starting a tradition that saw the Cowboys compile winning records for 20 consecutive years until 1986. During that span, they won 14 divisional championships and NFC championships in 1970, 1971, 1975, 1977,

Tom Landry was fired as head coach of the Dallas Cowboys in February 1989, after 29 consecutive seasons in charge. His tenure equaled the record of Earl (Curly) Lambeau in Green Bay. Landry had had been under fire as the Cowboys endured three straight losing seasons, culminating in the worst record in the NFL in 1988.

and 1978. The Cowboys defeated Miami 24-3 in Super Bowl VI and Denver 27-10 in Super Bowl XII. Through 1988, Landry's overall record, including postseason games, stood at 270-178-6. Only George Halas and Don Shula have won more games.

Landry is a University of Texas graduate. He played pro football as a defensive back and punter with the New York Yankees of the AAFC in 1949 and the New York Giants of the NFL from 1950 to 1955. He was a player-coach in 1954-55 and served as a full-time assistant coach with the Giants from 1956 to 1959, before moving to the Cowboys.

Lane, Dick (Night Train)

b. Austin, Texas, 16 April 1928.
Hall of Fame: 1974

Unhappy working in a factory, Dick Lane was out seeking work of any kind when he dropped into the Los Angeles Rams office in 1952 to ask for a tryout. His only credential was an ageing scrapbook that outlined his brief experience at Scottsbluff, Nebraska, Junior College and in the Army. Rams coach Joe Stydahar saw enough good clippings to give the 6-2, 210-pound newcomer a trial. During his first training camp, Lane not only earned a spot on the Rams team but he also acquired his nickname. He often visited with Tom Fears who was continually playing the hit record "Night Train" on his phonograph. One day, a teammate saw Lane in

Fears' room and blurted out: "Hey, there's Night Train." The nickname stuck.

As a cornerback, Lane was blessed with outstanding speed, agility, reflex actions, and fierce determination. He intercepted 14 passes in his 12-game rookie season, a single-season record that still stands. He was also a fierce tackler. Lane played two years with the Rams before being traded to the Chicago Cardinals. Six years later, he was sent to Detroit, where he had his finest years from 1960 to 1965. Lane was all-pro five times, as a Cardinal in 1956 and four times as a Lion. He also played in six Pro Bowls. In 14 seasons, Lane intercepted 68 passes, which he returned for 1,207 yards and five touchdowns.

Langer, Jim

b. Little Falls, Minnesota, on 16 May, 1948.
Hall of Fame: 1987

Jim Langer, a graduate of South Dakota State University, was signed as a free agent by the 1970 Cleveland Browns, waived after a few weeks, and quickly picked up by the Miami Dolphins. For the next two years, he languished as a special teams player and little-used reserve center and guard. Then in 1972, coach Don Shula decided to pit the 6-2, 255-pound Langer against the veteran Bob DeMarco in a head-to-head battle for the starting center job. Langer easily prevailed.

Langer went on to play every offensive down in Miami's perfect 1972 season. In a postseason film study, the Dolphins' coaches determined that he needed help on only three of more than 500 blocking assignments. Starting in 1973, he won all-pro honors six consecutive years, and his fellow players selected him for the AFC Pro Bowl squad every year from 1973 to 1978. After 10 seasons with the Dolphins, Langer finished his career with the Minnesota Vikings in 1980 and 1981. Langer was elected to the Hall of Fame in his first year of eligibility.

Lanier, Willie

b. Clover, Virginia, 21 August 1945.
Hall of Fame: 1986

For 11 seasons from 1967 to 1977, middle linebacker Willie Lanier made many critical defensive plays for the Kansas City Chiefs. Best remembered is a goal-line stand he generated in the 1969 AFL championship game that stopped the New York Jets three straight plays at the Chiefs' one-yard line. Kansas City defeated the Jets and then upset the Minnesota Vikings in Super Bowl IV.

The 6-1, 245-pound Lanier, who played his college football at Morgan State College, was

Dick (Night Train) Lane was a quick defensive back with an eye for the ball. Twice in his first three seasons he led the league in both interceptions and return yards.

the first black in pro football to excel at middle linebacker. In 11 seasons, Lanier intercepted 27 passes and recovered 15 fumbles but he was best known for his aggressive tackling, which earned him the nickname "Contact." Lanier was named all-AFL/AFC seven times and picked for eight Pro Bowls.

Largent, Steve

b. Tulsa, Oklahoma, 28 September 1954.

Steve Largent, a 5-11, 191-pound end from the University of Tulsa, was the fourth-round pick of the Houston Oilers in 1976. During summer camp that year, he was traded to the Seattle Seahawks, with whom he developed into the NFL's all-time leading pass receiver. Largent has caught more than 50 passes in 10 seasons and had more than 1,000 receiving yards in eight seasons. He also has 791 receptions, an all-time record, and early in the 1988 season, he became the all-time leader in receiving yardage. He is only two touchdown receptions shy of the fabled Don Hutson's record of 99.

Largent also has a string of 168 consecutive games in which he had caught at least one pass. He was named All-AFC in 1978 and all-pro in 1983, and has been picked for seven Pro Bowls.

Lary, Yale

b. Fort Worth, Texas, 24 November 1930.
Hall of Fame: 1979

Yale Lary was a different kind of triple-threat star during his 11-year career with the Detroit Lions. The 5-11, 189-pounder from Texas A&M was a superb safety, one of history's great punters, and a break-away threat as a punt returner. He first played in Detroit in 1952 and 1953, spent the next two years in the US Army, then returned for a second tenure in the NFL from 1956 to 1964. There is no question, however, that Lary's defensive play was a prime factor in his Hall of Fame election. He was all-pro four years, and he played in nine Pro Bowls. He intercepted 50 passes, which he returned for 787 yards and two touchdowns.

Lary added another 752 yards and three touchdowns on 126 punt returns. His 44.3-yard career average on 503 punts is among the best in history. In 1963, he averaged 48.94 yards punting, the second-highest season total ever. He won three NFL punting titles and missed a fourth by an average of 3.6 inches. Although Lary was comparatively small by pro football standards, he proved to be a major factor in making the Lions one of the league's most dominant teams in the 1950s, as they won NFL championships in 1952, 1953, and 1957.

Lateral

A toss that is not forward – it can be backward or parallel to the line of play.

Latrobe, Pennsylvania, YMCA

On September 3, 1895, John Brallier, an 18-year-old quarterback from Indiana Normal in Pennsylvania, accepted $10 and "cakes" (expenses) to play for the Latrobe (Pennsylvania) YMCA team against the neighboring Jeannette Athletic Club. Based on the belief that Brallier was the first pro football player and Latrobe was the sport's birthplace, that western Pennsylvania city was granted site designation for a pro football hall of fame in 1947.

Latrobe citizens, however, did not follow through on their plan for a hall of fame. Sixteen years later, the Pro Football Hall of Fame was established in Canton, Ohio. Perhaps this was appropriate because evidence discovered in the late 1960s also proved that Pittsburgh, Pennsylvania was pro football's birthplace.

Lavelli, Dante

b. Hudson, Ohio, 23 February 1923.
Hall of Fame: 1975

Dante Lavelli played only three games as an Ohio State freshman halfback in 1942 before leaving for army service in World War II. He returned four years later to compete for a job with the Cleveland Browns of the newly formed All-America Football Conference. Lined up against him at right end on the Browns' depth

Right: The proper name for the winners' trophy at the Super Bowl is the Vince Lombardi Trophy, named after the famed Green Bay coach of the Sixties.

Far Right: Yale Lary was in his element on long-yardage downs, either as a defensive back, punter or return specialist. His powerful hitting was a major factor in Detroit's domination of the NFL in the early 1950s.

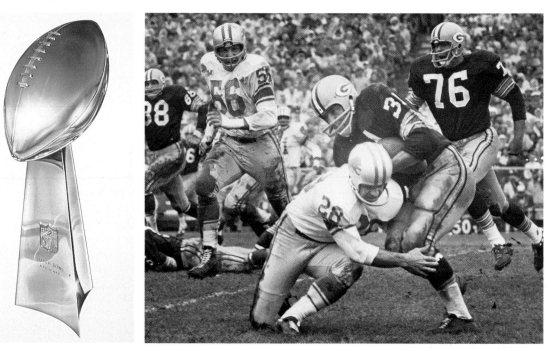

chart were four highly-touted and experienced players. The 6-0, 199-pounder somehow won the battle, quickly proving that head coach Paul Brown had made a good choice.

In 1946, Lavelli led the AAFC in receptions, made the all-league team, and caught the winning touchdown pass in the first AAFC title game against the New York Yankees. He was all-AAFC again in 1947. After the Browns moved to the NFL in 1950, he was all-pro two more years and a starter in three of the first five Pro Bowl games. In the 1950 NFL championship game against the Los Angeles Rams, Lavelli caught 11 passes and scored two touchdowns in a classic 30-28 triumph. He became a particular favorite of quarterback Otto Graham; all but 20 of his 386 career receptions came with Graham throwing. Lavelli caught 62 touchdown passes.

Layne, Bobby

b. Santa Anna, Texas, 19 December 1926;
d. 1 December 1986. Hall of Fame: 1967

An All-America from the University of Texas, Bobby Layne was one of the most successful of all quarterbacks during his 15 seasons in the

Another completion adds to his NFL record, and Steve Largent looks downfield to add to his record receiving yardage. Largent won the inaugural Bart Starr Trophy for NFL Man of the Year in 1988.

National Football League. His career began with the 1948 Chicago Bears and the 1949 New York Bulldogs. But it was with the Detroit Lions (1950-58) that he had his greatest years. He moved to the Pittsburgh Steelers during the 1958 season and played until 1963. Although he was never outstanding statistically, he was rich in the intangibles – leadership, determination, competitiveness, and coolness under fire.

The 6-2, 190-pounder used these qualities to guide the Lions to the 1952 and 1953 NFL championships and a third Western conference title

in 1954. Layne was a key figure in both championship victories, but almost single-handedly accounted for a 17-16 Detroit triumph in 1953. With the Lions trailing 16-10 and time running out, Layne completed three of his first five passes in just 60 seconds, then threw a 33-yard scoring pass to little-used end Jim Doran. The extra point gave Detroit the championship.

Layne completed 1,814 passes for 26,768 yards and 196 touchdowns. He also rushed for 2,451 yards and scored 372 points on 25 touchdowns, 120 extra points, and 34 field goals.

Bobby Layne not only was an accomplished passer, but a dangerous runner and competent kicker. His career figures show 196 touchdown passes, 25 touchdowns rushing, 120 extra points, and 34 field goals, plus two NFL championships with Detroit.

Leemans, Alphonse (Tuffy)

b. Superior, Wisconsin, 12 November 1912;
d. 19 January 1979. Hall of Fame: 1978

Alphonse (Tuffy) Leemans was a do-everything running back from George Washington University who began his postgraduate career by winning Most Valuable Player honors in the 1936 Chicago College All-Star game. This was particularly ironic because the 6-0, 200-pounder would not even have played in the game if a Washington, DC, sportswriter hadn't wrapped legitimate ballots around bales of hay to assure Leemans' success in the nationwide fan balloting. As the sportswriter suspected, the game's sponsor simply weighed the ballots as they came in.

Leemans carried his fast pace right into the pro ranks when he joined the New York Giants in 1936. He led the NFL in rushing, and was the only rookie named to the all-pro team. For the next seven years (through 1943), he was a key figure on a team that won three division titles and the 1938 NFL championship. Leemans played both fullback and halfback with the Giants, a team with a unique two-platoon system that saw each unit play just half of each game. As a result, his statistics were not overwhelming. He rushed for 3,142 yards and 17 touchdowns and passed for 2,324 yards and 25 touchdowns. Leemans was elected to the Hall of Fame 35 years after his final NFL game.

Lilly, Bob

b. Olney, Texas, 26 July 1939.
Hall of Fame: 1980

As a key man in the vaunted "Doomsday Defense" that helped make the Dallas Cowboys a dominant NFL power in the 1960s and 1970s,

defensive tackle Bob Lilly compiled a long list of honors and records. He was selected for 11 Pro Bowls and was a consensus all-pro choice eight times. In all, Lilly played in 292 pro games, including five NFL/NFC championship games and Super Bowls V and VI. In 14 years, he missed just one game.

A graduate of Texas Christian University, the 6-4, 260-pound Lilly was the Cowboys' first-ever draft pick in 1961, their first Pro Bowl selection in 1962, and their first all-pro choice in 1964. He began his pro career as a defensive end but head coach Tom Landry figured that his speed, strength, agility, and intelligence made him better suited for the tackle position. Lilly had his biggest thrill when the Cowboys won their first championship by defeating Miami 24-3 in Super Bowl VI. He entered the Super Bowl record book that day when he sacked Dolphins quarterback Bob Griese for a 29-yard loss. In his first year of eligibility, Lilly became the first player who spent his entire pro career with the Cowboys to be elected to the Hall of Fame.

Linebacker

The position behind the defensive line and in front of the secondary. In a 3-4 defense, there are four linebackers.

Little, Floyd

b. New Haven, Connecticut, 4 July 1942.

Floyd Little was the first first-round pick to sign with the Denver Broncos in the first AFL-NFL combined draft in 1967. Although hampered by injuries his first three seasons, the halfback from Syracuse University proved he could run, catch passes, and return kicks with the best. The 5-10, 195-pound Little won the 1967 AFL punt-return championship with a 16.9-yard average. He led the AFC in rushing with 901 yards in 1970 and the NFL with a career-high 1,133 yards in 1971. Little played in two AFL All-Star games and three Pro Bowls. He finished his nine-year career with 6,323 yards rushing, 2,418 yards on 215 pass receptions, 893 yards on punt returns, and 2,523 yards on kickoff returns. Little scored 54 touchdowns.

Locker Room

Each team is assigned a locker room at the stadium on game day. The locker room is used before the game, at halftime, and after the game. Facilities include dressing cubicles and/or lockers for each player, a coaches' dressing area, showers, rest rooms, and areas for the trainer's activities and the dispensing of equipment.

Lombardi Trophy

The winning team in each Super Bowl receives permanent possession of the game trophy named after legendary coach Vince Lombardi and created by Tiffany and Company. The sterling silver trophy represents an angled, regulation-sized football mounted on a three-sided base. It stands 20 inches high and weighs approximately seven pounds.

Lombardi, Vince

b. Brooklyn, New York, 11 June 1913;
d. 3 September 1970. Hall of Fame: 1971

As an assistant coach with the New York Giants, Vince Lombardi gained a reputation as a thorough and imaginative offensive mentor who seemed to have all the credentials to be a successful head coach. In 1959, the former member of the famous Fordham University "Seven Blocks of Granite" offensive line was named head coach of the Green Bay Packers. Few teams in pro football history have been in a more desperate situation than the Packers of the 1950s. Incredibly, Lombardi proved to be an instant cure for the Packers, who improved from 1-10-1 in 1958 to 7-5 in 1959. The next eight years, Green Bay was in a class by itself, winning six divisional and five NFL championships, plus victories in Super Bowls I and II.

Lombardi retired as the Packers' coach in 1968, retaining his general manager's assignment. But he wasn't happy on the sidelines and, in 1969, moved to the Washington Redskins, a team that had been almost as dormant as the Packers. With the Redskins, Lombardi repeated his first-year Green Bay feat by guiding his new team to a 7-5-2 record. But a "second miracle" was not to be. Cancer struck him down at 57. In just one decade in the NFL limelight, Lombardi became the symbol of excellence for the entire sport with a 105-35-6 record.

Los Angeles Raiders

Minneapolis was one of the original cities to be awarded a franchise when the American Football League was founded in August, 1959. However, Minnesota elected to play in the National Football League, leaving the AFL with one spot to fill. Faced with an ultimatum from Los Angeles Chargers owner Barron Hilton that he would withdraw if another franchise were not placed on the West Coast, the AFL turned to Oakland for its eighth team.

The Oakland Raiders' first problem was to find a stadium. They settled on Kezar Stadium in San Francisco, the home of the rival 49ers of the NFL. In 1961, the Raiders played in Candlestick Park in South San Francisco. The next year, they moved to Frank Youell Field, a high school stadium in Oakland that with temporary stands could seat 20,000. No matter what stadium the Raiders played in, attendance was meager.

Center Jim Otto, guard Wayne Hawkins, and quarterback Tom Flores gave the Raiders some respectability but they won only nine of 42 games in their first three seasons.

Oakland's fortunes changed sharply in 1963 when Al Davis, a San Diego Chargers assistant coach, was hired as the head coach-general manager. The 1963 Raiders improved to 10-4 and Davis was a unanimous choice for AFL Coach of the Year. For the next 25 years, the Raiders were one of the dominant teams in pro football. From 1963 to 1987, the Raiders experienced only three losing seasons and amassed a cumulative 242-109-11 record, the best winning percentage of any NFL team, while winning three Super Bowls.

Davis left the Raiders briefly in 1966 to serve as the AFL commissioner but, after the AFL-NFL merger, he was back as the team's managing general partner, a position he still holds. In the 10-year period between 1967, when they won their first AFL championship, through 1976, the Raiders won nine AFL/AFC Western Division championships, finishing second only in 1971. In 1967, coached by John Rauch, they lost to the Green Bay Packers 33-14 in Super Bowl II. In 1976, coached by John Madden, they followed up their first AFC championship with a 32-14 rout of the Minnesota Vikings in Super Bowl XI. From 1969-1978, Madden coached the Raiders to a 112-39-7 record.

In 1980, the Raiders managed a wild-card finish in the AFC West, then marched through the playoffs under head coach Tom Flores, to win the AFC championship and defeat the Philadelphia Eagles 27-10 in Super Bowl XV. AFC West championships in 1981 and 1983 were sandwiched around the Raiders' first-place finish in the AFC in the strike-shortened 1982 season when division standings were not kept. The Raiders played in Super Bowl XVIII following the 1983 season and overwhelmed the Washington Redskins 38-9, their second Super Bowl victory under Flores. The Raiders won another divisional championship in 1985 but dropped to 8-8 in 1986 and to 5-10 in 1987, their poorest season since 1963, and Flores was replaced by Mike Shanahan.

The Raiders' unprecedented record was made possible by a succession of talented football players acquired both through the college draft and by trades. Stars such as quarterbacks Daryle Lamonica and Jim Plunkett, cornerback Willie Brown, and quarterback-kicker George

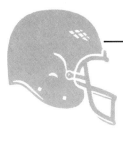

Blanda originally played for other pro teams. On the other hand, players such as wide receivers Fred Biletnikoff and Cliff Branch, quarterback Ken Stabler, tackle Art Shell, and guard Gene Upshaw were high-round draft picks.

As the Raiders improved on the field, things also looked up on the stadium front. In 1966, the team moved into the new Oakland-Alameda County Coliseum. The fans turned out in large numbers for 16 seasons until Davis transferred his team in 1982 to Los Angeles, where the Raiders could play in the much larger Los Angeles Coliseum.

Members of the Hall of Fame:

(7) Fred Biletnikoff, George Blanda, Willie Brown, Ron Mix, Jim Otto, Art Shell, Gene Upshaw.

Championships Won:

Super Bowl: XI (1976), XV (1980), XVIII (1983)
AFL: 1967
AFL Western Division: 1967, 1968 (tie), 1969
AFC Western Division: 1970, 1972, 1973, 1974, 1975, 1976, 1983, 1985

Overall Record:

AFL Regular Season	77	58	5	.568
AFL Postseason	3	3	0	.500
NFL Regular Season	181	93	6	.657
NFL Postseason	16	9	0	.640
Total	277	163	11	.626

Los Angeles Rams

On February 13, 1937, the National Football League granted a franchise to a Cleveland syndicate headed by Homer Marshman. The Cleveland Rams did not experience a winning season until 1945. However, in 1939, rookie tail-

back Parker Hall won the NFL's official Most Valuable Player award. In 1941, Marshman and his associates sold the team for $100,000 to Fred Levy, Jr., and Daniel F. Reeves, who at 29 became the youngest NFL owner. In 1943, Reeves become sole owner of the Rams, and in 1944 they made a major player acquisition by drafting UCLA quarterback Bob Waterfield as a future choice.

In 1945, with Adam Walsh coaching, Waterfield led the Rams, who had switched to the T-formation attack, to a 9-1 record. On November 22, he completed 10 passes to end Jim Benton for 303 yards, an NFL yardage record that lasted for 40 years. Waterfield, who was named the NFL's Most Valuable Player, threw two touchdown passes to defeat the Washington Redskins 15-14 for the 1945 NFL championship.

But only 32,178 turned out in Cleveland's Municipal Stadium for the championship game, and Reeves lost $50,000 during the season. Despite strong initial opposition from fellow NFL owners, Reeves moved his team to Los Angeles, where he could play in the 101,296-seat Coliseum. Reeves thus became the first owner to locate an established professional sports franchise on the West Coast.

The 1946 Rams finished 6-4-1 on the field but made big news by signing former UCLA All-America Kenny Washington, a running back, and Woody Strode, an end, as the first two blacks to play in the NFL since 1933. Reeves continued to lose money and, in 1947, added four new partners to help keep the franchise afloat. The Rams had to battle head-to-head with the Los Angeles Dons of the new All-America Football Conference.

The AAFC folded in 1949 just as the Rams were improving dramatically on the field. Tom Fears, who won NFL pass receiving titles in 1948, 1949, and 1950, and Elroy (Crazylegs) Hirsch were perfect targets for Waterfield and newcomer Norm Van Brocklin, who turned the Rams into one of history's highest scoring teams. The Rams won conference titles in 1949, 1950, and 1951. They lost NFL championship games to the Philadelphia Eagles 14-0 in 1949 and to the Cleveland Browns 30-28 in 1950. But in 1951, under new head coach Joe Stydahar, the Rams won their second and last NFL championship. They defeated Cleveland 24-17 in the championship game on a 73-yard touchdown pass from Van Brocklin to Fears.

The Rams lost a playoff with the Detroit Lions for the 1952 conference title. In 1955, under head coach Sid Gillman, they won their fourth Western Conference championship in seven years but were stunned by the Cleveland Browns 38-14 before an NFL championship game record crowd of 85,693 in the Coliseum.

Right: Vince Lombardi once said that winning was not the most important thing, it was the *only* thing. His record at Green Bay and Washington suggests he got his way more often than not.

Opposite top: The Los Angeles Rams have been one of the most consistent teams in the NFL in the 1980s, but their record is not quite as good as San Francisco's, so they have not won many NFC West titles.

Opposite bottom: Bo Jackson (34) sets off downfield for the Los Angeles Raiders. Jackson also plays major league baseball for the Kansas City Royals. The 1985 Heisman Trophy winner is a real game-breaker on NFL fields.

only once in
...ce excellent
...f 102,368 for a
...turnouts in
...ed 80,000 on
...two decades

...head coach
...g records in
...y have won
...pionships,
i... 1979.
H... five
(1... avasi, the
Ra... 1979 but
los... their only
Sup... the early
195... owess
bu... s were
buil... nd
Dav... n Olsen
form... ed
"Fea... unning
back...
yard... nd NFL
seaso... son set
an all-... 05
yards... olis
Colts a...

In 19... sea-
son wit... y

coach in the franchise's 52-year history.

Reeves, who lost control of his team in an ownership dispute in 1956, regained control in 1962. He died in 1971. The next year, Robert Irsay purchased the Rams from the Reeves estate for $19 million. He then traded the team to Carroll Rosenbloom in exchange for the Baltimore Colts franchise and $3 million. Rosenbloom operated the club until he died in 1979. The franchise has been operated since that time by his widow, Georgia Frontiere.

Members of the Hall of Fame:
(13) Tom Fears, Bill George, Sid Gillman, Elroy (Crazylegs) Hirsch, David (Deacon) Jones, Dick (Night Train) Lane, Ollie Matson, Joe Namath, Merlin Olsen, Dan Reeves, Andy Robustelli, Norm Van Brocklin, Bob Waterfield.

Championships Won:
NFL (pre-1970): 1945, 1951
NFC: 1979
NFL Western Conference: 1945, 1949, 1950, 1951, 1955
NFL Coastal Division: 1967, 1969
NFC Western Division: 1973, 1974, 1975, 1976, 1977, 1978, 1979, 1985

Overall Record:
NFL Regular Season	364	287	20	.556
NFL Postseason	11	19	0	.367
Total	375	306	20	.549

Luckman, Sid

b. Brooklyn, New York, 21 November 1916. Hall of Fame: 1965

Sid Luckman was a triple-threat tailback at Columbia University who excelled as a runner. However, Bears' owner-coach George Halas envisioned the 6-0, 195-pounder as the ideal candidate to run the T-formation attack he was creating in Chicago. Halas drafted him in the first round in 1939, but it took Luckman almost a year to take command of the complex new offense. Once he did, he came through in a big way. The showcase game for the T-formation was the 1940 NFL championship game in which the Bears overwhelmed the Washington Redskins 73-0. Almost immediately, many other pro teams frantically switched to the new attack. Luckman not only became a big-play and big-game star but he made Chicago into a winner. The Bears won four more divisional titles, and the NFL championships in 1941, 1943, and 1946. Luckman was an all-pro five times between 1941 and 1947, and the league's Most Valuable Player in 1943. He had many outstanding games but two in 1943 stand out. In November, he passed for a record-tying seven touchdowns in a 56-7 rout of the New York Giants. He followed with a five-touchdown passing performance in a 41-21 victory over the Washington Redskins in the NFL championship game.

When Luckman retired after the 1950 season, his career figures showed 904 pass completions for 14,683 yards and 137 touchdowns. He also did the Bears' punting, and intercepted 17 passes as a defensive back.

Lyman, William Roy (Link)

b. Table Rock, Nebraska, 30 November 1898; d. 28 December 1972. Hall of Fame: 1964

William Roy (Link) Lyman, a 6-2, 252-pound tackle from the University of Nebraska, began his NFL career with the champion Canton Bulldogs in 1922 and 1923. He moved to the Cleveland Bulldogs in 1924 and played with both the Canton Bulldogs and Frankford Yellow Jackets in 1925. Lyman joined the Chicago Bears on their long barnstorming tour in January, 1926, and remained with them through the rest of his career, which was concluded after the 1934 season. He took two one-year leaves of absence, one to play semi-pro football in 1929, the other to settle business problems in 1932.

Link played on just one losing team in 16 seasons of college and professional football. In his final two seasons, he was still a major contributor as the Bears won the 1933 NFL title and the 1934 Western Division championship. Lyman was the pioneer of a sliding, shifting style of defensive line play that confused his opponents and made him one of the most respected players of his time.

 ★

Mack, Tom

b. Cleveland, Ohio, 1 November 1943.

An All-America guard at the University of Michigan, Tom Mack was a first-round selection of the Los Angeles Rams in the 1966 NFL draft. Mack became a starter at left offensive guard in his rookie season and remained at that spot throughout his 13-season career. The 6-3, 250-pounder played in 184 consecutive games. Mack earned the first of 11 Pro Bowl invitations after his second season in 1967. Only Jim Otto, Ken Houston, and long-time teammate Merlin Olsen played in more Pro Bowls.

Mackey, John

b. New York City, NY, 24 September 1941.

Tight end John Mackey, who joined the Baltimore Colts as a second-round draft pick in 1963, quickly established himself as a star at his position. He was a strong blocker but also had the breakaway speed that made him a long-distance threat. The 6-2, 224-pound Syracuse University graduate averaged 30.1 yards on kickoff returns as a rookie. Mackey played in five Pro Bowls. In a 1969 poll, he was named the outstanding tight end in the NFL's first 50 years. Mackey played nine seasons with Baltimore and then ended his career with the San Diego Chargers in 1972. His lifetime record shows 320 pass receptions for 5,126 yards and 38 touchdowns.

Madden, John

b. Austin, Minnesota, 10 April 1936.

In 10 seasons as head coach of the Oakland Raiders from 1969 to 1978, John Madden enjoyed almost unparalleled success, guiding the Raiders to seven AFL/AFC Western Division titles, including five in a row from 1972 to 1976. The Raiders won the 1976 AFC championship and followed with a 32-14 victory over the Minnesota Vikings in Super Bowl XI. Madden's Raiders never finished below second. His .750 winning percentage (130-32-7) ranks Madden number one among coaches with 100 or more games in pro football. He is one of only four coaches to win 100 games his first 10 years.

Madden starred as a two-way tackle for Cal Poly (San Luis Obispo). He was drafted by the Philadelphia Eagles in 1959 but a knee injury in training camp ended any hopes of a pro playing career. He joined the Raiders' staff as an assistant in 1967. Three years later, at 33, he became head coach.

Man-for-Man

A type of pass defense in which each linebacker and defensive back is assigned a potential receiver to cover individually. Also called "single coverage."

Man-in-Motion

In 1930, head coach Ralph Jones of the Chicago Bears added the man-in-motion to the Bears' T-formation attack. The tactic, which had been used earlier with both the single-wing and double-wing offenses, spread the defense and put little, fast men outside where they could get running room. In the T-formation, the left halfback usually was the man-in-motion who, after setting up, would run to his right parallel to the line of scrimmage and be into open territory by the time the ball was snapped.

George Preston Marshall did much to make the NFL the crowd-pleasing game it is today; his public relations skill helped promote football as entertainment.

Mara, Tim

b. Brooklyn, New York, 29 July 1887;
d. 17 February 1959. Hall of Fame: 1963

When a New York bookmaker, Tim Mara, learned he could buy a National Football League franchise in 1925 for $500, he was enthusiastic. "A New York franchise to operate anything ought to be worth $500," he exclaimed. The New York Giants' first season was a financial flop, however, until the Red Grange-led Chicago Bears played in the Polo Grounds in December, 1925. More than 70,000 saw the game, and Mara netted $143,000. The future of pro football in New York seemed assured.

The very next year, however, Mara faced a stern challenge from the New York Yankees of the rival American Football League. Mara lost heavily, but the AFL and Yankees lost more and went out of business. In 1927, the Giants went 11-1-1 and presented Mara with his first championship. Mara had known hard times as a youngster, so when New York Mayor Jimmy Walker approached him about staging a charity game, he agreed to play the Notre Dame All-Stars. The game netted $115,153 for the New York City Unemployment Fund. For the next three decades, Mara's Giants were perennial championship contenders in the NFL. They won three NFL and eight divisional titles in his 34 years. He had to endure another inter-league war, this one with the All-America Football Conference, in the late 1940s. Once again, Mara and the NFL won.

Marchetti, Gino

b. Smithers, West Virginia, 2 January 1927.
Hall of Fame: 1972

Gino Marchetti was a second-round draft pick of the 1952 New York Yanks, but the team moved to Dallas before the season started. Within a year, the Texans folded, and the 6-4,

John Madden's career as a coach lasted 10 seasons, but his intensity forced him into retirement because it was dangerous to his health. His team's playing style was definitely damaging to opponents' playing records.

245-pound defensive end found himself in Baltimore with a new Colts franchise that was founded in 1953. The Colts quickly built toward championship status and Marchetti, who spent his collegiate career at the University of San Francisco, developed into a great player. He was an all-round brilliant defender, best as a pass-rusher but also adept at stopping the run. He was also the team captain through much of his career.

Marchetti was named all-pro seven years and selected for 11 consecutive Pro Bowl games. In 1969, one panel picked him as the finest defensive end in the NFL's first 50 years. Marchetti retired after the 1964 season, but returned for four games in response to a Colts emergency in 1966. In his first year of eligibility, he was elected to the Hall of Fame.

Marino, Dan

b. Pittsburgh, Pennsylvania, 15 September 1961.

The Miami Dolphins selected Dan Marino from the University of Pittsburgh in the first round of the 1983 NFL draft. Since that time, the 6-4, 214-pound Marino has been pro football's most dominating passer. In his first five NFL seasons, he won three AFC passing championships. He had passed for more than 300 yards 32 times

and thrown four or more touchdown passes in 17 games. In 1984, he passed for 5,084 yards and 48 touchdowns, both NFL records. Other personal highs included six touchdown passes against the New York Jets in 1986 and 521 yards passing against the New York Jets in early 1988. Marino was named all-pro in 1984, 1985, and 1986. He was selected for the Pro Bowl from 1983-1987, but knee injuries limited his actual participation to just one game. Marino has a 91.5 passing rating, completing 1,866 passes for 23,856 yards and 196 touchdowns.

Marshall, George Preston

b. Grafton, West Virginia, 11 October 1897;
d. 9 August 1969. Hall of Fame: 1963

George Preston Marshall bought the Boston Braves NFL franchise in 1932, changed the team name to Redskins in 1933, and moved the club to Washington in 1937. Marshall's teams, particularly in the years from 1936 through 1945, were very successful. They won NFL championships in 1937 and 1942, and six divisional titles over that 10-year period.

One of Marshall's biggest legacies came at the management level. He formed pro football's first team band and introduced gala halftime shows. He was the first to genuinely promote his team through the use of professional public relations methods. In 1937, Marshall's publicity campaign made Sammy Baugh the most famous pro football player before he threw his first NFL pass.

The flamboyant owner was also a significant force in improving the playing rules to open up the game and make it more crowd-pleasing. He championed the idea of splitting the NFL into two divisions and staging an annual playoff to determine the title. He was also controversial. In 1936, Marshall was so disdainful of the fan support for his divisional champion Boston Redskins team that he shifted the title game to the neutral Polo Grounds in New York.

Marshall, Jim

b. Danville, Kentucky, 30 December 1937.

Jim Marshall, a 6-4, 240-pound All-America tackle from Ohio State, began his pro football career with Saskatchewan of the Canadian Football League in 1959. The next year, he joined the Cleveland Browns as their fourth-round draft pick. In 1961, he was traded to the Minnesota Vikings, with whom he played for 19 years, the longest service with one club by any player in pro football history. Marshall became a key member of the "Purple People Eaters" defensive line that helped to make Minnesota a dominant team in the 1970s. He played 282 consecutive games, an all-time record. Marshall recovered 29 opponents' fumbles, an all-time record. He played in the Pro Bowl following the 1968 and 1969 seasons. In spite of his excellent career, Marshall may be best remembered for returning a San Francisco fumble 66 yards the wrong way for a safety in 1964.

Massillon Tigers

In 1903, the Massillon Tigers were organized as the first pro team in Ohio. In 1904, many other Ohio cities started pro football teams but Canton and Massillon, located just seven miles apart, became fearsome rivals from the beginning. In a two-game series that ended the 1906 season, Canton won the first game 10-5, but Massillon retaliated 13-6 in the second game. After the game, the Massillon Independent revealed a gambling scandal involving the Canton coach and at least one Bulldog player. Massillon toned down its program, and Canton did not play again until 1912. From then until 1919, Massillon-Canton showdowns were the highlight of every pro football season. While Massillon had a representative at the American Professional Football Association (forerunner of the NFL) organizational meeting in 1920, it did not play pro football again. Canton went on to play in the new league for six years, folding at the end of the 1936 season. Today, the intense Canton-Massillon competition continues in one of America's most noted high school rivalries.

Matson, Ollie

b. Trinity, Texas, 1 May 1930.
Hall of Fame: 1972

Ollie Matson, an All-America at the University of San Francisco and a 1952 Olympics bronze medal winner in track (400 meters), played 14 seasons in the NFL, beginning with the Chicago Cardinals in 1952. After a year in the Army in 1953, he returned to the Cardinals, with whom he stayed until 1959, when he was traded to the Los Angeles Rams for a stunning total of nine players. He finished his career with the Detroit Lions (1963) and the Philadelphia Eagles (1964-66).

With both the Cardinals and the Rams, Matson was hailed as the fleet-footed halfback who would lead his teams to championships. Through no fault of his own, Matson never had the supporting cast to back up his brilliant abilities. In 14 seasons, the combined record of his four teams was a dismal 58-117-5, and only twice did they finish above .500.

Yet his career record was exceptional. The 6-2, 220-pound Matson gained 12,844 yards on rushing, receiving, and returns. He scored 40

touchdowns running, 23 on receptions, and nine on kick returns. Few NFL greats ever exhibited such versatility. A Co-Rookie of the Year in 1952, Matson was all-pro four consecutive years and played in the Pro Bowl after each of his first five seasons. Although he didn't play in a championship game, his sport's ultimate honor came his way when he was elected to the Hall of Fame in his first year of eligibility.

Matte, Tom

b. Pittsburgh, Pennsylvania, 14 June 1939.

Tom Matte, a 6-0, 214-pound halfback from Ohio State University, was the Baltimore Colts' first-round draft choice in 1961. He was a dependable ball carrier and pass receiver who rushed for 4,509 yards and caught 235 passes for 1,687 yards in 12 seasons. Matte is best remembered for the 1965 season when the Colts'

Dan Marino is the most dangerous passer in the NFL today. His quick release makes him almost impossible to sack and his offensive line gives him enough time to pick out his quick receivers.

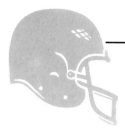

top two quarterbacks, Johnny Unitas and Gary Cuozzo, were injured. In desperation, the team turned to Matte, who had played quarterback in college at Ohio State. Matte wore a wristband with play numbers written on it and led the Colts over the Los Angeles Rams to give Baltimore a tie for the NFL Western conference championship. He quarterbacked the team again in the Colts' overtime loss to Green Bay in the conference playoff game.

Don Maynard was one of Joe Namath's favorite receivers. Here, he is about to catch a pass and take it 72 yards for a touchdown against Cincinnati in a 1971 game at Shea Stadium.

Maynard, Don

b. Crosbyton, Texas, 25 January 1937.
Hall of Fame: 1987

When Don Maynard retired in 1973, he ranked as the leading pass receiver in pro football history with 633 receptions. He spent the bulk of his 15-year career in New York, first with the Giants in 1958 and then with the Titans/Jets from 1960 to 1972. The 6-1, 185-pound Texas Western College product also played briefly with the 1973 St. Louis Cardinals.

Maynard's first pro experience with the Giants was unsuccessful. He spent a year in the Canadian Football League before returning to New York in 1960 as the first signee of the Titans in the new American Football League. Maynard had 72 receptions in his first year as a Titans wide receiver and never less than 38 catches in any of his 10 AFL seasons. He still holds the NFL record for most 100-yard receiving games (50).

The Titans/Jets used numerous quarterbacks in their first five seasons. It wasn't until Joe Namath arrived in 1965 that Maynard was able to get some kind of order into his receiving life. Namath-to-Maynard became one of pro football's most exciting and productive pass-catch combos the next several years. In all, Maynard gained 11,834 yards on his 633 catches and scored 88 touchdowns.

Maynard was the first player to have more than 10,000 yards in pass reception with one team and his 11,732 yards with the Titans/Jets was only passed by Steve Largent in 1987.

McAfee, George

b. Ironton, Ohio, 13 March 1918.
Hall of Fame: 1966

Although George McAfee measured just 6-0 and 177 pounds, he could do everything on a football field. The Duke University graduate, who played with the Chicago Bears in 1940 and 1941, and from 1945 to 1950, was an exceptional runner, a sure-handed pass receiver, and one of history's finest punt-return specialists. His 12.8-yard average on 112 punt returns was an NFL career mark for many years. McAfee also played defense, making 21 interceptions.

McAfee established himself as a game-breaker in his first preseason outing as a rookie by returning a punt 75 yards with 37 seconds left to defeat the Brooklyn Dodgers. In the regular-season opener that year, he ran back a kickoff 93 yards and threw a touchdown pass in a 41-10 Bears victory. In Chicago's 73-0 win in the 1940 NFL title game, he contributed a 34-yard touchdown on an interception return. An all-pro pick in 1941, McAfee spent three years in the Navy at what would have been the peak of his pro career.

McCormack, Mike

b. Chicago, Illinois, 21 June 1930.
Hall of Fame: 1984

After a fine career at the University of Kansas, Mike McCormack was the second-round draft

pick of the New York Yanks in 1951. The Yanks had a terrible season but McCormack earned a trip to the Pro Bowl, and, most importantly, made a lasting impression on a rival head coach, Paul Brown of the Cleveland Browns. The 6-4, 250-pound tackle spent the next two seasons in the US Army, but, while he was still a year away from civilian life, Brown engineered an amazing trade – a 15-player exchange that brought McCormack to Cleveland.

McCormack spent his first year in Cleveland in 1954 as a middle guard on defense, an emergency move brought about by the unexpected retirement of Bill Willis. Brown had McCormack targeted for right tackle on the offensive line, however, and he made the switch the next year. McCormack handled the job with distinction for eight years until his retirement after the 1962 season. He was selected for the Pro Bowl five times in that period, and served as the Browns' team captain from 1956 on. Brown often called McCormack "the finest offensive lineman I ever coached."

McCormack went on to be a head coach in Philadelphia from 1973 to 1975, Baltimore 1980 to 1981, and Seattle in 1982.

McElhenny, Hugh

b. Los Angeles, California, 31 December 1928. Hall of Fame: 1970

Hugh McElhenny was the number one draft choice of the San Francisco 49ers in 1952. Almost immediately, the 6-1, 198-pound halfback displayed the open-field style of running that had made him an All-America at the University of Washington. McElhenny ran 42 yards for a touchdown on his first play in preseason. He had the longest punt return in the NFL in 1952 – 94 yards – and the longest run from scrimmage – 89 yards. He wound up his brilliant rookie season with two touchdowns in the Pro Bowl. "The King," as he was nicknamed, was named Rookie of the Year and Player of the Year.

After nine outstanding seasons in San Francisco, McElhenny was an expansion-draft pick of the Minnesota Vikings in 1961. He had one of his finest pro seasons with the Vikings that year. He concluded his career playing one year each with the New York Giants (1963) and the Detroit Lions (1964). When he retired after the 1964 season, McElhenny was one of three players to have gained more than 11,000 all-purpose yards. In 14 seasons, he rushed for 5,281 yards and caught 264 passes for 3,247 yards. He was also outstanding as a punt and kickoff returner. He scored 60 touchdowns, 38 on rushes, 20 on receptions, and two on punt returns. He was elected to the Hall of Fame in his first year of eligiblity.

McGee, Max

b. Sefton City, Texas, 16 July 1932.

Max McGee, a 6-3, 210-pound offensive end with the Green Bay Packers, caught only four passes in the 1966 season. But in Super Bowl I, following that season, the veteran from Tulane University caught seven passes for 138 yards and two touchdowns to lead the Packers to a 35-10 victory over the Kansas City Chiefs. McGee was a fifth-round draft pick of the Packers in 1954. He spent the next two years in military service before returning to Green Bay in 1957. In 12 years, he caught 345 passes for 6,346 yards and 50 touchdowns. He played in one Pro Bowl, six NFL championship games, and Super Bowls I and II.

McNally (Blood), John

b. New Richmond, Wisconsin, 27 November 1903; d. 28 November 1985. Hall of Fame: 1963

Johnny Blood (McNally), a graduate of St. John's College of Minnesota, played with five different teams – the Milwaukee Badgers, Duluth Eskimos, Pottsville Maroons, Green Bay Packers, and Pittsburgh Pirates – during his 15-season NFL career from 1925 to 1939. His finest years came with the Packers, with whom he was a major contributor to four championship teams. The 6-0, 185-pounder was a superb halfback and possibly the finest receiver in the league. He could also throw passes and punt. On defense, he was a ball hawk and a deadly tackler.

His off-the-field antics, however, constantly captured the headlines and tended to dim his playing accomplishments. The way he acquired his adopted name, "Blood," is a good example. He decided to try pro football while he was still a student. To protect his remaining college eligibility, he needed an alias and found it when he saw a theater marquis announcing the movie Blood and Sand. "That's it," he exclaimed to a friend. "You be Sand, I'll be Blood." McNally tended to break training rules and ignore curfews. Once, he missed the team train but caught up with it by driving his car on the track and then gleefully joining his mates on the train.

Miami Dolphins

In 1965, the American Football League decided to expand to nine teams by placing a franchise in Miami, where the AFL had received a guarantee it could play in the Orange Bowl. The franchise was awarded to Minneapolis attorney Joseph Robbie and entertainer Danny Thomas for $7.5 million. The team nickname, Dolphins,

was chosen from more than 20,000 entries in a fan contest. Joe Thomas of the Minnesota Vikings was named general manager, and George Wilson, who had coached the Detroit Lions for nine years, was named the Dolphins' head coach.

The Dolphins opened the 1966 season at home against the Oakland Raiders, and Joe Auer thrilled the 26,776 fans by returning the opening kickoff 95 yards for a touchdown. But Miami won only three games in 1966. Wilson coached the team for four years but his teams did not win more than five games in one any season. During his tenure, however, the Dolphins did draft quarterback Bob Griese in 1967, and running backs Larry Csonka and Jim Kiick and safety Dick Anderson in 1968. All would prove to be outstanding stars in the future.

A new era began for the Dolphins in 1970 when Don Shula left Baltimore to become

Miami's head coach and vice president. Shula claimed he was no miracle worker but immediately proved to be just that. In his 19 seasons as head coach, the Dolphins have compiled a 190-88-2 record, a .682 winning percentage, best in the post-merger NFL. The Dolphins have fallen below .500 only twice (1976 and 1988) during Shula's tenure.

In 1970, Shula's first year, the Dolphins won 10 of 14 games. Miami then won four straight AFC Eastern Division championships from 1971 to 1974. The Dolphins lost to the Dallas Cowboys 24-3 in Super Bowl VI, but, in 1972, enjoyed the only perfect season (17-0-0) in NFL history. Miami culminated the historic season with a 14-7 victory over the Washington Redskins in Super Bowl VII. The Dolphins lost only two regular-season games in 1973 and repeated as world champions with a 24-7 victory over the Minnesota Vikings in Super Bowl VIII. In 1974, their championship string came to an end when they lost to the Oakland Raiders 28-26 in a dramatic first-round AFC playoff game.

In their championship years, the Dolphins relied on outstanding balance both on offense and defense, but that balance was destroyed in March, 1974, when three of the team's finest offensive players – Csonka, Kiick, and wide receiver Paul Warfield – signed a $3.3 million package deal to play in the World Football League in 1975. Except for the 1976 season, Shula kept the Dolphins in contention every

Troy Stradford runs behind Woody Bennett's block. Stradford's arrival in 1987 gave Miami the balanced offense that a team needs, but injuries on both sides of the ball have hampered the Dolphins' progress.

year but they didn't win another AFC Eastern Division championship until 1979, when Griese led the Miami attack with help from Csonka, who returned after a four-season absence. In the 1979 playoffs, the Dolphins lost to the Pittsburgh Steelers 34-14.

Although Griese and all-pro guard Larry Little retired in 1981, Shula coached the Dolphins to another AFC Eastern Division championship. In a classic playoff struggle, Miami lost to San Diego 41-38 in overtime. In the strike-shortened 1982 season, the Dolphins finished with a 7-2 record, second best in the AFC, then won the AFC championship with a 14-0 win over the New York Jets. They lost to the Washington Redskins 27-17 in Super Bowl XVII. Quarterback Dan Marino of the University of Pittsburgh joined the Dolphins in 1983 and led the team to three straight AFC East titles and the 1984 AFC championship. In 1984, with Mark Clayton and Mark Duper as his primary receivers, Marino set an all-time record with 48 touchdown passes and 5,084 yards passing. In Super Bowl XIX, however, the San Francisco 49ers defeated the Dolphins 38-16.

In 1987, the Dolphins moved from the Orange Bowl to 75,000-seat Joe Robbie Stadium, named for the team's owner. It is the only privately funded stadium in pro football.

Members of the Hall of Fame:

(3) Larry Csonka, Jim Langer, Paul Warfield.

Championships Won:

Super Bowl: VII, VIII
AFC: 1971, 1972, 1973, 1982, 1984
AFC Eastern Division: 1971, 1972, 1973, 1974, 1979, 1981, 1983, 1984, 1985

Overall Record:

AFL Regular Season	15	39	2	.286
NFL Regular Season	190	88	2	.682
NFL Postseason	14	10	0	.583
Total	219	137	4	.614

Michalske, Mike

b. Cleveland, Ohio, 24 April 1903;
d. 26 October 1983. Hall of Fame: 1964

An All-America at Penn State, Mike Michalske began his pro career with the New York Yankees of the American Football League in 1926. The 6-0, 209-pound guard moved to the NFL with the Yankees in 1927, but when the Yankees folded after the 1928 season, he waived $400 in salary due him in return for his free agency. Michalske then signed with the Green Bay Packers, with whom he finished his pro career after the 1937 season. He was an all-pro choice four times in eight years in Green Bay.

Michalske was known as "Iron Mike" because he played 60 minutes every game and was never injured. Michalske, who played fullback, guard, end, and tackle in high school and at Penn State, pioneered the idea of using former fullbacks at guard because they were fast and explosive. He was the first guard to be elected to the Hall of Fame.

Middle Guard

Before the advent of modern 3-4 and 4-3 defenses, many defensive lines consisted of two ends, two tackles, and a fifth man known as the middle guard, who lined up directly in front of the offensive center. As middle guards became more mobile and often involved in pass defense, the position of middle linebacker evolved.

Midfield Stripe

The 50-yard line.

Million Dollar Backfield

The offensive backfield of the San Francisco 49ers in 1954, 1955, and 1956 was known as the "Million Dollar Backfield." It consisted of Y.A. Tittle at quarterback, Hugh McElhenny and John Henry Johnson at halfback, and Joe Perry at fullback. In 1954, Perry and Johnson finished first and second and McElhenny eighth in the NFL in rushing. All four are now members of the Pro Football Hall of Fame.

Max McGee has a step on a Kansas City defender and makes an easy catch of Bart Starr's pass for one of his two touchdowns in Super Bowl I. Green Bay comfortably overcame the challenge of the Chiefs to win the first World Championship 35-10.

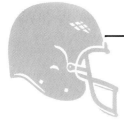

Millner, Wayne

b. Roxbury, Massachusetts, 31 January 1913;
d. 19 November 1976. Hall of Fame: 1968

Wayne Millner, a two-time Notre Dame All-America, joined the Boston Redskins in 1936. He moved with the team to Washington a year later, played until he was called into military service after the 1941 season, and then returned for a final year in 1945. At the time of his retirement, he had amassed 124 catches, the most for a Redskins receiver up to that time. Millner was an outstanding two-way end with cat-like reflexes and sure hands. He was at his best when the pressure was the greatest. A good example was his eight-catch performance in the Redskins' 28-21 victory over the Chicago Bears in the 1937 NFL championship game. Millner caught 55- and 75-yard touchdown bombs from Sammy Baugh, and then decoyed perfectly when the Redskins quarterback went to another receiver for the winning touchdown.

The 6-0, 191-pound Millner is also remembered for his last-second touchdown reception that gave Notre Dame an 18-13 upset over Ohio State in a 1935 game many still refer to as the most memorable college game in history.

Minnesota Vikings

A group of Minneapolis businessmen headed by Bill Boyer and Max Winter were granted a charter franchise in the American Football League in 1959. Early in 1960, they withdrew from the AFL, knowing they would be granted an NFL franchise that would begin play in 1961. To avoid conflict between Minneapolis and St. Paul, the team was to be known as Minnesota. Winter became the first team president, Bert Rose was named general manager, and Joe Thomas was hired as the chief talent scout. Rose coined the team name "Vikings" and hired Norm Van Brocklin, who had quarterbacked the Philadelphia Eagles to the 1960 NFL championship, as head coach.

In their first game in 1961, the Vikings upset the Chicago Bears 37-13 as rookie quarterback Fran Tarkenton came off the bench to throw four touchdown passes and score a fifth. The Vikings lost their next seven games and finished 3-11. During the next few seasons, Minnesota slowly assembled a squad of quality players such as fullback Bill Brown, center Mick Tingelhoff, and defensive ends Carl Eller and Jim Marshall.

The flamboyant and controversial Van Brocklin grabbed many of the headlines, however, with his feuds with Rose and some of his players. Van Brocklin resigned in 1967. A few days later, Tarkenton was traded to the New York Giants for two first- and two second-round draft choices. The trade insured another bountiful crop of rookies that included defensive tackle Alan Page and wide receiver Gene Washington. General manager Jim Finks also hired Bud Grant, a veteran from the Canadian Football League, as his head coach.

The Vikings were 3-8-3 in 1967 but won the NFL Central Division championship in 1968 and again in 1969. Quarterback Joe Kapp was the hero of the 1969 team that compiled a 12-2 record and defeated the Cleveland Browns 27-7 for the NFL championship. But in Super Bowl IV, the heavily favored Vikings were surprised by the Kansas City Chiefs 23-7. In the first 11 seasons after the NFL-AFL merger in 1970, the Vikings, under Grant, won the NFC Central Division championship nine times, missing only in 1972 and 1979. Minnesota was famous for its outstanding defense led by the "Purple People Eaters" line of Eller, Page, Marshall, and Gary Larsen. Embroiled in a contract dispute, Kapp did not play after his excellent 1969 season but the Vikings reacquired Tarkenton in 1972 in another multi-player trade with the Giants. Running back Chuck Foreman and wide receivers John Gilliam and Ahmad Rashad joined with Tarkenton to give the Vikings a lethal offense to complement their standout defensive unit.

Minnesota won NFC championships in 1973, 1974, and 1976 but lost in the Super Bowl each year. The Miami Dolphins defeated the Vikings 24-7 in Super Bowl VIII, and the Pittsburgh Steelers won 16-6 in Super Bowl IX. In Super Bowl XI, the Oakland Raiders prevailed 32-14. Minnesota also lost to the Dallas Cowboys 23-6 in the 1977 NFC championship game.

The Vikings' ranks were depleted with the retirement of Tarkenton, Tingelhoff, and Marshall in 1979. Another fine quarterback, Tommy Kramer, replaced Tarkenton, but the Vikings' era of dominance was over. They finished 7-9 in 1979, their first losing season since 1967. In 1980, they won the division title with a 9-7 record but lost to Philadelphia 31-16 in the first playoff game. In the strike-shortened 1982 season, the Vikings advanced to the second round of the NFC's postseason championship tournament.

After the 1983 season, Grant retired and was replaced by assistant Les Steckel. But the 1984 Vikings won only three games, and Grant came back for a final season in 1985. In his 18 years as the Minnesota coach, he compiled a 158-86-5 record, won 11 NFL/ NFC Central Division championships, and one NFL and three NFC championships. In 1986, Grant was replaced by his long-time aide, Jerry Burns, and Burns led the Vikings to a wild-card playoff spot in 1987.

They advanced to the NFC championship game before losing to the Washington Redskins 17-10. The 1988 Vikings went 11-5 and earned another wild-card spot. They beat the Rams in the wild-card game, but lost to the 49ers 34-9.

During their first 25 seasons, Minnesota played outdoors in Metropolitan Stadium in suburban Edina. In 1986, they moved indoors to the 63,000-seat Hubert H. Humphrey Metrodome.

Members of the Hall of Fame:
(4) Jim Langer, Hugh McElhenny, Alan Page, Fran Tarkenton

Championships Won:
NFL (pre-1970): 1969
NFC: 1973, 1974, 1976
NFL Central Division: 1968, 1969
NFL Western Conference: 1969
NFC Central Division: 1970, 1971, 1973, 1974, 1975, 1976, 1977, 1978, 1980

Overall Record:

NFL Regular Season	218	179	9	.548
NFL Postseason	13	14	0	.481
Total	231	193	9	.544

Misdirection

A deceptive running play that the blockers feign is headed one way while the ball carrier heads in the other direction.

Mitchell, Bobby

b. Hot Springs, Arkansas, 6 June 1935.
Hall of Fame: 1983

Bobby Mitchell played halfback with the Cleveland Browns from 1958 to 1961. He teamed with the incomparable Jim Brown to give the Browns one of history's most lethal running duos. The University of Illinois graduate was not only a big-yardage rusher, he was also an excellent pass receiver and a breakaway threat as a punt- and kickoff-return specialist.

In 1962, he was traded to the Washington Redskins, where he in effect embarked on a second pro career, that of a full-time flanker. When the 6-0, 195-pound Mitchell retired after the 1968 season, his record of 14,078 combined net yards was the third highest ever. His 91 touchdowns ranked fifth all-time. Eighteen of his touchdowns came by rushing, 65 on receptions, three on punt returns, and five on kickoff returns. Mitchell won the NFL receiving title in 1962 with 72 catches. He never caught fewer than 58 passes his first six years in Washington. Mitchell was also the first black to play regularly with the Redskins.

With a 98-yard kickoff return, a 232-yard rushing game, and a 78-yard punt return his first two NFL seasons, Mitchell gained a

deserved and lasting reputation as a big-play threat. He was named all-pro in 1962 and 1964 and played in four Pro Bowls.

Mix, Ron

b. Los Angeles, California, 10 March 1938.
Hall of Fame: 1979

Ron Mix chose to sign with the Los Angeles Chargers of the new American Football League instead of the NFL's Baltimore Colts in 1960 simply because the Chargers offered him a far better deal. Playing in his home town was not an important consideration because the 6-4, 250-pound University of Southern California graduate didn't really like football well enough to think of playing for more than a year or two. The Chargers moved from Los Angeles to San Diego in 1961, but Mix improved as a player, began to like the game, and stayed around the entire 10 years of the AFL, plus a final year (1971) with the Oakland Raiders. Nicknamed the "Intellectual Assassin" because he was articulate off the field as well as devastating in action, Mix was an all-AFL selection eight times as a tackle and once as a guard. He played in seven AFL All-Star games and five of the first six AFL championship games. Incredibly, he was called for holding only twice in his first 10 seasons. Mix was unanimously chosen for the AFL's all-time team in 1969.

Monday Night Football

In 1970, the American Broadcasting Company signed a contract to televise 13 regular-season NFL games that would be played on Monday night. The Cleveland Browns defeated the New York Jets 31-21 in the inaugural Monday night game in the 1970 season opener. The experiment proved to be an immediate success. Television ratings have remained consistently high, and capacity in-stadium crowds have made Monday Night Football a gala event every week. In 1987-1988, Monday Night Football ranked as the fourteenth most-watched series on television.

Monk, Art

b. White Plains, New York, 5 December 1957.

Art Monk, a 6-3, 209-pound wide receiver from Syracuse University, was the Washington Redskins' first-round draft choice in 1981. After nine NFL seasons, Monk, who still is playing, ranked among history's top 20 receivers with 576 receptions for 7,979 yards and 39 touchdowns. His finest season came in 1984, when he caught an all-time record 106 passes for 1,372 yards and seven touchdowns. The next year he had 91

receptions. Monk was all-pro in 1984 and 1985 and a Pro Bowl selection from 1984 to 1986.

Monsters of the Midway

Beginning with their 73-0 victory over the Washington Redskins in the 1940 NFL championship game, the Chicago Bears dominated pro football over a seven-year period and were known as "The Monsters of the Midway."

Montana, Joe

b. Monongahela, Pennsylvania, 11 June 1956.

Joe Montana, a third-round draft choice of the San Francisco 49ers in 1979, played as a backup to Steve DeBerg for a year before earning the regular quarterback job in 1980. The Notre Dame graduate, who still is active, won NFC passing championships in 1981, 1984, and 1985 and the NFL title in 1987. A four-time All-NFC selection, Montana was the Most Valuable Player in Super Bowl XVI when he directed the 49ers to a 26-21 victory over the Cincinnati Bengals, and in Super Bowl XIX, when he and the 49ers defeated the Miami Dolphins 38-16. In Super Bowl XXIII, he passed for a record 357 yards and threw the game-winning touchdown pass in the final minute as the 49ers beat the Bengals again, this time 20-16. He has been a five-time Pro Bowl selection. In 10 NFL seasons, Montana has passed for more than 300 yards 30 times. He has completed 2,322 passes for 27,533 yards and 190 touchdowns. His 92.0 passing rating is the highest in NFL history.

Moore, Lenny

b. Reading, Pennsylvania, 25 November 1933.
Hall of Fame: 1975

When Lenny Moore joined the Baltimore Colts in 1956, the 6-1, 198-pound Penn State star was a combination flanker-halfback who rushed for a career-high 649 yards but caught only 11 passes. But in the next five seasons, as the Colts became one of the NFL's premier teams, Moore teamed with quarterback Johnny Unitas to give Baltimore a devasting pass-catch combination.

In the Colts' drive to their first championship in 1958, Moore contributed 1,536 rushing-receiving yards and 14 touchdowns, and was named all-pro for the first time. In the championship game against the New York Giants, Moore caught six passes for 101 yards. Moore did not fare as well when he shifted back "inside" a few years later. His injuries increased and his yardage production decreased. To his credit, he rebounded with a 20-touchdown performance in 1964 to win NFL Comeback Player of the Year acclaim.

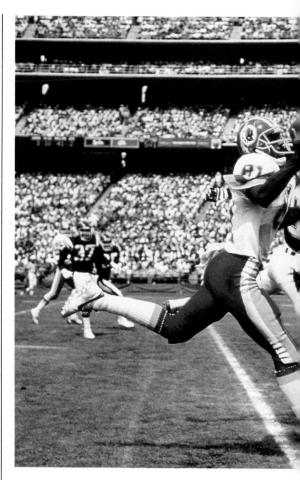

Art Monk grabs a long pass from Jay Schroeder on the San Diego 15-yard line. Wayne Davis made the tackle, but Monk still caught passes for 174 yards in this 1986 game.

Moore retired after the 1967 season with exceptional career totals – 12,449 combined net yards, 5,174 yards rushing, 363 pass receptions for 6,039 yards, and 678 points on 113 touchdowns. He was named all-pro five times and played in seven Pro Bowls.

Morrall, Earl

b. Muskegon, Michigan, 17 May 1934.

Earl Morrall, a 6-2, 210-pound All-American quarterback from Michigan State, played in the NFL for 21 years, longer than any other player except George Blanda. He began his career with the 1956 San Francisco 49ers, then played with the Pittsburgh Steelers, Detroit Lions, New York Giants, Baltimore Colts, and Miami Dolphins before retiring after the 1976 season. With the Colts in 1968, he won the NFL passing title as a replacement for the injured Johnny Unitas, was named NFL Player of the Year, and led Baltimore to Super Bowl III. In 1972, he took charge when Dolphins ace Bob Griese was injured, played a major role in Miami's perfect (17-0) season, and won the AFC passing championship. Morrall totaled 1,379 completions for 20,809 yards, 161 touchdowns, and 148 interceptions. He played in two pro Bowl games.

Motley, Marion

b. Leesburg, Georgia, 5 June 1920.
Hall of Fame: 1968

In the eight seasons he played with the Cleveland Browns from 1946 to 1953, Marion Motley, a 6-1, 238-pound fullback, was a devastating pass-protection blocker who became famous for his running of the Browns' draw play. The maneuver called for Browns' quarterback Otto Graham to drop back to pass but to hand off to Motley when the enemy rush line drew close. Motley would then barrel around or over opponents who blocked his path. Defenses could never again concentrate solely on Graham.

Motley played college football at South Carolina State College and the University of Nevada. Cleveland head coach Paul Brown first observed Motley in action at McKinley High School in Canton, Ohio, when he was coaching arch-rival Massillon. During World War II, Motley played for Brown's Great Lakes Navy team. Thus, Brown had good reason to sign Motley, whom many insist was the finest all-round football player during Cleveland's era of dominance. Motley was a three-time all-AAFC fullback and the leading rusher in the league's four-year history. In 1950, his first season in the NFL, Motley was all-pro, as well as the individual rushing champion. In his career, he rushed for 4,720 yards and averaged 5.7 yards each carry, an all-time record. He also caught 85 passes and scored 38 touchdowns.

Above: Tommy Kramer stands over center awaiting the snap. The Minnesota Vikings, under head coach Jerry Burns, are returning to their days as a powerhouse in the NFC, and it may not be long before they make their fifth Super Bowl appearance.

Left: Joe Montana started the 1988 season with a fight on his hands to remain as the 49ers' starting quarterback; he ended it with a third Super Bowl winner's ring on his finger, and accolades pronouncing him the greatest quarterback ever.

Muff

The touching of the ball by a player in an unsuccessful attempt to gain possession of a free ball; no possession is established.

Musso, George

b. Collinsville, Illinois, 8 April 1910.
Hall of Fame: 1982

George Musso played with the Chicago Bears from 1933 to 1944 when "The Monsters of the Midway" were the dominant team in the NFL. At 6-2, 270-pounds, the Millikin College graduate was the biggest Bear and also one of the best. The Bears' owner-coach, George Halas, first offered Musso $90 a game and sent him $5 expense money to seal the deal. When he faltered early, his salary was cut to $45 a game.

Musso, however, improved so rapidly the salary cut never took effect. Over the next 12 seasons, he was a standout as a middle guard on defense and first at tackle and later at guard on offense. "Big Bear" became the epitome of the powerful linemen who made the Bears successful. A quality 60-minute performer who was the first to be all-pro at two positions, as a guard in 1935 and a tackle in 1937, Musso also proved to be an exceptional team leader. He was the team captain his last nine seasons. Musso was elected to the Hall of Fame 38 years after his final NFL game.

N

★ ★

Nagurski, Bronko

b. Rainy River, Ontario, Canada, 3 November 1908. Hall of Fame: 1963

Bronko Nagurski already was a legend by the time he joined the Chicago Bears in 1930. At the University of Minnesota, the 6-2, 225-pounder was an All-America pick both as a tackle and a fullback in his senior season. Stories of his remarkable prowess both on and off the field captivated fans everywhere. With the Bears, the legend grew. Nagurski was a bull-like fullback, the symbol of powerful and rugged play at the NFL level. He was also a peerless blocker and a bone-jarring tackler as a linebacker on defense. Nagurski played with the Bears for eight seasons through 1937, when he retired to begin a more lucrative career as a professional wrestler. But in 1943, he answered the Bears' call for help, necessitated by the manpower shortages of World War II, and returned for one final season.

In his prime, Nagurski was even a threat as a forward passer. He had a favorite play that would call for him to fake a plunge, then retreat a step or two and lob a pass to a waiting receiver. His touchdown pass to Red Grange gave the Bears a victory over Portsmouth in the 1932 championship game. A year later, Nagurski used the same play twice to lead Chicago to a 23-21 victory in the 1933 NFL title contest.

Even after his layoff, Nagurski could still contribute to the Bears. He was used mostly as a tackle but carried the ball on key plays. In his final game in the 1943 title showdown, Nagurski plowed through the line for the touchdown that put the Bears ahead to stay in a 41-21 victory over the Washington Redskins.

Bronko Nagurski, a powerful full-back-linebacker, was one of the greatest players ever to play professional football. Giants head coach Steve Owen said the only way to stop Nagurski was "to shoot him before he leaves the dressing room."

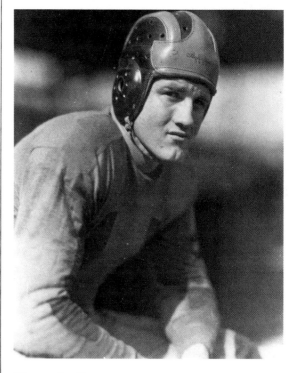

Namath, Joe

b. Beaver Falls, Pennsylvania, 31 May 1943. Hall of Fame: 1985

From the moment when Joe Namath signed a reported $400,000 contract with the New York Jets in 1965, the touted quarterback from the University of Alabama attracted universal attention to his every action, both on and off the field. Many insist his decision to join the AFL instead of accepting the offer of the NFL's St. Louis Cardinals marked the turning point in the costly inter-league struggle of the 1960s.

Although his playing career was hampered by a string of injuries, the 6-2, 200-pounder had the knack of making exciting things happen on the football field. Namath is best remembered for guiding the Jets to a stunning upset of the Baltimore Colts in Super Bowl III after personally guaranteeing the victory a few days before the game.

Namath had a long list of accomplishments. In 1967, he became the first player to pass for more than 4,000 yards in one season. He regularly produced 300-yard games when such feats were rarities. His 266-yard, three-touchdown performance against Oakland in the 1968 AFL title game put the Jets into Super Bowl III. His career totals show 1,886 completions for 27,663 yards and 173 touchdowns. Namath was the 1968 AFL Player of the Year and a unanimous all-pro quarterback in 1972. In 1969, he was named to the AFL's all-time team. After 12 seasons with the Jets, Namath moved to the Los Angeles Rams for a final season in 1977.

Nance, Jim

b. Indiana, Pennsylvania, 30 December 1942.

Jim Nance, a 6-1, 240-pound fullback from Syracuse University, was selected by the Boston Patriots in the nineteenth round of the 1965 AFL draft. In 1966, he set an all-time AFL record with 1,457 yards rushing, and he led the league again with 1,216 yards in 1967. Nance was named all-AFL in 1966 and 1967. After seven years with the Patriots, Nance missed the 1972 season with injuries, then concluded his career with the New York Jets in 1973. In eight years, he rushed for 5,401 yards and 45 touchdowns. He caught 133 passes for 879 yards and one touchdown.

National Football Conference

With the completion of the AFL-NFL merger in 1970, all the teams of the National Football League except Baltimore, Cleveland, and Pittsburgh made up the 13-team National Football Conference. The Dallas Cowboys, New York Giants, Philadelphia Eagles, St. Louis (moved to Phoenix in 1988) Cardinals, and Washington Redskins made up the NFC Eastern Division. The Chicago Bears, Detroit Lions, Green Bay Packers, and Minnesota Vikings made up the NFC Central Division. The Atlanta Falcons, Los Angeles Rams, New Orleans Saints, and San Francisco 49ers made up the NFC Western Division. In 1976, the Seattle Seahawks joined the Western Division, but in 1977 shifted to the American Football Conference and the Tampa Bay Buccaneers became a permanent member of the NFC Central and the fourteenth team in the conference.

The NFC championship summary:

Dallas Cowboys	(5)	1970, 1971, 1975, 1977, 1978
Washington Redskins	(4)	1972, 1982, 1983, 1987
Minnesota Vikings	(3)	1973, 1974, 1976
San Francisco 49ers	(3)	1981, 1984, 1988
Los Angeles Rams	(1)	1979
Philadelphia Eagles	(1)	1980
Chicago Bears	(1)	1985
New York Giants	(1)	1986

National Football League

Pro football was in a disorganized state when representatives of the nation's top pro teams met in Canton, Ohio, on September 17, 1920, to form the American Professional Football Association, the direct forerunner of the National Football League. Charter memberships were extended to 10 teams from four states. A membership fee of $100 was established, but no club ever paid it.

The mere existence of an organized league did not bring an immediate end to the chaos. During the NFL's first decade, 36 cities were members at one time or another. When the 1930 season opened, just 10 of those 36 teams still were in business. Only four teams from the 1920s remain in the NFL today. They are the Chicago Bears, Green Bay Packers, New York Giants, and Chicago/St. Louis/Phoenix Cardinals.

After five discouraging seasons, the NFL's fortunes began to turn in 1925 with the formation of the New York Giants franchise, and the signing of Harold (Red) Grange by the Chicago Bears. Both events gave the NFL much-needed exposure. When Grange and the Bears staged a coast-to-coast barnstorming tour after the

Joe Namath was more than just a football player, he was a media star with a comment always close to hand. He "guaranteed" the underdog New York Jets' victory in Super Bowl III.

season, large crowds turned out to see pro football games for the first time. In 1926, the NFL had to fight off the challenge of the first rival American Football League in a costly but brief battle. The AFL played only one season.

With a more-or-less stable membership for the first time, the NFL concentrated on making pro football more appealing to the fans in the 1930s. Rules changes included moving the goal posts to the goal line, making a forward pass legal anywhere behind the line of scrimmage, and moving the ball in 10 yards for the next scrimmage play if the previous play ended within five yards of the sidelines. In 1933, the NFL was divided into two divisions with the leaders meeting each year for the overall championship, which became an instant hit. Two exceptional super-stars – end Don Hutson and quarterback Sammy Baugh also helped transform pro football into an exciting offensive spectacle.

Immediately after World War II, the NFL faced its own "war," a costly inter-league struggle with the new All-America Football Conference. After four years, the battle ended with the Cleveland Browns, Baltimore Colts, and San Francisco 49ers joining the NFL and the rest of the AAFC disbanding. The Colts failed after the 1950 season, and the New York Yanks threw in the towel a year later. In 1952, the Dallas Texans became the last NFL franchise to fail. A new Baltimore Colts franchise was admitted in 1953, and, for the rest of the 1950s, the same 12 teams took the field every year.

In 1951, Commissioner Bert Bell contracted for the 1951 championship game to be televised coast-to-coast by the DuMont network. It was the introduction of the NFL to the television age. Attendance showed dramatic gains from 25,356 per game in 1950 to 43,617 in 1959. One game more than any other, the 1958 championship game between the Baltimore Colts and New York Giants, raised pro football interest to the boiling point. The heart-stopping action in the Colts' 23-17 overtime victory captivated the large national television audience that saw it.

In 1960, Pete Rozelle was named commissioner to replace Bert Bell, who had died in 1959. The Dallas Cowboys in 1960 and the Minnesota Vikings in 1961 became new NFL members. Still another rival, the fourth American Football League, began play in 1960. A bitter six-year struggle ensued before an AFL-NFL merger agreement was signed in June, 1966. Meanwhile, the Atlanta Falcons in 1966 and the New Orleans Saints in 1967 became NFL expansion teams. In 1970, the merged NFL consisted of 26 teams divided into the American and National Football Conferences. The NFL expanded again with the addition of the Seattle

Earle (Greasy) Neale transformed the Philadelphia Eagles from doormats into a dominant force in the 1940s. His Eagle defense, lining up in a 5-2 formation, was particularly effective against the run.

Seahawks and Tampa Bay Buccaneers in 1976.

The 1970s and 1980s have brought new and, often, much more serious problems to the NFL. There have been player strikes and threats of strikes, and many court and legislative challenges. The NFL also had to repel the challenges of two more rival leagues, the World Football League (1974-75) and the United States Football League (1983-85). Three teams changed cities in the 1980s. In 1982, the Oakland Raiders moved to Los Angeles. The Colts transferred from Baltimore to Indianapolis in 1984, and the Cardinals, who moved from Chicago to St. Louis in 1960, made a second shift, this one to Phoenix in 1988. Through it all, NFL football has continued to grow in popularity. Attendance, which averaged more than 55,000 per game since 1971, soared over the 60,000 mark in both 1981 and 1986. The Super Bowl has evolved into the premier event of the entire sports world. In response to the growing popularity of NFL football overseas, NFL owners in 1985 voted to stage at least one pre-season game in England/Europe and/or Japan each year.

Neale, Earle (Greasy)

b. Parkersburg, West Virginia, 5 November 1891; d. 2 November 1973. Hall of Fame: 1969

Earle (Greasy) Neale coached pro football for just 10 years, all of them with the Philadelphia

New England Patriots quarterback Doug Flutie takes the snap. Hero-worshipped in Boston since his college days, Flutie was described by Chicago quarterback Jim McMahon as 'America's favorite midget.' Flutie led the Patriots to within one victory of the AFC wild card game in 1988.

Eagles (1941 to 1950). Before Neale joined the club, the Eagles had been perennial losers in the NFL. Under his guidance, Philadelphia finished second in its division in 1944, 1945, and 1946, and then won three consecutive Eastern Division titles, as well as NFL championships by shutout scores in both 1948 and 1949. Although Neale compiled a 66-44-5 record and made the Eagles the NFL's dominant team in the late 1940s, he was fired after the 1950 season.

Neale was a brilliant star at West Virginia Wesleyan College. He once played pro football with the Canton Bulldogs while using an assumed name. Neale coached six different college teams and the semi-pro Ironton, Ohio, Tanks before joining the NFL ranks. His first NFL project was to learn the new T-formation attack, which he then utilized successfully as he developed the Eagles into a championship caliber team.

The Nesser Brothers

In 1904, Joe Carr, who later would become president of the National Football League, re-

organized the Columbus Panhandles pro football team. Most of the players were employees of the Panhandle division of the Pennsylvania Railway so they could travel free to road games. The team rarely played at home so stadium rental fees were not a problem. The team operated for more than 20 years but rarely was successful.

The Panhandles were one of the best known of the early day pro football teams. This was because most of their top players came from one family. Six Nesser brothers – John (quarterback), Phil (tackle), Ted (halfback), Fred (tackle-end), Frank (fullback), and Al (guardend) – were long-term Panhandles. For a game or two in 1921, a seventh Nesser brother – Raymond, the youngest of the clan – also wore the maroon-and-gold Columbus uniform. Legend also claims that Mother Nesser busied herself patching Panhandle uniforms, and Papa Nesser, who brought his family to America from Trier, Germany, in the early 1880s, served as the team's water boy. Curiously, the largest Nesser brother, 350-pound Pete, did not play football. In the early 1920s, Ted's son Charles also

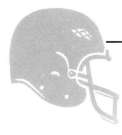

played for the Panhandles, making them the only father-son duo to appear in an NFL lineup together.

Neutral Zone

The space (the length of the ball) between the offensive and defensive line.

Nevers, Ernie

b. Willow River, Minnesota, 11 June 1903; d. 3 May 1976. Hall of Fame: 1963

When Red Grange bolted from the National Football League to the new American Football League in 1926, the NFL desperately searched for a name star to replace him as a gate attraction. The solution came in the form of 6-1, 205-pound Ernie Nevers, an All-America from Stanford who had been a hero in the 1925 Rose Bowl. Nevers, who also signed pro basketball and pro baseball contracts, agreed to play with the Duluth Eskimos for $15,000 and 25 percent of the gate. Nevers proved to be the superstar the NFL was seeking. Duluth played a 29-game schedule that year, and the multi-talented fullback played all but 26 minutes of a 1,740-minute season. In the one game he didn't start, he came off the bench to throw the winning touchdown pass.

Possessed with an indomitable competitive spirit, Nevers ran, passed, caught passes, returned kicks, punted, placekicked, called signals, played outstanding defense, and eventually became a player-coach. Nevers played a second year in Duluth, sat out the 1928 season with a broken tranverse process, and then returned in 1929 with the Cardinals, for whom he served as player-coach in 1930-31, and again in 1939. On Thanksgiving Day, 1929, Nevers enjoyed his finest game, a 40-point outburst in a 40-6 victory over the cross-town Bears. A week later, he scored all 19 points in a shutout victory over Dayton. Thus, in two weeks, he scored 59 consecutive points for his team, one of the most remarkable feats in sports history.

New England Patriots

In 1959, the American Football League awarded its eighth franchise to a group of 10 New England businessmen headed by William H. Sullivan, Jr., who was named the team president. The franchise, representing Boston, was named the Boston Patriots. It appropriately adopted red, white, and blue as the official colors. Sullivan selected Lou Saban as head coach and picked Boston University Field as the team's home stadium. The Patriots finished with a 5-9 record in their first season, and Sulli-

van reported losses of $350,000.

In 1961, the team acquired quarterback Vito (Babe) Parilli. For the next seven years, he teamed with receiver-kicker Gino Cappelletti, who became the highest scorer in AFL history. Mike Holovak, the Patriots' director of player personnel, replaced Saban as head coach in midseason. The 1961 Patriots finished 7-1-1 under Holovak, who kept the Patriots in constant championship contention for the next several years.

In 1963, Boston tied for the AFC Eastern Division title, defeated Buffalo in a playoff, and then lost to San Diego 51-10 in the AFL championship game. The 1964 Patriots had a 10-3-1 record, their best under Holovak, but finished second behind the Buffalo Bills. However, the Patriots, who had moved to 38,000-seat Fenway Park in 1963, finished in the black for the first time in 1964.

Jim Nance, a powerful runner from Syracuse, joined the team in 1965, and a year later, he rushed for an AFL-record 1,458 yards. The Patriots slipped badly in 1967 and 1968, and Holovak was replaced by Clive Rush before the 1969 season. The Patriots fared no better under Rush, who was fired in mid-1970.

In addition to their troubles on the field, the Patriots faced stadium problems as well. They moved from Fenway Park to Boston College Alumni Stadium in 1969 and to Harvard Stadium in 1970. In August, 1971, the Patriots moved into new Schaefer Stadium in Foxboro, Massachusetts, and the team was renamed the New England Patriots. The facility was renamed Sullivan Stadium in 1983.

Although the Patriots steadily built up a pool of talented players in the early 1970s, they didn't enjoy another winning season until 1976, the fourth year of head coach Chuck Fairbanks' tenure. Quarterback Jim Plunkett from Stanford was the 1971 NFL Rookie of the Year. Other quality newcomers in the early 1970s included guard John Hannah, wide receiver Darryl Stingley, quarterback Steve Grogan, and running backs Mack Herron and Sam Cunningham. The 1976 Patriots were the only team to defeat the eventual Super Bowl champion Oakland Raiders. New England's 11-5 record brought a wild-card playoff berth but the Patriots lost to Oakland 24-21 in the first round. The 1978 Patriots won their first divisional championship since 1963 with an 11-3 record, but Fairbanks's late-season announcement that he was leaving for a college coaching job demoralized the team and eliminated any championship hopes.

In the strike-shortened 1982 season, the Patriots' 5-4 record gave them a berth in the AFC postseason tournament but they lost to Miami in the first round. Midway into the 1984 season, head coach Ron Meyer was fired and replaced by the former Baltimore Colts Hall of Fame receiver, Raymond Berry, who immediately turned the Patriots into winners. In Berry's first full season in 1985, New England earned a wild-card berth with an 11-5 record and then defeated the New York Jets, Los Angeles Raiders, and Miami Dolphins to win its first AFC championship. In Super Bowl XX, the Patriots were beaten by the Chicago Bears 46-10. New England won the AFC East with another 11-5 record in 1986 but lost to the Denver Broncos 22-17 in the first playoff game. In Berry's third full season in 1987, his team fell one game short of another divisional championship. In 1988, Victor Kiam purchased a controlling interest in the club from Sullivan.

Members of the Hall of Fame:
(1) Raymond Berry

Championships Won:
AFC: 1985
AFL Eastern Division: 1963
AFC Eastern Division: 1978, 1986

Overall Record:

AFL Regular Season	63	68	9	.482
NFL Postseason	1	1	0	.500
NFL Regular Season	139	141	0	.496
NFL Postseason	3	5	0	.375
Total	206	215	9	.490

New Orleans Saints

The NFL awarded an expansion franchise to New Orleans on All Saints Day, November 1, 1966. John W. Mecom, Jr., from Houston, Texas, was designated majority stockholder and president of the franchise. Among his limited partners was Al Hirt, the Bourbon Street trumpet player. The team was named the Saints in honor of the Dixieland classic, "When the Saints Go Marchin' In." Tom Fears, formerly with the Los Angeles Rams, was hired as head coach.

Several veteran NFL players, including defensive end Doug Atkins from the Chicago Bears, fullback Jim Taylor from the Green Bay Packers, and quarterback Gary Cuozzo from the Baltimore Colts, provided the nucleus for the first New Orleans team, and the Saints won five of their six preseason games. In the 1967 regular-season opener, before more than 80,000 fans in Tulane Stadium, the Saints' John Gilliam returned the opening kickoff against the Rams for a 94-yard touchdown. The Saints finished with a 3-11 record. Dave Whitsell tied for the NFL lead with 10 interceptions. Rookie end Dan Abramowicz, destined to become the leading receiver in team history, had 50 receptions. Home attendance averaged 77,000.

The bright hopes generated in 1967 failed to materialize in the years ahead. The Saints improved to 4-9-1 in 1968 and to 5-9 in 1969 but Fears was fired midway through the 1970 season. He was replaced by J.D. Roberts, who led his team to a 19-17 upset of the Detroit Lions in the first game. The winning points came on the game's last play, an NFL record-setting 63-yard field goal by Tom Dempsey, who was born without a right hand or toes on his right foot. Roberts failed to produce a winner, however, and was fired after the 1972 season.

John North led the Saints to 5-9 seasons in 1973 and 1974 before he was fired in 1975, the year the team moved into the 72,000-seat Louisiana Superdome. Hank Stram had a 7-21 record in 1976 and 1977. Dick Nolan, a former San Francisco 49ers coach, then led the Saints to a 7-9 record in 1978 and a break-even 8-8 record in 1979. Quarterback Archie Manning, running back Chuck Muncie, and wide receiver Wes Chandler gave the Saints unprecedented offensive punch. With 370 points in 1979, they finished second in the entire NFC in scoring. But the Saints fell to 1-15 in 1980 and Nolan was fired after 12 games.

O.A. (Bum) Phillips, who had made the Houston Oilers into a winning team, was hired in New Orleans in 1981. With quarterback Ken Stabler and running back George Rogers creating excitement, the Saints improved under Phillips, but his best record was 8-8 in 1983. Phillips resigned after 12 games in 1985. His son Wade finished out the season.

In June 1985, Mecom sold the Saints to New Orleans car dealer Tom Benson for $70.2 million. The next year, Benson named Jim Finks, who had been successful in building winners in Minnesota and Chicago, as general manager. Finks hired Jim Mora, who had coached two United States Football League championship teams, as head coach. The Saints improved to 7-9 in Mora's first season, then enjoyed their finest year ever in 1987. Paced by new stars such as quarterback Bobby Hebert, running back Rueben Mayes, and kicker Morten Andersen, the Saints won 12 of 15 games, the second best record in the NFL. In their first playoff appearance they were upset by Minnesota 44-10.

Members of the Hall of Fame:
(2) Doug Atkins, Jim Taylor.

Championships Won:
None

Overall Record:

NFL Regular Season	112	205	5	.356
NFL Postseason	0	1	0	.000
Total	112	206	5	.354

New York Giants

Saying "a franchise of any kind in New York should be worth $500," Tim Mara became the owner of an NFL team in 1925. He named his

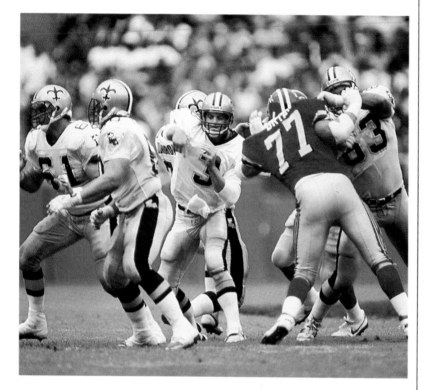

New Orleans Saints suffered 21 consecutive seasons of below .500 football until 1987, when it had not only it first winning season, but also saw its first playoff action. Led by Bobby Hebert (3) the Saints won 10 games in 1988, but failed to make the playoffs.

team the Giants after the baseball club with which it would share the Polo Grounds. Today the Giants still exist as the fourth oldest franchise in pro football, with the Mara heirs, son Wellington and nephew Tim, still in control.

During their six-decade history, the Giants have been one of the NFL's most successful teams both on and off the field. The senior Mara experienced at least two difficult years, however, before the Giants' future in pro football was assured. Faced with competition from college football which captured fan and media attention in New York, the Giants were $40,000 in the red as the 1925 season drew to a close. Then on December 6, the Chicago Bears brought their storied rookie, Red Grange, to New York. A record crowd of 73,000 jammed the Polo Grounds, and Mara recouped all of his losses in one day. Mara faced an even bigger challenge in 1926, when the rival American Football League established a New York Yankees team with Grange as the principal attraction. Mara lost $40,000 but the Yankees lost $100,000 and the AFL folded. The Giants finished sixth in the 22-team NFL and then defeated the AFL champion Philadelphia Quakers 31-0 in history's first inter-league postseason game.

Buoyed by tackles Steve Owen and Cal Hubbard and halfback Joe Guyon, the 1927 Giants, coached by Earl Potteiger, won the NFL championship with an 11-1-1 record. Their defense permitted an all-time low 20 points in 13 games. After the 1930 season, the Giants became the first NFL team to play in a major charity game, defeating the Notre Dame All-Stars 22-0 before 55,000 fans. The game raised $115,153 for the New York City Unemployment Fund.

In 1931, Owen was named head coach. He played for two more seasons but coached the Giants for 23 years until after the 1953 season. Under Owen, the Giants were consistent championship contenders. They won eight NFL Eastern Conference championships, including NFL championships in 1934 and 1938. Owen's cumulative record was 153-108-17.

In the 1930s, Owen's teams were led by center Mel Hein, end Morris (Red) Badgro, halfback Ken Strong, and tailback Ed Danowski. The Giants lost to the Chicago Bears 23-21 in the first NFL championship game in 1933. The 1934 championship game was played on an icy field at the Polo Grounds, but the Giants donned basketball shoes at halftime to gain the footing needed to upset the Bears 30-13. Owen unveiled his A-formation offense in 1937 and the Giants won Eastern championships in 1938 and 1939. In 1938, they defeated the Packers 23-17 for the NFL championship but they lost to the Packers 27-0 the next year.

In the 1940s, the Giants played in three more NFL championship games but lost each time – 37-9 to the Bears in 1941, 14-7 to the Packers in 1944, and 24-14 to the Bears in 1946.

In 1950, Owen introduced his "Umbrella" defense, and he had stars such as defensive tackle Arnie Weinmeister and safety Emlen Tunnell to make it effective. The Giants defeated the Cleveland Browns twice to tie for the division title but lost a playoff game to the Browns that year. They were a close second again in 1951 and 1952 but slumped badly in 1953. Owen was fired and assistant coach Jim Lee Howell was promoted to head coach.

Howell stayed with the team until his retirement in 1960. Led by players such as halfback Frank Gifford, tackle Roosevelt Brown, defensive end Andy Robustelli, and middle linebacker Sam Huff, the Giants won six Eastern Conference championships in eight seasons, beginning in 1956. Three were under Howell and three under coach Allie Sherman (1961-63). They won the 1956 NFL championship with a 47-7 victory over the Bears but lost their next five NFL championship games to Baltimore in 1958 and 1959, to Green Bay in 1961 and 1962, and to the Chicago Bears in 1963. In 1961, Y.A. Tittle replaced long-time favorite Charlie Conerly at quarterback; Tittle won NFL Most Valuable Player honors in 1961 and 1963.

Fortunes changed dramatically for the Giants after the 1963 season. Under six coaches in the next 25 years, they managed to finish above .500 only six times. Fran Tarkenton came to New York in a multi-player trade with Minnesota in 1967 but the prolific passer could not transform the Giants. He led his team to four consecutive second-place finishes from 1967 to 1970.

The Giants didn't finish as high as second again until 1984 and 1985. They advanced to the second playoff round each year. In 1986, led by head coach Bill Parcells and stalwarts such as quarterback Phil Simms, running back Joe Morris, and linebackers Carl Banks, Harry Carson, and Lawrence Taylor, the Giants won their first NFC championship with a 14-2 regular-season record and a 17-0 victory over Washington in the championship game. Then they defeated the Denver Broncos 39-20 in Super Bowl XXI.

The Giants, who moved from the Polo Grounds to Yankee Stadium in 1956, played both in the Yale Bowl in New Haven, Connecticut, and Shea Stadium in New York in 1973, 1974, and 1975 before moving to their present home, 76,000-seat Giants Stadium in East Rutherford, New Jersey. The Giants had 86 consecutive sellouts before moving to the Yale Bowl and have led the NFL in attendance seven of 12 seasons since moving to Giants Stadium.

Members of the Hall of Fame:
(24) Morris (Red) Badgro, Roosevelt Brown, Larry Csonka, Ray Flaherty, Frank Gifford, Joe Guyon, Mel Hein, Wilbur (Pete) Henry, Arnie Herber, Cal Hubbard, Sam Huff, Alphonse (Tuffy) Leemans, Vince Lombardi, Tim Mara, Don Maynard, Hugh McElhenny, Steve Owen, Andy Robustelli, Ken Strong, Fran Tarkenton, Jim Thorpe, Y.A. Tittle, Emlen Tunnell, Arnie Weinmeister.

Championships Won:
Super Bowl: XXI
NFL (pre-1970): 1927, 1934, 1938, 1956
NFC: 1986
Eastern Conference: 1933, 1934, 1935, 1938, 1939, 1941, 1944, 1946, 1956, 1958, 1959, 1961, 1962, 1963
NFC Eastern Division: 1986

Overall Record:
NFL Regular Season	442	366	32	.545
NFL Postseason	10	16	0	.385
Total	452	382	32	.540

New York Jets

Harry Wismer was granted a charter franchise at the American Football League's organizational meeting on August 14, 1959. His team was to be known as the New York Titans and would play in the Polo Grounds. Sammy Baugh, the record-setting quarterback from the Washington Redskins, was hired as head coach. Don Maynard, a free agent wide receiver from Canada, became the first player to sign a Titans contract.

The Titans, who drew only 9,607 fans in their first home game, were 7-7 the first two years but fell to 5-9 in 1962 under new head coach Clyde (Bulldog) Turner. Wismer, who had lost $2.1 million in the first two years, could not

Phil Simms lines up behind the offensive line of the New York Giants. In Super Bowl XXI, Simms completed 22 of 25 passes for three touchdowns; his 88 percent completion rate is a Super Bowl record.

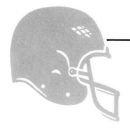

meet his payroll, and the AFL took over the club's operation for the rest of the year. In 1962, the Titans drew just 36,161 in seven home games.

In 1963, a five-man syndicate headed by David (Sonny) Werblin purchased the franchise for $1 million. Weeb Ewbank was chosen head coach and the team name was changed to Jets. The colors, which had been blue and gold, were changed to green and white. The next year, the Jets moved into new Shea Stadium and set an AFL attendance record when 45,665 saw them beat Denver 30-6 in the season opener. In 1965, Werblin signed Joe Namath, the heralded quarterback from Alabama, to a reported $400,000 contract. Even with Namath, New York did not become a winner until 1967, when it finished second in the AFL East with an 8-5-1 record.

In 1968, the Jets won the AFL Eastern Division with an 11-3 record and the AFL championship with a 27-23 victory over the Oakland Raiders. Joe Namath was the Most Valuable Player as the Jets upset the NFL's Baltimore Colts 16-7 in Super Bowl III. In the AFL's last season in 1969, the Jets again won the AFL East with a 10-4 record but were defeated by the Kansas City Chiefs 13-6 in a first-round playoff game. Four Jets – Ewbank, Namath, Maynard, and defensive end Gerry Philbin – were named to the AFL's all-time team that was selected after the season.

The Jets did not experience a winning season in the first 11 years after the AFL-NFL merger. Even Namath, who had an exceptional season in 1972, lost much of his effectiveness due to injuries. Ewbank resigned as head coach after the 1973 season and Charley Winner was selected to take his place. When Winner did not produce a winning team, Lou Holtz (1976) and Walt Michaels (1977-1982) directed the Jets. Michaels's 1981 Jets won 11 of 16 games and earned a wild-card playoff berth but lost in the first playoff round. New York won six of nine games in the strike-shortened 1982 season and won two postseason tournament games before falling to the Miami Dolphins 14-0 in the AFC championship game. The defensive line, led by ends Joe Klecko and Mark Gastineau, became known as the "New York Sack Exchange," and running back Freeman McNeil gave the Jets a solid offensive punch.

Michaels resigned after the 1982 season and was replaced by Joe Walton. Walton and the Jets earned a wild-card berth with an 11-5 record in 1985 but lost to New England in the first playoff round. The Jets were a wild-card playoff team again in 1986, defeating Kansas City before losing to the Cleveland Browns in double-overtime in the divisional playoff game.

In 1984, the Jets left Shea Stadium, their home for 20 years, to move to New Jersey to share Giants Stadium with the Giants.

Members of the Hall of Fame:
(3) Weeb Ewbank, Don Maynard, Joe Namath

Championships Won:
Super Bowl: III
AFL: 1968
AFL Eastern Division: 1968, 1969

Overall Record:

AFL Regular Season	69	65	6	.514
AFL Postseason	2	1	0	.667
NFL Regular Season	122	156	2	.439
NFL Postseason	3	4	0	.429
Total	196	226	8	.465

Newsome, Ozzie

b. Muscle Shoals, Alabama, 16 March 1956.

A 6-2, 232-pound All-America wide receiver at the University of Alabama, Ozzie Newsome was a first-round draft choice of the 1978 Cleveland Browns. With the Browns, he was converted into a tight end. After 11 seasons, Newsome, who still is playing, had 610 receptions for 7,416 yards and 44 touchdowns. He ranked among the top 10 lifetime receiving leaders and led all tight ends in receptions. In 1983 and 1984, Newsome had back-to-back 89-reception seasons. He won all-pro honors in 1979 and 1984 and played in three Pro Bowl games.

NFL Alumni Association

Formed in 1967 to help care for players not covered by pensions and other ex-pros down on their luck, the NFL Alumni Association was reorganized in 1977 for the purpose of "serving youth through sports and sports through youth." Made up of former professional football players and other interested businessmen, the NFL Alumni Association is headquartered in Fort Lauderdale, Florida.

NFL Champions, 1920-1932

1920	Akron Pros
1921	Chicago Staleys
1922	Canton Bulldogs
1923	Canton Bulldogs
1924	Cleveland Bulldogs
1925	Chicago Cardinals
1926	Frankford Yellow Jackets
1927	New York Giants
1928	Providence Steam Roller
1929	Green Bay Packers
1930	Green Bay Packers
1931	Green Bay Packers
1932	Chicago Bears

NFL Championship Games, 1933-1969

(Home team in bold)

1933 **Chicago Bears** 23, New York Giants 21
1934 **New York Giants** 30, Chicago Bears 13
1935 **Detroit Lions** 26, New York Giants 7
1936 Green Bay Packers 21, Boston Redskins 6*
1937 Washington Redskins 28, **Chicago Bears** 21
1938 **New York Giants** 23, Green Bay Packers 17
1939 **Green Bay Packers** 27, New York Giants 0
1940 Chicago Bears 73, **Washington Redskins** 0
1941 **Chicago Bears** 37, New York Giants 9
1942 **Washington Redskins** 14, Chicago Bears 6
1943 **Chicago Bears** 41, Washington Redskins 21
1944 Green Bay Packers 14, **New York Giants** 7
1945 **Cleveland Rams** 15, Washington Redskins 14
1946 Chicago Bears 24, **New York Giants** 14
1947 **Chicago Cardinals** 28, Philadelphia Eagles 21
1948 **Philadelphia Eagles** 7, Chicago Cardinals 0
1949 Philadelphia Eagles 14, **Los Angeles Rams** 0
1950 **Cleveland Browns** 30, Los Angeles Rams 28
1951 **Los Angeles Rams** 24, Cleveland Browns 17
1952 Detroit Lions 17, **Cleveland Browns** 7
1953 **Detroit Lions** 17, Cleveland Browns 16
1954 **Cleveland Browns** 56, Detroit Lions 10
1955 Cleveland Browns 38, **Los Angeles Rams** 14
1956 **New York Giants** 47, Chicago Bears 7
1957 **Detroit Lions** 59, Cleveland Browns 14
1958 Baltimore Colts 23, **New York Giants** 17 (OT)
1959 **Baltimore Colts** 31, New York Giants 16
1960 **Philadelphia Eagles** 17, Green Bay Packers 13
1961 **Green Bay Packers** 37, New York Giants 0
1962 Green Bay Packers 16, **New York Giants** 7
1963 **Chicago Bears** 14, New York Giants 10
1964 **Cleveland Browns** 27, Baltimore Colts 0
1965 **Green Bay Packers** 23, Cleveland Browns 12
1966 Green Bay Packers 34, **Dallas Cowboys** 27
1967 **Green Bay Packers** 21, Dallas Cowboys 17
1968 Baltimore Colts 34, **Cleveland Browns** 0
1969 **Minnesota Vikings** 27, Cleveland Browns 7

*Played at neutral site, Polo Grounds, New York

NFL Charities

In 1973, NFL Charities, a non-profit organization, was formed by the NFL member teams to enable them collectively to make grants to charitable causes. The money for NFL Charities activities is generated from NFL Properties' licensing of NFL trademarks and team names. Since 1973, more than 100 different needy organizations have received grant commitments totaling nearly $8 million from NFL Charities. The largest is a $1 million, 10-year commitment to the Vince Lombardi Cancer Research Center at Georgetown University.

NFL Films

NFL Films is recognized as the premier film-making organization in the world of sports. Its staff of almost 150 includes award-winning cameramen, technicians, soundmen, and script writers. NFL Films, which was organized in 1964, has received 55 television Emmy awards. From February through August, NFL Films concentrates it efforts on creating highlight films for each of the 28 NFL teams. During each season, NFL Films is responsible for filming every play and processing the film virtually overnight for use all over the world that week.

NFL Players Association

The National Football League Players Association was organized in 1956 and formally recognized by the NFL owners in 1957. In 1959, the Bert Bell Pension Plan was instituted. The Association was relatively inactive until 1968, when a lengthy dispute over pre-season game pay, higher minimum salaries, and pension and insurance plan increases turned into a combination players' strike/owners' lockout that lasted two weeks. The players staged preseason strikes in 1970 and 1974, but no regular-season games were missed.

Neither the players nor the owners were as fortunate in 1982, when a strike that lasted 57 days interrupted the regular season. NFL teams wound up playing a nine-game regular-season schedule and a special playoff tournament was devised to determine the teams that would meet in Super Bowl XVII. In the new collective bargaining agreement that followed, the free-agent system was left unchanged, but a minimum salary schedule based on years of experience was established. A severance pay plan was introduced along with improved pension and insurance benefits.

In 1987, unrestricted free agency became the principal issue. As in 1982, an in-season strike began after the second week but the owners retaliated by staging games between replacement teams with the results counting in the final standings. After 24 days, the strike ended. No agreement was reached but the players continued to perform under most of the 1982 agreement while the NFL Players Association pursued an anti-trust suit.

NFL Properties

NFL Properties was established in 1963 to fill a need for quality control in the use of NFL trademarks on souvenir items. NFLP now serves as the licensing, marketing, and publishing arm of the National Football League. NFL Properties

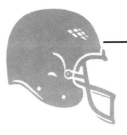

acts as the quality control guardian for any commercial use of league and club trademarks. The licensing and marketing divisions of NFL Properties are headquartered in New York.

The Creative Services division of NFL Properties is the publisher of official NFL books and printed materials in addition to the in-stadium GameDay magazine.

Nickel Defense

A defensive formation in which an extra (fifth) pass defender, the Nickel back, is brought into the game, usually in place of a linebacker.

1932 Championship Game

Because tie games did not count in the standings, the Chicago Bears (6-1-6) and Portsmouth Spartans (6-1-4) tied for first place in 1932. A hastily scheduled playoff game, the first ever for the NFL, was played indoors in Chicago Stadium. The field was only 80 yards long and the sidelines were close to the stands.

Out of this game came three significant rules changes that helped to make pro football a more offense-oriented game. The changes included moving the goal posts to the goal line and the hashmarks 10 yards inbounds, and

making a forward pass legal anywhere behind the line of scrimmage. The NFL owners liked the idea of a season-ending championship game, so they split the league into two divisions in 1933, with the two first-place teams playing for the NFL championship.

Nitschke, Ray

b. Elmwood Park, Illinois, 29 December 1936. Hall of Fame: 1978

A ferocious middle linebacker, 6-3, 235-pound Ray Nitschke was the heart of the Green Bay Packers defense during their dynasty in the 1960s. The University of Illinois graduate was a savage but clean-playing performer, equally adept at stopping the run or defending against passes. In his 15-year NFL career from 1958 to 1972, he recorded 25 interceptions. A three-time all-pro selection, Nitschke was the Most Valuable Player in the 1962 NFL title game. He was picked as the top middle linebacker of his day by former NFL linebackers in a poll conducted in the 1960s. In 1969, he was named the outstanding linebacker in the NFL's first 50 years. Nitschke became the first Green Bay defensive player primarily from the 1960s to be elected to the Hall of Fame.

Nitschke was an all-state quarterback in high

JoJo Townsell (83) and Joe Klecko (73) combine to stop a New England player on a punt return. The New York Jets have suffered black Decembers for the past few seasons that have seen them drop out of contention.

Below: As the hub of Green Bay's defensive alignment for 15 seasons, Ray Nitschke struck terror into the hearts of ball carriers. Orphaned at a young age, the middle linebacker used sporting technique as a method of learning discipline.

school. At Illinois, he played both fullback on offense and linebacker on defense. The Packers wisely eyed him as a middle linebacker when they drafted him in the third round in 1958. Nitschke soon established himself as one of the hardest-hitting and most skilled of all pro football players.

No Shows

The term applied to fans who purchase tickets but do not attend a game.

Nobis, Tommy

b. San Antonio, Texas, 20 September 1943.

A consensus All-America and the Outland Trophy winner as a senior at the University of Texas, linebacker Tommy Nobis was drafted by both Atlanta of the NFL and Houston of the rival AFL in 1965. American astronauts orbiting the Earth used their radio communications to urge Nobis to sign with the Oilers, but the 6-2, 240-pound Nobis opted for the Falcons. Nobis won Rookie-of-the-Year acclaim in 1966 and all-pro honors in 1967. He was selected for five Pro Bowl games in his first seven seasons. He retired after the 1976 season.

Noll, Chuck

b. Cleveland, Ohio, 5 January 1932.

Chuck Noll began his pro football career as a linebacker and offensive guard with the Cleveland Browns from 1953 to 1959. He spent 10

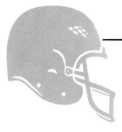

years as an assistant coach with the Los Angeles/San Diego Chargers and Baltimore Colts before being named head coach of the Pittsburgh Steelers in 1969. His first Pittsburgh team finished 1-13, but Noll initiated a building program that would turn the Steelers into the dominant team of the 1970s. In 1972, the Steelers won the AFC Central Division championship, their first championship in 40 years of NFL play. Pittsburgh then won six more AFC Central championships between 1974 and 1979, and AFC championships in 1974, 1975, 1978, and 1979. They also set a record by winning Super Bowls IX, X, XIII, and XIV.

The retirement of many stars of the Super Bowl years forced another rebuilding program, one that produced two more AFC Central Division championships in 1983 and 1984. Through 1988, Noll's 20-year regular-season record in Pittsburgh was 168-125-1. His teams had won 15 of 22 playoff games, and his 183 victories ranked fifth among all NFL coaches.

Head coach Chuck Noll looks on unconcernedly. He has been under pressure in recent seasons as his Steelers have aged and fallen from their pedestal.

Nomellini, Leo

b. Lucca, Italy, 19 June 1924.
Hall of Fame: 1969

In the San Francisco 49ers' first NFL draft in 1950, their first pick was Leo Nomellini, a 6-3, 264-pound All-America tackle from the University of Minnesota. Nomellini proved to be everything the 49ers envisioned – and more. He played for 14 years from 1950 to 1963 and saw action in 174 consecutive regular season games, and, counting 10 Pro Bowl appearances, preseason and playoff games, 266 pro contests in all. "The Lion," as he was known, became one of the few men ever to be named all-pro both on offense and defense. He was all-league on the offensive unit twice and on the defensive side four times. In his first year of eligibility he was elected to the Hall of Fame.

Nomellini grew up in Chicago's tough west side, passing up high school sports to work in a factory to help support his family. His first taste of football was with the Cherry Point, North Carolina, Marines team in 1942. On his return from service, he was offered a scholarship at Minnesota. Freshmen were eligible in 1946, and, in the first college game he ever saw, Nomellini was a starting guard for the Gophers.

Nose Tackle

The position in the middle of a three-man defensive line. He normally lines up directly across from the center.

Offense

1. The team with the ball.
2. The tactics of that team.

Officials

The NFL utilizes seven-man officiating teams to administer and control its games. A capsulized summary of the duties of each official follows:

REFEREE – Responsible for control of the game. Gives signals for all fouls and is final authority for rules interpretations. Takes a position in the offensive backfield 10 to 12 yards behind the line of scrimmage. Responsible for determining legal snap, legal motion, legality of blocks on passing plays. Adjusts final position of ball at end of play.

UMPIRE – Primary responsibility is to rule on players' equipment as well as their conduct and actions on scrimmage line. Lines up approximately four to five yards downfield. Observes legality of blocks by offensive linemen and warding off of blocks by defensive linemen.

HEAD LINESMAN and LINE JUDGE – Each straddles line of scrimmage on opposite side of the field from the other. Each is responsible for ruling on offside, encroachment, and actions pertaining to scrimmage line prior to or at the snap. Each is responsible for ruling on out-of-bounds plays on his side of field. HEAD LINESMAN helps determine forward progress of ball and assists on rulings on passing plays. LINE JUDGE directs his attention toward activities that occur behind the umpire.

BACK JUDGE and SIDE JUDGE – Back judge operates on same side of field as line judge, side judge on same side of field as head linesman. Each is 17 yards deep, and keys on wide receiver on his side of field. Each concentrates on actions of offensive receivers, observing legality of potential block(s) or of actions taken against them by defenders. Each makes decisions involving catching, recovery, or illegal touching of loose ball beyond scrimmage line.

FIELD JUDGE – Takes a position 25 yards downfield. Concentrates on the tight end, his

actions, and actions taken against him. Times interval between plays on 45-second clock. Other responsibilities are similar to those of side judge and back judge. With back judge, rules whether conversions or field goals are successful.

During the first nine years of the NFL from 1920 to 1928, three-man officiating crews consisted of a referee, umpire, and head linesman. The NFL introduced the field judge position in 1929 and stayed with a four-man crew until 1947, when a fifth official, the back judge, was added. In 1965, a sixth official, the line judge, was added. Thirteen years later in 1978, the side judge position was created to complete the seven-man alignment that exists today.

Offside

A penalty called when any part of a player's body is across the line of scrimmage at the time the ball is snapped.

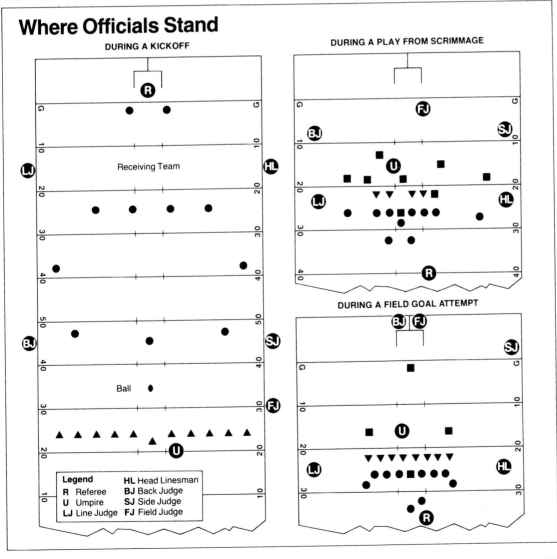

Olsen, Merlin

b. Logan, Utah, 15 September 1940.
Hall of Fame: 1982

Many highly touted rookies have trouble adjusting to pro football early in their careers but Merlin Olsen, the Los Angeles Rams' first-round draft choice in 1962, was an instant hit. The 6-5, 270-pound All-America and Outland Trophy winner from Utah State won the starting left defensive tackle job the third week of his rookie season and never gave it up. Olsen, a Phi Beta Kappa scholar, quickly learned that sheer brute strength was not as important in the NFL as it had been in college and high school, so he carefully mastered the intricacies of defensive line play.

During the 1960s and early 1970s, Olsen was a key element in the Rams' devastating "Fearsome Foursome" defensive line. He always was quiet and unpretentious, but deadly effective in game action. He was a consensus all-pro pick from 1966 to 1970 and again in 1973. He played in a record 14 consecutive Pro Bowls. Olsen was elected to the Hall of Fame in his first year of eligibility. Upon his retirement from the field, Olsen moved into the television commentary box, where he continues to be highly respected.

Onside

The side of a play toward the flow of the action.

Onside Kick

A short kickoff that carries at least 10 yards, allowing the kicking team a chance to recover the free ball.

Oorang Indians

The Oorang Indians existed as a National Football League franchise in 1922 and 1923 solely because the team owner, Walter Lingo, wanted to promote the sale of the Airedale, a new hunting dog he was breeding in his Oorang Kennels. Lingo had another passion – American Indians – and so he hired Jim Thorpe, the most famous of all Indian athletes, to serve as the team's player-coach. Thorpe lined up an entire team of either full-blooded or part-blooded Indians. One team member was Joe Guyon, who, like Thorpe, was destined for a future berth in the Pro Football Hall of Fame. The rest of the roster was filled with names such as Big Bear, Bobolash, Dick Deer Slayer, Xavier Downwind, Eagle Feather, Long-Time Sleep, Wrinkle Meat, and Joe Little Twig.

The team called Marion, Ohio, home, but it played most of its games on the road. It was a big gate attraction for a while. Halftime shows always were flamboyant, with Indian dancing, hunting acts, and Airedale exhibitions. But the on-field Indians, who never were too successful, had a 2-6 NFL record in 1922 and fell to 1-10 in 1923, then disbanded.

Option Pass

A play in which the quarterback or running back has the option to run or pass, and then passes.

Option Run

A running play in which the quarterback moves down the line and has the option to hand off, pitch, or run.

Option Runner

A running back adept at rushing without pre-determining the hole in the line he will use, allowing him to run wherever he sees open space – or "to daylight."

Orange Crush

In 1977, the Denver Broncos won their first AFC championship largely on the strength of an outstanding defensive unit known as the "Orange Crush." The Broncos allowed just 148 points in 14 games. In 1978, when the NFL schedule increased to 16 games, the Orange Crush permitted 198 points, the second best mark in the NFL that season.

Otto, Jim

b. Wausau, Wisconsin, 5 January 1938.
Hall of Fame: 1980

Jim Otto weighed only 205 pounds in 1960, when he finished his college career at the Uni-

Jim Otto stands impassively on the sidelines. It was a pose his opponents rarely saw once the ball was snapped – the Raiders' center was an immensely strong blocker.

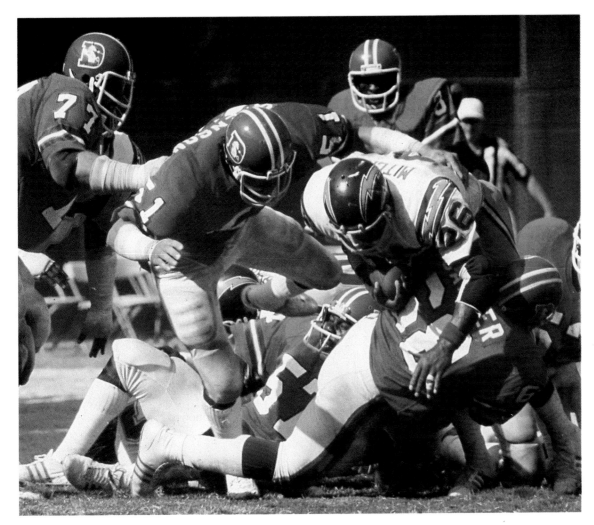

A San Diego ball carrier runs into the unyielding Denver defense. The Orange Crush was one of the most successful units in recent NFL history.

versity of Miami, Florida. No NFL team was willing to give him a chance so he signed with the Oakland Raiders of the new American Football League. Few felt either he or his team had much chance of success. But the intensely determined Otto built his weight up to 255 pounds and earned a berth on the Raiders' team. He started every game for Oakland for the next 15 seasons and was named all-AFL 10 consecutive times and all-AFC in 1970, 1971, and 1972. Otto was picked for all nine AFL All-Star games and the first three AFC-NFC Pro Bowl games. Altogether, he played 308 games as a Raider.

Otto was a sure-handed ball-snapper, a superior blocker, and a tower of strength on the Raiders' perennially outstanding lines. He was elected to the Hall of Fame in his first year of eligibility.

Out of Bounds

The ball or a player is out of bounds if it (he) touches or crosses the six-foot wide, solid white boundary line that rims the playing field.

Overtime

The extra 15-minute period added on to regular-season games to try to break ties. Also called "sudden death" overtime, because the first team to score in any manner wins the game. In postseason games, as many overtime periods as needed to determine a winner are played.

Owen, Steve

b. Cleo Springs, Oklahoma, 21 April 1898;
d. 17 May 1964. Hall of Fame: 1966

Steve Owen began his pro football career as a 6-0, 235-pound tackle with the 1924 Kansas City Blues. He moved to the New York Giants in 1926. As the Giants' captain in 1927, he led a championship team that allowed an all-time record low 20 points in 13 games. Owen played seven years with the Giants and, in 1931, he also became the team's coach. It was a job he held for 23 years until 1953. Owen's credo as a player was that football was a no-frills sport and he coached the Giants the same way.

In the 1930s and 1940s, New York was among the most feared teams in the NFL. Owen's Giants won eight Eastern Division titles, NFL championships in 1935 and 1938, and tied for division leads in 1943 and 1950. His 23-year career record was 153-108-17. Owen was often criticized for being too conservative but he was actually one of the game's great innovators. His development of the Umbrella defense in the post-World War II era is a prime example. In 1937, he introduced the A-formation offense and developed a unique two-platoon system in which each unit was equally adept at both offense and defense. The idea worked well; Giants players didn't tire as easily and became less prone to injuries.

★ ★ ★ Pads ★ ★ ★

All NFL players must wear the following equipment of suitable protective nature:

1. Helmet with chin strap fastened
2. Shoulder pads
3. Hip pads
4. Thigh pads
5. Knee pads
6. Stockings
7. Acceptable shoes – barefoot kicking is permitted

Protective equipment may be worn unless, in the opinion of the officials, endangers other players.

NFL PROTECTIVE EQUIPMENT

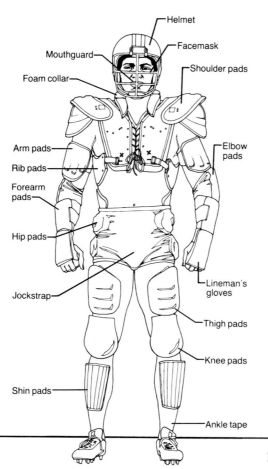

Helmet
Facemask
Mouthguard
Shoulder pads
Foam collar
Arm pads
Elbow pads
Rib pads
Forearm pads
Hip pads
Lineman's gloves
Jockstrap
Thigh pads
Knee pads
Shin pads
Ankle tape

Page, Alan

b. Canton, Ohio, 7 August, 1945.
Hall of Fame: 1988

A consensus All-America at Notre Dame, 6-4, 275-pound Alan Page was a first-round pick of the Minnesota Vikings in the 1967 NFL draft. Extremely fast and strong, with cat-like reflexes, Page won a starting job in the fourth week of his rookie season and never missed a start again in 11½ years with the Vikings and a final 3½ seasons with the Chicago Bears. Overall, he played in 238 regular season and post-season games, including Super Bowls IV, VIII, IX, and XI. Page played in nine Pro Bowls and was named all-pro nine times. He was selected as the NFC Defensive Player of the Year four times in the 1970s.

Page amassed some amazing career defensive statistics: 23 opponents' fumbles recovered, 28 blocked kicks, and 173 sacks. He became the first home-town native of Canton to be elected to the Hall of Fame.

Parker, Clarence (Ace)

b. Portsmouth, Virginia, 17 May 1912.
Hall of Fame: 1972

Clarence (Ace) Parker was the second-round draft pick of the Brooklyn Dodgers after he finished his college career at Duke University in 1937. But he really wanted to be a professional baseball player, so he signed a contract with the Philadelphia Athletics baseball team. After the baseball season, Parker decided to join the Dodgers for just one season. That one year proved to be only the start of his pro football career, because injuries suffered in baseball made it impossible for Parker to continue in his favorite sport.

Parker stayed with the Dodgers through the 1941 season. After a three-year service tenure in World War II, he played with the Boston Yanks of the NFL in 1945 and the New York Yankees of the All-America Football Conference in 1946. Although he was comparatively

small at 5-11 and 168 pounds, Parker was a triple-threat offensive star who also excelled on defense. In 1940, he was named the NFL's Most Valuable Player.

Parker, Jim

b. Macon, Georgia, 3 April 1934.
Hall of Fame: 1973

Although Jim Parker had been a two-way tackle, an All-America, and the Outland Trophy winner as the nation's top lineman at run-oriented Ohio State, he had very little pass-blocking experience when the Baltimore Colts chose the 6-3, 275-pounder in the first round of the 1957 draft for the specific purpose of protecting the team's great quarterback, Johnny Unitas.

Parker did the job expected of him so well that he earned a number of nicknames – Johnny Unitas' bodyguard, the mother hen, the den mother, the guardian. Parker divided his career almost evenly between guard and tackle. In his 11 years of NFL play, which concluded after the 1967 season, he was all-pro four times as a tackle and four times as a guard. From 1959 to 1966, he played in eight consecutive Pro Bowls. Parker became the first man who played solely on the offensive line to be elected to the Hall of Fame.

Parker, Raymond K. (Buddy)

b. Kemp, Texas, 16 December 1913.

Raymond (Buddy) Parker's pro coaching career began in 1949 when he was a co-coach of the Chicago Cardinals and ended in 1965 with a bizarre week-before-the-season resignation at Pittsburgh. In between, he terminated a successful six-year tenure with the Detroit Lions with a stunning resignation at a "Meet the Lions" banquet two days before the first 1957 pre-season game. He led the Lions to three consecutive Western Conference championships (1952-54) and NFL titles in 1952 and 1953. After his departure, he was hired immediately by the Steelers. His 51-47-6 eight-year record in Pittsburgh was the best for any Steelers coach up to that time. Overall, Parker's coaching record was 107-76-9.

Parker was a star running back at Centenary College. He played NFL football for nine years with the Detroit Lions and Chicago Cardinals from 1935 to 1943.

Pass

A pass may be thrown either forward or backward. A forward pass is a legal scrimmage play. The pass is usually thrown by the quarterback, and it may be caught and advanced by other backs, the wide receivers, and the tight end. The forward pass may be intercepted and returned by an opponent. If the forward pass is not caught by either team, it is ruled incomplete, and the ball is brought back to the original scrimmage line.

A backward pass, also called a lateral, may be thrown (usually underhanded) to a teammate who may advance the ball. If the backward pass is not caught, it becomes a free ball which may be recovered by either team.

Pass Pattern

The route a receiver runs on his way to catch a pass.

Pass Rush

The charge by any defensive player to tackle (sack) or pressure the quarterback as he attempts to pass.

Passer Rating System

The NFL rates its forward passers for statistical purposes against a pre-fixed performance standard based on statistical achievements of qualified pro passers since 1960. The system now in use was adopted in 1973 and is the longest-used of nine methods of rating passers since official statistics first were kept in 1932. The current system removes inequities that existed in former methods and, at the same time, provides a means of comparing passing

Clarence (Ace) Parker won the NFL Player of the Year award in 1940 despite playing the first three weeks of the season wearing a 10-pound brace from knee to ankle, to protect the lower joint he had damaged playing baseball.

performances from one season to the next.

Four categories are used as a basis for compiling a rating: 1 – Percentage of touchdown passes per attempt 2 – Percentage of completions per attempt 3 – Percentage of interceptions per attempt 4 – Average yards gained per attempt. The statistical accomplishment in each category earns a specific rating point. Rating points from the four categories are added and then converted to a 100-point table to make the rating more understandable.

The maximum score possible is 158.3. However, experience has proven that only the finest passers finish a season with an over-100 rating. The highest-rated passer in a single season was Milt Plum, who had a 110.4 rating with the Cleveland Browns in 1960 (the system was not in effect at that time).

Payton, Walter

b. Columbia, Mississippi, 25 July 1954.

In 13 years with the Chicago Bears, halfback Walter Payton compiled a list of records that clearly establishes him as one of the great players in NFL history. His major records include most rushing yards, 16,726; most 100-plus yards rushing games, 77; most rushing touchdowns, 110; most 1,000-plus yards rushing seasons, 10; most single-game rushing yards, 275; and most combined net yards, 21,803.

The 5-10, 202-pound graduate of Jackson State University was the first-round draft choice of the Bears in 1975. He rushed for 679 yards as a rookie and then ran for more than 1,000 yards 10 of the next 11 seasons. In 1977, he had career highs with 1,852 rushing yards and 2,216 combined net yards. Payton was named all-pro five times and chosen NFL Player of the Year in 1976 and 1977. He was selected for nine Pro Bowl games. In spite of the pounding he took on 4,347 rushes, receptions, and kick returns, Payton missed only one game of 190 in his NFL career. He retired after the 1987 season.

Penalty

An infraction of the rules that can result in loss of yardage and/or down, or nullification of a play.

Penalty Marker

The yellow flag thrown by officials to indicate a penalty.

Penetration

Movement of defensive linemen across the line of scrimmage.

Perry, Joe

b. Stevens, Arkansas, 27 January 1927.
Hall of Fame: 1969

Joe Perry played football only one year at Compton (California) Junior College before he entered the US Navy. John Woudenberg, a San Francisco 49ers' tackle, spotted him one day running wild for the Alameda (California) Naval Station team and highly recommended him to 49ers owner Tony Morabito. The 6-0, 200-pound Perry picked up his nickname, "The Jet," in his second season, when 49ers quarterback Frankie Albert raved about his quick starts. "He's strictly jet-propelled," Albert said.

Originally a straight-ahead runner with little breakaway ability, Perry quickly adjusted to the demands of pro football. He teamed with Hugh McElhenny and briefly with John Henry Johnson to give the 49ers a knockout punch on the ground. He became only the fourth runner in NFL history to rush for more than 1,000 yards, a feat he accomplished in both 1953 and 1954, making him the first player to do it in consecutive seasons. His 9,723 yards rushing in combined AAFC-NFL play placed him first all-time when he retired. Perry was traded to the Baltimore Colts in 1961 but the 49ers brought him back to San Francisco for a final season in 1963. In his first year of eligibility, he was elected to the Hall of Fame.

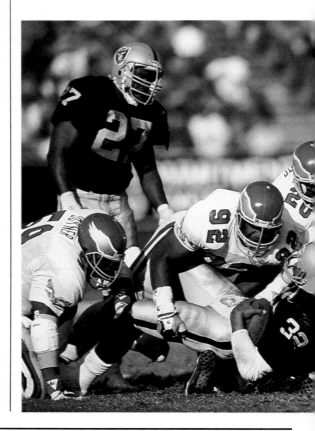

Philadelphia Eagles

Knowing that Pennsylvania state laws banning sports on Sunday were about to be repealed, Bert Bell and Lud Wray petitioned for a National Football League franchise in Philadelphia in 1933. Bell named the team in honor of the eagle, the symbol of the National Recovery Administration of the New Deal. Bell became the team's general manager and ticket sales-

man, Wray the coach. The Eagles were rudely introduced to the NFL with a 56-0 loss to the New York Giants, and they did not experience a winning season in their first decade.

Financial losses were heavy. In 1934, a disillusioned Wray sold his interest to Bell. In 1939, the Eagles signed Davey O'Brien, a 5-7, 150-pound Heisman Trophy-winning quarterback for $12,000. The former Texas Christian star played brilliantly but the Eagles won only two games during his two years with the team.

In 1941, Bell engineered a unique deal in which Philadelphia and Pittsburgh traded franchises, and Alexis Thompson took over as Eagles' owner. Thompson immediately hired Earle (Greasy) Neale as head coach. Neale installed the new T-formation attack with quarterback Tommy Thompson as the field leader and slowly began to build for the future. Financial and manpower shortages caused by World War II forced the Steelers and Eagles to join forces as Phil-Pitt in 1943. The "Steagles" won

Above: Joe (the Jet) Perry's speed made him a double threat rushing or receiving. In addition to his 9,723 yards on the ground, he also caught 260 passes for more than 2,000 yards and 12 touchdowns. Perry also was an emergency kicker.

five games and finished just one game out of first place.

The arrival of halfback Steve Van Buren in 1944 signaled the start of the most successful years in Philadelphia's history. The Eagles had their first winning seasons in 1944, 1945, and 1946 and finished second in the NFL East each year. By 1947, Neale's building program had climaxed with the addition of end Pete Pihos, linebacker Alex Wojciechowicz, fullback Joe Muha, and halfback Bosh Pritchard. That season, the Eagles won the NFL Eastern Division championship but lost a 28-21 thriller to the Chicago Cardinals in the NFL championship game.

In 1948, the Eagles won their second NFL East championship, then edged the Cardinals 7-0 in the snow in the NFL championship game. Philadelphia had its best season in 1949 with an 11-1 regular-season record and a 14-0 victory over the Los Angeles Rams in the NFL championship game. In the 1950 season opener, the NFL-champion Eagles were matched against the Cleveland Browns, who had dominated the All-America Football Conference. The Browns won 35-10 before 71,237 at Philadelphia's Municipal Stadium. The 1950 Eagles finished 6-6, and Neale was fired. In his final seven seasons, Neale's teams had a 54-22-3 record.

The Eagles remained competitive in the early 1950s but did not win another NFL championship until 1960, when they won 10 of 12 games and defeated Green Bay 17-13 in the title game. Coached by Buck Shaw, the Eagles were led by quarterback Norm Van Brocklin and center-linebacker Chuck Bednarik, who played both offense and defense during much of the season.

The 1961 Eagles finished second to the New York Giants with a 10-4 record under new head coach Nick Skorich, but they did not win another championship for 20 years. They had losing records 14 of the next 16 seasons. In 1971, the Eagles changed playing sites when they moved to the new 66,052-seat Veterans Stadium.

Dick Vermeil became head coach in 1976, and, in his third season in 1978, guided the Eagles to a 9-7 record and a wild-card playoff berth. Philadelphia lost to Atlanta in the first round. An 11-5 record gave the Eagles another wild-card spot in 1979, and they defeated the Chicago Bears before falling to Tampa Bay in playoff action.

In 1980, Wilbert Montgomery provided running punch while quarterback Ron Jaworski and wide receiver Harold Carmichael combined to form a lethal passing attack. The Eagles finished with a 12-4 record and the NFC Eastern Division championship. In the NFC championship game, they defeated the Dallas Cowboys 20-7 and advanced to Super Bowl XV, where they lost to the Oakland Raiders, 27-10. In 1981, Vermeil had his team in the playoffs for the fourth straight season but they lost to the New York Giants in the first round. Vermeil resigned after the 1982 season.

Marion Campbell followed Vermeil as the Philadelphia coach but was fired late in the 1985 season. Buddy Ryan was selected as the new head coach in 1986, and in 1988, his Eagles won the NFC Eastern Division with a 10-6 record before losing to the Chicago Bears in the playoffs, 20-12.

Members of the Hall of Fame:
(11) Chuck Bednarik, Bert Bell, Bill Hewitt, Sonny Jurgensen, Ollie Matson, Earle (Greasy) Neale, Pete Pihos, Jim Ringo, Norm Van Brocklin, Steve Van Buren, Alex Wojciechowicz

Championships Won:
NFL (pre-1970): 1948, 1949, 1960
NFC: 1980
NFL Eastern Conference: 1947, 1948, 1949, 1960
NFC Eastern Division: 1980, 1988

Overall Record: (incl. Phil-Pitt)

NFL Regular Season	305	395	24	.438
NFL Postseason	7	6	0	.538
Total	312	401	24	.440

Phil-Pitt

Because of financial and manpower problems during World War II, the Philadelphia Eagles and Pittsburgh Steelers merged for the 1943 season. The team officially was known as Phil-Pitt, but the team was popularly known as the Steagles. Earle (Greasy) Neale of the Eagles and Walt Kiesling of the Steelers served as co-head coaches. With some talented rookies and star end Bill Hewitt, who returned after four years of retirement, Phil-Pitt finished in third place with a 5-4-1 record, just one game out of first place. The Phil-Pitt merger was dissolved after the 1943 season.

Phoenix Cardinals

The oldest professional football team, the Cardinals were organized in 1899 by a painting and decorating contractor named Chris O'Brien. The team played at Normal Field on the corner of Normal Boulevard and Racine Avenue in Chicago, Illinois. In 1901, O'Brien found some second-hand jerseys discarded by the University of Chicago, which were faded maroon in color, and he labeled them "cardinal." Thus the team became the Racine Cardinals.

When the American Professional Football Association, the forerunner to the National Football League, was organized in 1920, the Cardinals were included as a charter member. The team, which soon was known as the Chicago Cardinals, became a big rival of the Staleys, who moved to Chicago from Decatur, Illinois, in 1921 and became the Bears in 1922.

In 1925, the Cardinals battled the Bears to a scoreless tie in Red Grange's professional debut. The next week, they became involved in one of the NFL's first big controversies. After losing to Pottsville to fall behind the Maroons in the championship race, the Cardinals played and won games against Milwaukee and Hammond, teams that had been disbanded and regrouped on short notice. When NFL president Joe Carr learned that Milwaukee had used high school players in its game with the Cardinals, he fined the Chicago team $1,000. Meanwhile, Carr had suspended Pottsville for violating Frankford's territorial rights. Thus, the Cardinals, who were coached by Norm Berry, were the 1925 NFL champions with an 11-2-1 record.

In 1926, O'Brien sold star quarterback John (Paddy) Driscoll to the Bears, and the Cardinals slipped into the second division. They experienced only two winning seasons in the next 20 years. However, in 1929, player-coach Ernie Nevers etched a permanent place in history by scoring all 40 points in the Cardinals' 40-6 Thanksgiving Day victory over the Bears.

A Chicago dentist, David Jones, bought the team for $25,000 that year, and in 1933, he sold it to Charles W. Bidwill, Sr., for $50,000. For the rest of the decade, the Cardinals were big losers on the field and at the gate, but Bidwill's faith in pro football never wavered. In 1944, World War II manpower shortages forced the Cardinals to merge with the Steelers for one season.

At war's end, the Cardinals' fortunes began to change. Bidwill acquired an outstanding quarterback, Paul Christman, in 1945, and the team switched to the T-formation. In 1946, Bidwill signed fullback Pat Harder and halfback Elmer Angsman, and lured Jimmy Conzelman, who had led Providence to the 1928 NFL title as a player-coach, back to the NFL as the head coach. Bidwill completed his "Dream Backfield" in 1947 when he signed Charley Trippi, a Georgia All-America, for an unprecedented $100,000. A fifth top-notch back, Marshall Goldberg, who had first joined the Cardinals in 1939, helped lead the defense. Bidwill died in April, 1947, before he could see his prized unit in action. The 1947 Cardinals won the NFL Western Conference and defeated the Philadelphia Eagles 28-21 for their first NFL championship since 1925. In 1948, the Cardinals were even better with an 11-1 regular-season record but they lost to Philadelphia 7-0 in the NFL

championship game.

Although the Cardinals boasted two of history's greatest performers – halfback Ollie Matson and defensive back Dick (Night Train) Lane – for several years in the 1950s, they only had one winning season in the decade. In 1951, Bidwill's two sons, Charles, Jr. (Stormy), and Bill, were selected to operate the club. Poor attendance at Comiskey Park in Chicago prompted the Bidwills in 1960 to move their team to St. Louis, where they would play in 34,000-seat Busch Stadium. In 1966, the Cardinals moved into a new home, 51,392-seat Busch Memorial Stadium.

In 1973, Don Coryell became the Cardinals' head coach, and, buoyed by stars such as quarterback Jim Hart, tackle Dan Dierdorf, and receiver Mel Gray, he turned the Cardinals into big winners in 1974, 1975, and 1976. They won NFC Eastern Division championships in 1974 and 1975 and fell one game short in 1976. In playoff action, St. Louis lost to Minnesota 30-14 in 1974 and to Los Angeles 35-23 in 1975.

Jim Hart's 18 seasons with the Cardinals from 1966 to 1983 represents ths second-longest playing career with one team in the NFL.

Coryell left the Cardinals after the 1977 season, and they have not been serious championship contenders since then. They did play in the NFC championship tournament in the strike-shortened 1982 season but lost to Green Bay in the first round.

In 1988, faced with dwindling income and the lack of an adequate stadium in St. Louis, Bill Bidwill, who had taken full control of the Cardinals in 1972, asked for and received NFL approval to move his team to Phoenix, Arizona, where it plays in 72,000-seat Sun Devil Stadium.

In the 1988 season, Phoenix were tied at the top of the NFC Eastern Division with a 7-4 record, but after losing quarterback Neil Lomax with an injury, the Cardinals lost its final five games and finished three games behind Philadelphia and New York.

Members of the Hall of Fame:
(12) Charles Bidwill, Sr., Guy Chamberlin, Jimmy Conzelman, John (Paddy) Driscoll, Walt Kiesling, Earl (Curly) Lambeau, Dick (Night Train) Lane, Ollie Matson, Ernie Nevers, Jim Thorpe, Charley Trippi, Larry Wilson

Championships Won:
NFL (pre-1970): 1925, 1947
NFL Western Conference: 1947, 1948
NFC Eastern Division: 1974, 1975

Overall Record: (incl. Card-Pitt)

NFL Regular Season	360	467	39	.438
NFL Postseason	1	4	0	.200
Total	361	471	39	.437

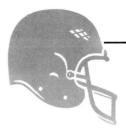

Piccolo, Brian

b. Pittsfield, Massachusetts, 21 October 1943;
d. 16 June 1970.

Brian Piccolo was the leading college scorer as a senior at Wake Forest in 1964. After the Chicago Bears signed him as a free agent in 1965, he became a backup to Hall of Fame half-back Gale Sayers, who became his roommate on team trips. Piccolo rushed for 450 yards after Sayers was injured in 1968 and played the first nine games of the 1969 season up to the Atlanta game on November 16. A persistent cough led to a chest x-ray that revealed a cancerous tumor in his chest. Piccolo won the hearts and prayers of sports fans everywhere during a try-ing ordeal of numerous operations and treat-ments that ended with his death at 26 exactly seven months after his last NFL game. His in-spirational fight for life became the subject of a movie, "Brian's Song," and a cancer research fund was established in his memory.

The Cardinals' special-team players are on their marks. Their move to Phoenix from St. Louis in 1988 was the first franchise move in the 1980s that was not met with strong criticism.

Pihos, Pete

b. Orlando, Florida, 22 October 1923.
Hall of Fame: 1970

In 1945, the Philadelphia Eagles drafted Pete Pihos, who had been outstanding as an end and fullback at the University of Indiana, even though they knew he would have to spend two years in military service before he could play in the NFL. The Eagles simply felt the 6-1, 210-pound Pihos was worth waiting for. When Pihos was ready to turn pro, Philadelphia paid him $17,000, an unusually high contract figure for the time. Originally a 60-minute player, Pihos earned every penny.

In his first three seasons, the Eagles won three divisional championships and the NFL title in 1948 and 1949. Pihos was a near 60-minute player on all three powerhouses and all-pro the last two seasons. In 1952, injuries forced the Eagles to move Pihos to defensive end on a full-time basis. He was named all-pro. A year

later, he was an offensive specialist for the first time. He responded by winning three consecutive NFL pass receiving championships with totals of 63, 60, and 62 catches. He was named to the all-pro offensive team each year, including his final season in 1955. Altogether, Pihos was named all-pro six times in nine years. His career record shows 373 receptions for 5,619 yards and 61 touchdowns.

Pitchout

A long, underhanded toss, usually from a quarterback to a running back.

Pittsburgh Steelers

Early in 1933, 32-year-old Art Rooney, a former boxer and semipro football player, spent $2,500 for a National Football League franchise in Pittsburgh. Rooney named his new team the Pirates after the city's baseball club. The NFL team's name was changed to Steelers in 1941. Today the Steelers operate as the sixth oldest franchise in the NFL and have played in the same market longer than all but three teams in pro football. Although Rooney was willing to try almost anything that would make his team a winner, the Steelers went longer without a

championship of any kind than any other team in pro football history. Rooney's first big pro football success did not come until the team's fortieth season in 1972, when the Steelers won the AFC Central Division.

From 1933 to 1971, the Steelers finished as high as second in their division only in 1936, 1942, 1947, 1949, and 1962. While the Steelers finished fourth with a 7-4-3 record in 1963, they could have won the divisional championship with a win over the New York Giants in the season finale. They lost 33-17.

Still, the Steelers made their share of news. In 1938, Rooney signed Byron (Whizzer) White

The Los Angeles Rams defender's dive is in vain as Pete Pihos catches a long pass. With halfback Steve Van Buren providing powerful running, Pihos formed a dangerous offensive tandem, commanding great respect from defenders.

Below: Terry Bradshaw drops back to pass against the Dallas Cowboys in Super Bowl X, a game Pittsburgh won 21-17. The Steelers were the last dynasty in the NFL, winning four NFL championships between 1974 and 1979.

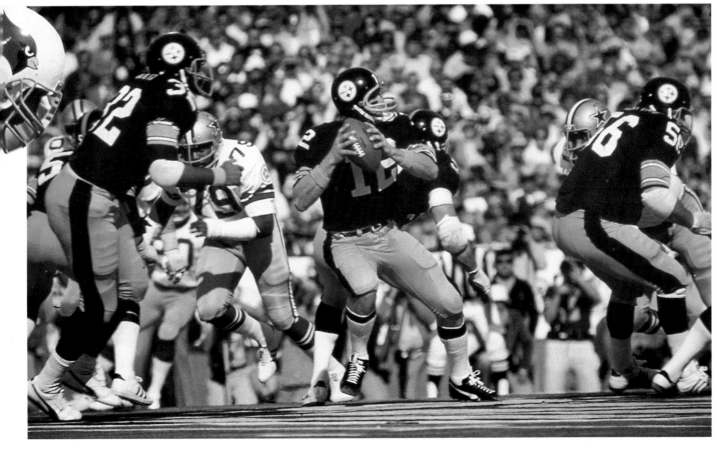

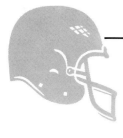

for $15,800, the largest contract in pro football history to that date. White, now a U.S. Supreme Court justice, played with the Steelers only two years before leaving for Oxford University in England to study as a Rhodes scholar. In 1942, rookie Bill Dudley led the Steelers to a 7-4 record, their best ever at that time. In 1946, Dudley returned from the service to lead the NFL in rushing, interceptions, and punt returns.

In 1962, quarterback Bobby Layne teamed with fullback John Henry Johnson to lead the Steelers to a best-ever 9-5 record, and Johnson became the first Pittsburgh back to rush for 1,000 yards in one season. In 1968, the Steelers experienced their fifth consecutive losing season with a 2-11-1 record.

Then Rooney hired Chuck Noll, a former Cleveland Browns guard and Baltimore Colts assistant, as head coach. Noll's building program began with the drafting of defensive tackle Joe Greene in 1969. In 1970, Pittsburgh added quarterback Terry Bradshaw and moved into its new 59,000-seat home at Three Rivers Stadium. In 1971, an outstanding draft produced future stars such as linebacker Jack Ham, safety Mike Wagner, and defensive end Dwight White. In 1972, a big running back from Penn State, Franco Harris, joined the fold and the Steelers enjoyed their first winning season under Noll. They won the AFC Central Division championship with an 11-3 record and defeated Oakland 13-7 in a first-round playoff game before losing to the Miami Dolphins 21-17 in the AFC championship game.

The Steelers had a 10-4 record in 1973, but had to settle for a wild-card playoff berth. In 1974, they began a string of six straight AFC Central Division championships that carried through the 1979 season. In four of those six seasons, the Steelers also won the AFC championship and the Super Bowl, a feat never matched by any other club. Pittsburgh's first world championship came with a 16-6 win over Minnesota in Super Bowl IX. The Steelers repeated with a 21-17 victory over Dallas in Super

Bowl X. Three seasons later, they whipped the Cowboys again, 35-31 in Super Bowl XIII. The Steelers' remarkable string concluded with a 31-19 win over the Los Angeles Rams in Super Bowl XIV.

In the 1980s, the Steelers have not matched their successes of the 1970s but they did play in the 1982 AFC championship tournament and won AFC Central Division championships in 1983 and 1984. In both 1982 and 1983, they lost first-round playoff games but, in 1984, they defeated Denver in the first playoff round before losing to Miami 45-28 in the AFC championship game.

Just before the start of the 1988 season, Rooney, one of pro football's most revered men, died at the age of 87. The Steelers continue as a family enterprise with president Dan Rooney and Art Rooney's other sons still in charge.

Members of the Hall of Fame:

(14) Bert Bell, Mel Blount, Terry Bradshaw, Bill Dudley, Joe Greene, Jack Ham, Cal Hubbard, John Henry Johnson, Walt Kiesling, Bobby Layne, Marion Motley, Johnny (Blood) McNally, Art Rooney, Ernie Stautner

Championships Won:

Super Bowl: IX, X, XIII, XIV
AFC: 1974, 1975, 1978, 1979
AFC Central Division: 1972, 1974, 1975, 1976, 1977, 1978, 1979, 1983, 1984

Overall Record:

NFL Regular Season	329	379	20	.466
NFL Postseason	15	8	0	.652
Total	344	387	20	.471

Plane of the Goal

The imaginary plane extending upward from the goal line that must be broken by a player in possession of the ball in order to score a touchdown.

Play Action

Plays in which the quarterback first fakes a handoff (a "play fake"), then passes.

Playbook

A confidential collection of a team's plays, diagrams, strategies, and terminologies.

Playoff Bowl

The Playoff Bowl between the two second-place teams in each conference of the National Football League was created in 1960 to help fund the Bert Bell players' pension fund, which had been instituted a year earlier. All 10 Playoff

---

★ ★ ★ Playoff Bowl scores: ★ ★ ★

7 January 1961	Detroit Lions 17, Cleveland Browns 16
6 January 1962	Detroit Lions 28, Philadelphia Eagles 10
6 January 1963	Detroit Lions 17, Pittsburgh Steelers 10
5 January 1964	Green Bay Packers 40, Cleveland Browns 23
3 January 1965	St. Louis Cardinals 24, Green Bay Packers 17
9 January 1966	Baltimore Colts 35, Dallas Cowboys 3
8 January 1967	Baltimore Colts 20, Philadelphia Eagles 14
7 January 1968	Los Angeles Rams 30, Cleveland Browns 6
5 January 1969	Dallas Cowboys 17, Minnesota Vikings 13
3 January 1970	Los Angeles Rams 31, Dallas Cowboys 0

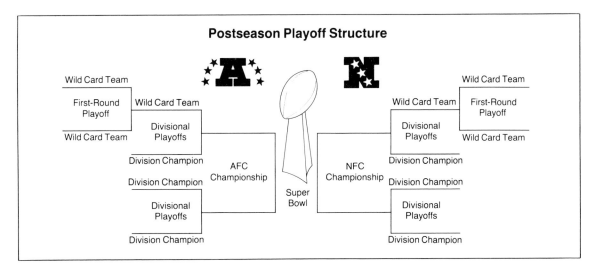

Postseason Playoff Structure

Bowls were played in the Orange Bowl in Miami. The series was discontinued with the completion of the AFL-NFL merger in 1970. Western Conference teams won eight of the 10 Playoff Bowl games. The biggest crowd of the series was 65,569 for the Baltimore-Dallas game following the 1965 season.

Playoffs

Under the NFL playoff format since 1970, the three divisional championship teams from both the AFC and NFC automatically qualify for the postseason playoffs. Two wild-card qualifiers (non-division winning teams with the next best records) from each division complete the playoff field. The wild-card teams play each other in a first-round game, with the winner playing the championship team with the best won-lost record in the divisional playoffs. The team with the second-best record plays the team with the third-best record in the other divisional playoff game. If the wild-card winner comes from the same division as the team with the best record, then the wild-card team plays the team with the second-best record. The two winners of the divisional playoffs then play for the conference championship. The two conference champions then meet in the Super Bowl to determine the NFL championship.

Pocket

The protected area around a quarterback, formed by his blockers, as he passes.

Pollard, Fritz

b. Chicago, Illinois, 27 January 1894; d. 11 May 1986.

As one of three black players to compete in the American Professional Football Association (forerunner to the NFL) in its first season in 1920, Fritz Pollard was one of pro football's true pioneers. Pollard helped coach as well as play for the Akron Pros, who won the first APFA championship. He also was the player-coach of the Hammond Pros in 1923, thus becoming the first black coach in pro football. Pollard, who starred as a 5-8, 175-pound halfback with Brown University's 1916 Rose Bowl team, commanded high pay for the time, as much as $1,500 a game. He also played briefly with the Milwaukee Badgers and Providence Steam Roller before retiring after the 1926 season with Akron.

Possession

Control of the ball, by an individual or a team.

Post Pattern

A pass receiver's route that goes straight downfield near the sideline, then breaks across the field toward the goalpost.

Pottsville Maroons

In 1925, their first NFL season, the Pottsville Maroons from the coal-mining region of northeastern Pennsylvania became embroiled in a controversy that lasted many decades. The Maroons stormed to a 9-2 record before defeating the Chicago Cardinals 21-7 in a game the Chicago newspapers, without official NFL authorization, billed as a championship game.

.In those days, teams were allowed to schedule late-season games in order to determine a league champion. The Maroons, who already had a scheduled game with Providence, also scheduled an exhibition game against the Notre Dame All-Stars, a team that included the famous Four Horsemen. The Car-

dinals, meanwhile, scheduled games against Milwaukee and Hammond.

In scheduling the exhibition game in Philadelphia's Shibe Park, the home territory of the Frankford Yellow Jackets, on a day the Yellow Jackets were playing, the Maroons were in direct violation of NFL rules. When NFL President Joe Carr heard of the Pottsville plans, he notified the team's management that he would take stern action, including forfeiting the franchise, if the Maroons went ahead with the game. Pottsville ignored Carr's warning.

On December 12, the Maroons defeated the All-Stars 9-7. That same day, Carr fined the club $500, suspended it from all rights and privileges (including the right to compete for the championship), and returned its franchise to the league. He also canceled Pottsville's scheduled game with Providence.

Meanwhile, the Cardinals, coached by Norman Barry, won both of their games, and with them the league title, with an 11-2-1 record. The Maroons, who weren't eligible for the title, finished in second place at 10-2.

Although the Cardinals legitimately won the NFL title, until this day, many people in Pottsville continue to argue that their team should have been named NFL champion in 1925 and that the championship was stolen from them.

Power Sweep

A run around end with both guards pulling to lead the blocking.

Preseason Games

When the NFL regular-season schedule was increased from 14 to 16 games in 1978, the number of preseason games was reduced from six to four. However, those teams playing in the AFC-NFC Hall of Fame game in Canton, Ohio, or in international games are allowed to play five preseason games that year.

Prevent Defense

A defense specifically designed to stop long passes.

Pro Bowl

The Pro Bowl game traces back to 1939 when the New York Giants defeated the "Pro All-Stars" 13-10 before an estimated 20,000 at Wrigley Field in Los Angeles. The series was discontinued after the 1942 season but revived in 1951 under a new format that matched the all-stars of the American (Eastern) and National (Western) conferences of the NFL. The Pro Bowl series continued as a season-ending fixture in Los Angeles for the next 20 years.

Meanwhile, the rival American Football League was staging its own all-star game. Nine games were played from 1962 to 1970 with the 1966 clash between the Buffalo Bills and AFL All-Stars the only break in the East vs. West schedule.

With the completion of the merger, the AFC-NFC Pro Bowl series was inaugurated in January, 1971. During the 1970s, the Pro Bowl was staged in seven different cities but, in 1980, the game was moved to Aloha Stadium in Honolulu, Hawaii, where it is played today. After the 1989 game, the NFC led the AFC 11-8.

Each 42-man squad, composed of 20 offensive and 17 defensive players plus four specialists and one extra player, is chosen in balloting among the 14 head coaches in each conference and the NFL Players Association members on each team. The players who receive the most votes at their positions are the designated starters.

The following players have been picked to appear in the Pro Bowl and/or the AFL All-Star Game 10 or more times:

14 games	Merlin Olsen, DT, Los Angeles Rams
12 games	Ken Houston, S, Houston Oilers, Washington Redskins
	Jim Otto, C, Oakland Raiders
11 games	Bob Lilly, DT, Dallas Cowboys
	Tom Mack, G, Los Angeles Rams
10 games	Joe Greene, DT, Pittsburgh Steelers
	Gino Marchetti, DT, Baltimore Colts
	Leo Nomellini, DT, San Francisco 49ers
	Mel Renfro, CB-S, Dallas Cowboys
	Jim Ringo, C, Green Bay Packers, Philadelphia Eagles
	Johnny Unitas, QB, Baltimore Colts

The Pro Football Hall of Fame at Canton. Every year the enshrinement of the new class is celebrated with a game. In 1989 the game was between Buffalo and Washington, in 1990 Chicago will play Denver.

Pro Football Hall of Fame

The Pro Football Hall of Fame, which was opened in Canton, Ohio, on September 7, 1963, celebrated its twenty-fifth anniversary in 1988. During its first quarter century, the Hall welcomed almost 4,500,000 visitors from every state in the United States and more than 100 other nations.

Latrobe, Pennsylvania, originally was awarded site designation for a pro football hall of fame in 1947. When Latrobe's plans stalled, Canton, with a rich pro football background, made its move. Canton was the National Football League's birthplace city. The city gained site designation from the NFL in 1961.

Election is the ultimate individual goal of every pro football player. The responsibility for electing new members rests with the 30-member Board of Selectors, which is made up of media representatives from the 28 NFL cities, an at-large member, and the president of the Pro Football Writers Association. To be eligible, players must be retired five years; coaches need only to be retired; and a contributor such as a commissioner or team administrator can be active or retired. Between four and seven new members are elected each year.

Providence Steam Roller

Providence, Rhode Island, made its mark in the National Football League in several ways. It was one of the first to omit the traditional "s" at the end of the team nickname and the only team to play its home games in a bicycle-racing stadium. Because of the curves of the racing track around the football field, the end zones were limited to five yards in depth. The stands were so close on the sidelines along the racing straightaways that players being tackled often were bounced into the seats. Still, the fans could see the action close at hand, and capacity crowds of 10,500 turned out to watch the Steam Roller play.

The Steam Roller played in the NFL from 1925 to 1931. In 1928, coached by Jimmy Conzelman, it made history by winning the league championship with an 8-1-2 record. Thus, Providence became the last of the small-city teams, except for Green Bay, to win an NFL title. The Steam Roller also was the last team not now in the NFL to win a championship.

Punt

A type of kick used primarily on fourth down that ordinarily results in change of possession.

Earnest Jackson, 43, on a power sweep behind two Pittsburgh blockers.

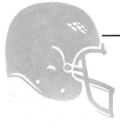

Purple People Eaters

In the late 1960s and early 1970s, the Minnesota Vikings featured an outstanding defense that was led by a mobile but rugged front four known as "The Purple People Eaters." At the ends were 6-6, 255-pound Carl Eller and 6-3½, 248-pound Jim Marshall, and at the tackles were 6-4, 255-pound Alan Page and 6-5, 255-pound Gary Larsen. In 42 games from 1969 to 1971, the Vikings permitted just 34 touchdowns on scrimmage plays. Their reign began to decline after Larsen's retirement in 1974.

Pylons

Padded markers with orange coverings that are placed at the intersections of the goal lines and the sidelines, and the back lines and the sidelines. Monitoring the pylons sometimes can determine whether a player was in or out of bounds as he entered or left the end zone.

★ ★

Quarter

A 15-minute playing period; four quarters make up a game.

Quarterback

The player who calls the signals at the line, determines if and when to change the play after he assesses the defense, takes the snap from center, and either hands off, pitches out, decides to run himself, or passes the football. He lines up close behind the center, except when using the Shotgun formation. The quarterback isnormally the focal point of a team's offense.

Quarterback Sneak

A short-yardage play in which the quarterback takes the snap and immediately runs forward behind the block of the center.

Quick Kick

A surprise punt that is designed to take the defensive team by surprise and create poor field position for the receiving team. The quarterback, lined up in the shotgun formation, usually is the player making the quick kick. Just before he receives the snap from center, he drops back two or three paces, then kicks before a defensive rush can be effective.

The Minnesota Vikings' offense is on the field as the Purple People Eaters defense watches. The Vikings' defense was largely responsible for their four Super Bowl appearances, but they always came up just short in the championship game.

Ray, Hugh (Shorty)

b. Highland Park, Illinois, 21 September 1884; d. 16 September 1956. Hall of Fame: 1966

At the urging of the Chicago Bears' George Halas, Hugh (Shorty) Ray was hired by the National Football League in 1938 not only to improve officiating but also to streamline the playing rules as well. A primary goal was to make the game safer for its players, but a secondary, perhaps more far-reaching, desire was to make the sport more appealing to fans.

Although Ray was only 5-6, 138 pounds, he had been a four-sport star at the University of Illinois. He had coached for 10 years and had considerable experience in both officiating and rules-making at the high school and college level before joining the NFL.

By improving time-saving officiating techniques, Ray added an average of 12 plays to every NFL game. Ray took more than 300,000 stopwatch notations and sponsored many progressive rules changes during his 15 years as the NFL's supervisor of officials. At the time of his retirement after the 1952 season, Halas insisted that his finest contribution to pro football was to bring Ray into the NFL.

Read

1. The quarterback's observation of the defensive alignment.
2. The observation of keys or the action of the offense by a defensive player.

Receive

1. At the start of each half, one team gets the choice of whether to kick off or receive (be kicked to).
2. To catch a pass.

Receiver

An offensive player eligible to catch a pass.

Red Dog

The term "Red Dog," the original nickname for the defensive maneuver now known as the blitz, came from the first man to attempt one. He was Don (Red) Ettinger, a New York Giants linebacker from 1948 to 1950. Ettinger had *red* hair and, as he explained, "I was just *doggin'* the quarterback a little."

Reeves, Daniel F.

b. New York City, 30 June 1912; d. 15 April 1971. Hall of Fame: 1967

Daniel F. Reeves became a part-owner of the Cleveland Rams in 1941, and became sole owner in 1943. Three years later, in January, 1946, just after the Rams had defeated the Washington Redskins 15-14 in the 1945 NFL championship game, Reeves announced he was moving his team to Los Angeles. Although fellow NFL owners were against the move, Reeves persisted and the transfer was completed. It marked the first time an established major sports league had fielded a team on the Pacific coast.

Reeves' move to California was triggered by the severe financial losses he had suffered in Cleveland. In Los Angeles, his initial deficits, fueled by a life-and-death struggle with the rival Dons of the All-America Football Conference, were even larger. But by the time the AAFC folded after the 1949 season, the Rams were on the verge of outstanding success on the playing field, and massive crowds began to fill the Los Angeles Coliseum. The Rams won divisional titles in 1949, 1950, 1951, and 1955, and the NFL championship in 1951. Rams' attendance topped 80,000 22 times during the first two decades in California. The innovative Reeves instituted a famed "Free Football for Kids" program that fostered an interest in pro football by youngsters. He became the first NFL owner since 1933 to have a black player on his team when he signed Kenny Washington and Woody Strode to 1946 contracts. Reeves' experimentation in the early days of television provided the groundwork for pro football's current successful TV policies. He was also a pioneer in many aspects of personnel work and the NFL draft.

Above left: Hugh (Shorty) Ray's meticulous eye and his almost fanatical attention to detail were crucial to his work for the NFL in the area of rules amendments, making him one of the most vital innovators in football history.

Above: Daniel F. Reeves saw the future of football as a truly national sport, so he moved his Rams from Cleveland to Los Angeles. After the initial struggle, he saw his team become one of the dominant teams of the late 1940s/early 1950s.

Renfro, Mel

b. Houston, Texas, 30 December 1941.

In 1964, the Dallas Cowboys drafted Mel Renfro, an All-America cornerback from the University of Oregon on the second round. The 6-0, 192-pounder intercepted seven passes his rookie season and also led the NFL in both punt-return and kickoff-return yardage. He led the NFL with 10 interceptions in 1969. In his 14-year career, Renfro intercepted 52 passes, had 842 yards on punt returns, and 2,246 yards on kickoff returns. Renfro was all-pro in 1965, 1969, and 1973; played 10 Pro Bowls from 1964 to 1973.

Reverse

A running gadget play in which the quarterback hands off to a ball carrier who has circled from an opposite direction from the flow of the play. There are a number of variations.

Ribbons

A ribbon is attached to the top of each goal post upright so that the teams may determine wind direction and strength.

Rice, Jerry

b. Starkville, Mississippi, 13 October 1962.

Jerry Rice, a 6-2, 200-pound All-America wide receiver from Mississippi Valley State University, was the first-round choice of the San Francisco 49ers in the 1985 NFL draft. In just four seasons, he already has claimed a place in the NFL record book. In 1987, he caught an all-time record 22 touchdown passes. He ended the season with a record string of 13 straight games with at least one touchdown reception and also scored 138 points to lead the NFL and set a new 49ers team record. (His consecutive-game touchdown streak was snapped in the first game in 1988.) Rice was named the NFL Player of the Year in 1987. He was named all-pro in

John Riggins races into the end zone for one of his two touchdowns in Super Bowl XVII. Known as 'the Diesel', his performance led some journalists to describe the one-back offense Washington used so successfully as 'Rigginomics.'

In a reverse the quarterback runs with the ball and hands off to a running back going the other way. If the running back hands off again, it becomes a double reverse.

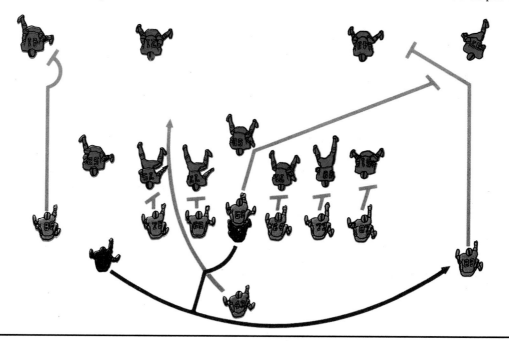

1986, 1987, and 1988, and was selected to play in the Pro Bowl each year. He equaled a record with 11 catches and set another with 215 receiving yards en route to earning Most Valuable Player honors in Super Bowl XXIII In his first four years he had 264 receptions for 4,881 yards and 49 touchdowns.

Richter, Les

b. Fresno, California, 6 October 1930.

Les Richter was a virtually unanimous All-America pick as an offensive guard and linebacker in both his junior and senior seasons at the University of California. In the 1952 NFL draft, he was the second player selected and the first choice of the Dallas Texans. Before he played even one game with the Texans, he was traded to the Los Angeles Rams for 11 players. The 6-3, 240-pound Richter served two years as an army lieutenant before reporting to the Rams in 1954. Richter played in eight Pro Bowls in nine years for the Rams. He retired in 1962.

Riggins, John

b. Centralia, Kansas, 4 August 1949.

John Riggins, a 6-2, 240-pound All-America running back from the University of Kansas, en-

tered the NFL as the first-round draft choice of the New York Jets in 1971. He played with the Jets for five seasons, then played out his option and signed with the Washington Redskins in 1976. With the Redskins, Riggins pounded out four 1,000-yard rushing seasons and scored a record 24 touchdowns in 1983. He was the Most Valuable Player in Super Bowl XVII with a 166-yard rushing performance against the Miami Dolphins. His career ended after the 1985 season. In 14 years, Riggins rushed for 11,352 yards, fifth in NFL history, and scored 104 touchdowns. His 116 total touchdowns have been surpassed only by Jim Brown and Walter Payton.

Riley, Ken

b. Bartow, Florida, 6 August 1947.

Ken Riley, a 6-foot, 183-pound quarterback from Florida A&M University, was selected in the sixth round of the 1969 AFL-NFL draft by the Cincinnati Bengals. Head coach Paul Brown immediately moved Riley to cornerback, where he played with distinction until 1983.

In 15 seasons, Riley intercepted 65 passes, which he returned for 596 yards and five touchdowns. Riley also recovered 18 fumbles. He was named All-AFC in 1975 and all-pro in 1983.

Jerry Rice is a picture of concentration as he hauls in another pass. As a boy he caught bricks while helping his father, who was a house builder, and this could be why he makes catching a football look so easy.

Jim Ringo listened to the advice of his wife and father and became one of the premier centers in the NFL. After 11 years in Green Bay, including 6 as an all-pro, he moved to Philadelphia and did not miss a game in his four seasons with the Eagles.

Ringo, Jim

b. Orange, New Jersey, 21 November 1932. Hall of Fame: 1981

At 211 pounds, Jim Ringo felt he was too small to make the Green Bay team when he joined the Packers in 1953 after a fine career at Syracuse University. But both his wife and father told him he shouldn't quit without trying. Ringo not only earned a spot with the Packers, he became a premier center for the next 11 years in Green Bay and four more seasons with the Philadelphia Eagles from 1964 to 1967. Ringo increased his weight to 235 pounds and reacted to the challenge of much bigger opponents by effectively utilizing his quickness and native football intelligence. A quiet but respected leader, he berated his teammates when necessary and instilled the will to win.

While the Packers of the mid-1950s struggled on the field, Ringo advanced to all-pro status, his first selection coming in 1957. He was named all-pro six of 11 years in Green Bay. Ringo was a Pro Bowl starter 10 times and one of a few players to start for both the East and West teams in the postseason series. He wound up his 15-season career with a string of 182 consecutive games as a starter, including 56 straight with the Eagles. Ringo was named coach of the Buffalo Bills in October 1976, but left at the end of the following season.

Robinson, Johnny

b. Delhi, Louisiana, 9 September 1938.

Johnny Robinson, a member of Louisiana State's 1959 national championship team, was a number-one draft pick of the Detroit Lions in 1960 but he signed with the Dallas Texans of the new AFL. The 6-1, 205-pound halfback played as a running back for two years, then was switched to safety. Robinson won All-AFL honors five years from 1965 to 1969 and All-AFC acclaim in 1970 and 1971. He was selected for six AFL All-Star games and the first two Pro Bowls, and in 1969, was named to the all-time AFL team. In 12 seasons, Robinson intercepted 57 passes and is tied for seventh among the all-time leaders. He twice led the league in interceptions, the AFL in 1966 and the NFL in 1972.

Robustelli, Andy

b. Stamford, Connecticut, 6 December 1925. Hall of Fame: 1971

When Andy Robustelli joined the Los Angeles Rams as the team's nineteenth-round draft choice in 1951, he was told his only chance to make the team was as a defensive end. Because he had been an excellent offensive player at Arnold College, Robustelli seriously considered passing up pro football for a high school coaching job. He didn't even unpack his bags for the first two weeks of training camp.

But the 6-0, 230-pounder did make the team, and he stayed around the NFL as a superb pass-rushing defensive end for the next 14 years. Robustelli enjoyed five outstanding seasons in Los Angeles, then was traded to the New York Giants in 1956. Happy to be near his home in Stamford, Robustelli played even better the next nine years, until his retirement after the 1964 season. Robustelli was named all-pro seven times, twice with the Rams and five times with the Giants, in his 14 seasons. He played in the Pro Bowl seven years. In 1962, he was selected the NFL Player of the Year by the Maxwell Club of Philadelphia.

Rollout

The action of the quarterback as he moves across the backfield toward the sideline to pass (as opposed to a straight dropback). Also a play based on this action.

Rooney, Art

b. Coulterville, Pennsylvania, 17 January 1901; d. 25 August 1988. Hall of Fame: 1964

In 1933, Art Rooney paid $2,500 for the Pittsburgh Pirates NFL franchise. His first Pirates teams – the club name was changed to Steelers in 1941 – were not much better than the semi-pro teams he once sponsored before he became involved with the NFL. The closest the Steelers came to a championship in their first 40 years was a tie for the Eastern Division title in 1947 (they lost a playoff game), and a close second-place finish in 1963. In 1938, Rooney signed Byron (Whizzer) White, the Colorado All-America, to a then-record $15,000 contract. Such devotion to pro football was demonstrated time and again by Rooney, who proved to be one of NFL's guiding lights during the depression years of the 1930s. Since the Steelers didn't win, they didn't draw crowds, either. Rooney's losses mounted but his resolve never wavered.

Finally, in the 1970s, the Steelers hit on the right combination of coaching and brilliant playing talent, and became the dominant team of pro football. They won four Super Bowls in a six-year period, a feat unmatched by any pro team. With the possible exception of the clubs Pittsburgh defeated, the entire sports world rejoiced with Rooney as he accepted the Vince Lombardi Trophy each year. One of the most revered of all sports personalities, the down-to-earth Rooney was loved and admired for the warmth and kindness and genuine personal interest he extended to everyone he met.

When Rooney died, tributes poured in from friends and admirers from every walk of life. The Dallas Cowboys, arch-rivals of Mr Rooney's teams in two Super Bowls, made a gesture believed to be unprecedented by an opposing team of wearing his initials, AJR, on their helmets during the 1988 season-opener against the Steelers.

★ ★ ★ Roster Size ★ ★ ★

In 1988, NFL teams were limited to 45 active players, plus a two-player inactive list, for each regular-season game. However, since roster limits first were imposed in 1925, NFL teams have followed many different roster ceilings:

1925	16	1951-1956	33	1985-1987	45
1926-1929	18	1957-1958	35	1988	47
1930-1934	20	1959	36	*35 for first three games.	
1935	24	1960	38		
1936-1937	25	1961-1962	36	**45 for first two games.	
1938-1939	30	1963	37		
1940-1942	33	1964-1973	40	**AFL roster limits:**	
1943-1944	28	1974	47		
1945-1946	33	1975-1977	43	1960-1961	35
1947	35*-34	1978-1981	45	1962-1963	33
1948	35	1982	45**-49	1964	34
1949-1950	32	1983-1984	49	1965	38
				1966-1969	40

Rotation

Shifting zone pass coverage to the left or right.

Roughing the Kicker

A 15-yard penalty assessed to any player who applies unnecessary roughness while running into a kicker or punter.

Roughing the Passer

A 15-yard penalty assessed to any defensive player who runs into the passer after the ball as left his hand.

Art Rooney was the grand old man of football. He endured years of losing in Pittsburgh with equanimity and good grace, and when at last the Steelers started to win, the football world rejoiced with him.

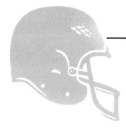

Rozelle, Pete

b. South Gate, California, 1 March 1926.
Hall of Fame: 1985

In 1960, Pete Rozelle, then 33, became the Commissioner of the National Football League, replacing the late Bert Bell, who had enjoyed a highly successful 14-year reign until his death in 1959. Rozelle, who went to the NFL owners' meeting that year as the general manager of the Los Angeles Rams, was clearly a compromise choice, his election coming on the twenty-third ballot. Whatever doubts the NFL owners might have had, however, were erased when Rozelle quickly took firm control, as his backers had predicted. In a few years, Rozelle was universally recognized as the most effective commissioner in professional sports.

The NFL's problems during Rozelle's long tenure are well-documented – periodic television negotiations, the war with the American Football League and the resulting merger, player unrest with strikes and threats of strikes, plus the numerous court and legislative challenges that have threatened the organizational structure of the sport. Through it all, Rozelle's firm leadership has remained a dominating factor. At the start of his commissionership, there were 13 NFL teams and 500 players. Today, 28 teams employ more than 1,500 players. NFL attendance has grown from 40,106 a game in 1960 to 60,663 in 1986. NFL per-team TV receipts have increased from $330,000 a year in 1962 to approximately $17 million today. The Super Bowl has developed into the leading American sports events. The list of impressive comparisons is long. The Commissioner's current contract runs through 1991, when he will be 65 and, he has stated, ready for retirement.

Pete Rozelle has been Commissioner of the NFL through almost three decades, during which time football has become one of the most popular spectator sports in the world.

Run

A scrimmage play in which a running back, quarterback, or an end (on a reverse) runs with the football after receiving it on a direct snap from center or on a handoff.

Running Back

A general classification for the fullbacks and halfbacks whose primary responsibility is to run with the football.

Rule Changes

A summary of the National Football League's most significant rules changes:

1933	Creation of hashmarks – ball to be moved in 10 yards whenever it is in play within five yards of the sidelines.
1933	Goal posts returned to goal lines.
1934	Forward passing legalized any spot behind scrimmage line.
1934	Fumbled ball (except on lateral pass) may be advanced by either team, whether ball strikes ground or not.
1950	Adoption of free substitution rule (first adopted as a war-time emergency measure in 1943, 1944, and 1945).
1955	Ball declared dead immediately if runner contacted by defensive player touches ground with any part of body except hands or feet.
1972	Hashmarks moved 70 feet, 9 inches (23 7/12 yards) inbounds.
1974	Goal posts returned to end lines.
1974	Field goals missed from beyond 20-yard-line will result in ball being put in play by opponent on prior scrimmage line.
1974	Tie games to extend into one 15-minute overtime period with first team to score winning. If there is no score, game ends in tie, except in playoff games where play continues until winner is determined.
1978	Defenders may contact pass receivers only once and then only in first five yards beyond scrimmage line.
1986	Limited use of instant replay as an officiating aid.

Running Lane

The lane parallel to and behind the line of scrimmage used by pulling offensive linemen.

Russell, Andy

b. Detroit, Michigan, 29 October 1941.

Andy Russell was the sixteenth-round draft pick of the Pittsburgh Steelers in 1963. The 6-2, 225-pound linebacker from the University of Missouri had an excellent rookie season before missing the next two years while serving in the army. He then returned in 1966 to become one of the best defenders in Steelers history. Russell played in 168 successive games through the 1976 season and was the Steelers' defensive captain for 10 years. He was named all-pro nine times and selected for seven Pro Bowls. He intercepted 18 passes in his 12-year career.

Saban, Lou

b. Brookfield, Illinois, 13 October 1921.

Lou Saban, a former Cleveland Browns center and assistant college football coach, was named head coach of the Boston Patriots in the new AFL in 1960. His checkerboard pro coaching career took him to the Buffalo Bills in 1962, to the Denver Broncos in 1967, and back to Buffalo in 1972. He was most successful during his first term in Buffalo when he coached the Bills to AFL championships in 1964 and 1965. Saban left the Bills to coach at the University of Maryland in 1966 but returned to pro football as head coach and general manager of the Broncos in 1967. In 1972, he returned to Buffalo. During Saban's tenure, O.J. Simpson set an all-time NFL single-season rushing record in 1973 (2,003 yards). After the fifth game of the 1976 season, Saban once again resigned. His cumulative regular-season record for 15 pro seasons was 97-101-7. Saban played at the University of Indiana before he began his career in 1946.

The Steel Curtain closes around another hapless quarterback as Joe Greene and L.C. Greenwood share another sack.

Sack

When a player attempting to pass is tackled on or behind the line of scrimmage by a defender.

Safety

1. A two-point scoring play most often caused by the tackling of a ball carrier, or a quarterback attempting to pass, in his own end zone. A punt blocked through the back of the kicking team's endzone is also a safety.
2. A player position in the defensive secondary.

John Elway has just seen a 25-yard pass to Clarence Kay ruled incomplete after instant replay; now he is firmly in the grasp of George Martin in his own end zone. The safety turned the game, reducing Denver's lead in Super Bowl XXI to 10-9, and the Giants went on to win 39-20.

Safety Valve

A receiver who remains near the line of scrimmage in case the quarterback is pressured by the defense and must get rid of the ball.

San Diego Chargers

The Los Angeles Chargers were founded in 1959 by hotel magnate Barron Hilton as one of the charter franchises of the American Football League. Sid Gillman, who just had been fired by the Los Angeles Rams, was named the head coach. A few months later, he also assumed the general manager's duties. With Gillman orchestrating a flashy offense featuring quarterback Jack Kemp, running back Paul Lowe, and end Dave Kocourek, the Chargers won the 1960 AFL Western Division championship but lost to the Houston Oilers 24-16 in the first AFL championship game. Only 9,928 showed up at the Los Angeles Coliseum to watch the Chargers clinch their division championship, so Hilton decided to move his team to San Diego, California in 1961.

In San Diego, the Chargers continued to win. They captured AFL Western Division titles in 1961, 1963, 1964, and 1965. In 1963, they routed the Boston Patriots 51-10 for their only AFL championship. The Chargers lost to Houston 10-3 in the 1961 AFL championship game and to the Buffalo Bills in both the 1964 and 1965 AFL championship games. A host of offensive standouts that included tackle Ron Mix, flanker Lance Alworth, running back Keith Lincoln, and quarterback John Hadl transformed the Chargers of the early 1960s into one of the most exciting teams in pro football.

Their fortunes began to turn in 1966 and, while they finished above .500 throughout the remaining AFL seasons, they didn't win another division championship until 1979. In 1966, Hilton sold the Chargers to a group headed by Eugene Klein for $10 million. Gillman retired in mid-1969 because of ill health but returned for a final season in 1971. His lifetime record with the Chargers was 83-51-6.

Harland Svare, Ron Waller, and Tommy Prothro followed Gillman as head coaches but the Chargers fell below .500 for seven straight seasons from 1970 to 1976. In 1978, Don Coryell moved from the St. Louis Cardinals to become the Chargers' head coach. With quarterback Dan Fouts throwing to receivers such as Kellen Winslow, Wes Chandler, and Charlie Joiner, the Chargers again became one of pro football's most exciting offensive teams. They scored more than 400 points in 1979, 1980, and 1981 and won AFC Western Division championships each year. San Diego lost to Houston 17-14

in a first-round playoff game in 1979 but advanced to the AFC championship before losing to Oakland 34-27 in 1980. The Chargers reached the AFC championship game again in 1981 with a classic 41-38 overtime victory over Miami, then lost to the Bengals 27-7 in 59-below-zero wind-chill weather in Cincinnati. In the 1982 AFC championship tournament, San Diego eliminated Pittsburgh but lost to Miami in the second round. Eight games into the 1986 season, Coryell resigned and was replaced by assistant Al Saunders. Coryell's record in San Diego was 72-60.

In 1984, Alex G. Spanos purchased the majority interest in the Chargers. In 1987, after starting with an 8-1 record and a first-place standing in the AFC West, the Chargers lost their final six games to fall out of contention. The Chargers' poor form continued in 1988 and following a 6-10 record Saunders was fired.

Members of the Hall of Fame:
   (5) Lance Alworth, Sid Gillman, David (Deacon) Jones, Ron Mix, Johnny Unitas

Championships Won:
   AFL: 1963
   AFL Western Division: 1960, 1961, 1963, 1964, 1965
   AFC Western Division: 1979, 1980, 1981

Overall Record:

AFL Regular Season	86	48	6	.636
AFL Postseason	1	4	0	.200
AFL Regular Season	124	151	5	.452
NFL Postseason	3	4	0	.429
Total	214	207	11	.508

San Francisco 49ers

Anthony J. (Tony) Morabito formed the San Francisco 49ers in 1946 as a charter member of the All-America Football Conference. Morabito, who had been unsuccessful in his attempts to buy an NFL franchise, signed 12 players from NFL teams. He also acquired two Bay area standouts – quarterback Frankie Albert and fullback Norm Standlee – and hired Lawrence (Buck) Shaw as head coach. During the next four seasons, the 49ers had an overall 38-14-2 record but finished second each year to the Cleveland Browns, who lost only four regular-season games in those four years. The 49ers administered two of those losses, 34-20 in 1946 and 56-28 in 1949. When the AAFC folded after the 1949 season, San Francisco was one of three teams accepted into the NFL.

In the supposedly faster company of the NFL, the 49ers continued to be a competitive team although they did not win a divisional championship until their twenty-first NFL season in 1970. Shaw continued to coach the 49ers until after the 1954 season, and his teams became noted for their offensive prowess. In 1954, the 49ers unveiled their "Million Dollar Backfield," which included quarterback Y.A. Tittle and three outstanding running backs – Joe Perry, Hugh McElhenny, and John Henry Johnson. All four are members of the Pro Football Hall of Fame. Throughout the 1950s, tackle Leo Nomellini, the 49ers' first-ever NFL draft choice, was a standout both on offense and defense.

The 49ers came close to a championship in 1957 when they tied Detroit for the NFL Western Conference lead. In the playoff game, the 49ers jumped to a 24-7 halftime lead but eventually lost 31-27. During a 1957 game against the Chicago Bears, Tony Morabito suffered a fatal heart attack. His brother Vic, who had joined him as a partner in 1947, took over full control of the team.

Quarterback John Brodie gave the 49ers firepower in the 1960s but a 7-5 record in 1960 was their best of the decade. Vic Morabito died in 1964, and the Morabito widows, Josephine and Jane, gave Lou Spadia full operating authority. In 1968, Dick Nolan became head coach, and, in just two years, led the 49ers to their first-ever division championship. The 49ers won NFC Western Division titles in 1970, 1971, and 1972. San Francisco advanced to the NFC championship game in both 1970 and 1971 but lost to the Dallas Cowboys each year. In the first playoff game in 1972, the 49ers led the Cowboys 28-16 but gave up two touchdown passes in the last two minutes to lose 30-28.

A new era began for the 49ers in 1977 when Edward J. DeBartolo, Jr., became the youngest team owner in the NFL. The first three seasons under DeBartolo were disappointing. The 49ers had 2-14 records in both 1978 and 1979. But Bill Walsh, who was named head coach in 1979, acquired quarterback Joe Montana and wide receiver Dwight Clark in the 1979 draft, and the 49ers were on the threshold of a much happier era. Several successful drafts turned the 49ers into a talent-laden team and in 1981 they marched to a 13-3 record and the NFC Western Division championship. They stunned Dallas 28-27 in the NFC championship game and then defeated the Cincinnati Bengals 26-21 in Super Bowl XVI.

San Francisco slipped to 3-6 in the strike-hit 1982 season but rebounded with NFC West championships in 1983 and 1984. The 49ers lost the 1983 NFC championship to Washington 24-21 but defeated the Chicago Bears 23-0 for the 1984 NFC title. They then overwhelmed Miami 38-16 in the Super Bowl XIX.

San Francisco won a wild-card berth in 1985 and NFC West championships again in 1986 and 1987, when their 13-2 record was the best pro football. The 49ers lost in the first playoff

round each year. They won the division again in 1988 and went on to their third NFL title, defeating Cincinnati again in Super Bowl XXIII, 20-16. From 1981 to 1988 under Walsh, who retired following the 1988 season and was replaced by 49ers assistant coach George Seifert, San Francisco had a .705 winning percentage (94-39-1).

Members of the Hall of Fame:
(6) John Henry Johnson, Hugh McElhenny, Leo Nomellini, Joe Perry, O.J. Simpson, Y.A. Tittle.

Championships Won:
Super Bowl: XVI, XIX, XXIII
NFC: 1981, 1984, 1988
NFC Western Division: 1970, 1971, 1972, 1981, 1983, 1984, 1986, 1987, 1988

Overall Record:

AAFC Regular Season	38	14	2	.722
AAFC Postseason	1	1	0	.500
NFL Regular Season	270	255	13	.514
NFL Postseason	12	8	0	.600
Total	321	278	15	.535

Sanders, Orban (Spec)

b. Temple, Oklahoma, 26 January 1920.

Orban (Spec) Sanders played only four years of pro football but his brilliant play in two leagues made a lasting impression on his sport. Sanders, a 6-1, 196-pound halfback from the University of Texas, joined the New York Yankees of the All-America Football Conference in 1946 and rushed for 1,432 yards and passed for 1,442 in 1947. He missed the 1949 season because of a severe knee injury. When he returned to the New York Yanks of the NFL in 1950, he was shifted to defense, and he led the league with 13 interceptions. Sanders was named All-AAFC in 1946 and 1947, and All-NFL in 1950.

Sayers, Gale

b. Wishita, Kansas, 30 May 1943.
Hall of Fame: 1977

Gale Sayers, a University of Kansas All-America and a Chicago Bears first-round draft choice in 1965, burst onto the NFL scene with a mercurial flourish rarely experienced in the NFL's long history. In his first preseason game, against the Los Angeles Rams, the 6-0, 200-pound halfback raced 77 yards on a punt return, went 93 yards on a kickoff return, and then startled everyone with a 25-yard, left-handed scoring pass. Midway through his rookie year, he scored four touchdowns against Minnesota, including one on a 96-yard kickoff return. Later that year, he scored a record-tying six touchdowns against San Francisco. In his sensational rookie-of-the-year season, he amassed 2,272 combined net

yards and scored a record 22 touchdowns.

Sayers got even better in his second season when he rushed for 1,231 yards, averaging 5.4 yards per carry. There is no telling what heights Sayers might have reached if he hadn't suffered a serious right knee injury in 1968. It was a foreboding of things to come, although Sayers did go through a torturous rehabilitation program and bounced back with a second 1,000-yard rushing season, when he led the NFL in 1969. A left knee injury early in 1970 effectively ended Sayers' career after just five years.

Sayers' career marks show 4,956 yards rushing, 1,307 yards on 112 pass receptions, 391 yards on punt returns, and 2,781 yards on kick-off returns. He scored 56 touchdowns and was named all-pro four times. He was Player of the Game in three Pro Bowls. In his first year of eligibility, Sayers, 34, became the youngest player elected to the Hall of Fame.

Schmidt, Joe

b. Pittsburgh, Pennsylvania, 19 January 1932.
Hall of Fame: 1973

Joe Schmidt was not highly regarded when he completed his college career at the University of Pittsburgh. He was picked in the seventh

round of the 1953 draft by the Detroit Lions but many on the Detroit staff doubted that he could make it in the pros. The 6-0, 220-pounder not only won a spot on the Lions' roster but, within two years, he was named all-pro. Schmidt was named all-pro eight consecutive years, selected for nine consecutive Pro Bowls, and picked by his teammates as the most valuable Lion four times.

Many considered Schmidt the ideal middle linebacker. As the Detroit defensive captain, a job he held for nine years, he had the uncanny knack of seemingly always knowing what the opposition was going to do. Schmidt was a ferocious tackler, fast enough to move laterally along the scrimmage line to follow a run or to drop back to cover a pass. He played with the Lions for 13 seasons until he retired after the 1965 campaign.

In 1967 Schmidt was named as head coach of the Lions, taking them to a wild card game in 1970. After four straight winning seasons, he left Detroit in 1972.

Scoreboard

Each stadium is equipped with at least one large, electrically operated scoreboard situated

Babe Laufenberg (12) was San Diego's starting quarterback in the 1988 season opener against the L.A. Raiders, for whom Steve Beuerlein was the starter. Almost uniquely, neither quarterback and been credited with a regular-season pass completion before the game.

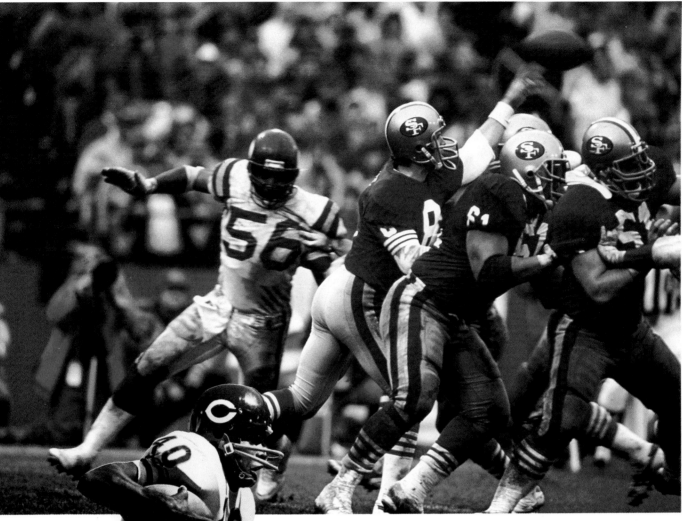

behind one end zone and two or more smaller scoreboards situated in areas of maximum visibility. Information on the scoreboard includes the scoring by quarters, the cumulative score, the time clock, and the number of time-outs remaining for each team. Most scoreboards also have a large area for use as a message board and/or an instant replay monitor.

Scoring

Points may be scored in football by four different methods:

Touchdown 6 points
Field goal 3 points
Safety 2 points
Point-after-touchdown 1 point
(Also known as conversion, or extra point)

Scramble

When the quarterback runs to avoid being sacked, at the same time still looking for an open receiver.

Above: Steve Young (8) releases a pass as the pocket breaks up around him. The left-hander is a direct descendant of the founder of the Mormon faith. The 49ers' backup quarterback would be a sure-fire starter on most other teams.

Left: Gale Sayers escapes from the grasp of Larry Wilson, the St. Louis Cardinals' Hall of Fame safety. The talented halfback was halted at his peak by crippling knee injuries.

Screen Pass

A delayed passing play in which the defensive line is allowed to penetrate the backfield and the ball is thrown to a running back or receiver who has a wall of blockers made up of offensive linemen who have pulled out of position.

Scrimmage (Line of)

The imaginary line running from sideline to sideline at the point where the ball is snapped; the line from which a play begins.

Seams

The areas between defensive zones where it is easier for receivers to make catches.

Seattle Seahawks

On December 5, 1974, the National Football League awarded an expansion franchise to Seattle Professional Football, Inc., whose majority partner was Lloyd W. Nordstrom. In anticipation of an NFL team, Seattle had begun construction of the 65,000-seat Kingdome two years earlier. A contest to name the team drew 20,365 entries, and Seahawks was the winner. Jack Patera, a Minnesota Vikings assistant, became the first head coach.

The Seahawks played in the NFC Western Division in 1976 before being assigned permanently to the AFC Western Division the next year. Seattle won only two of 14 games in 1976 but, in its third season in 1978, had a 9-7 record. With quarterback Jim Zorn connecting regularly with wide receiver Steve Largent, Seattle became one of the highest scoring teams in the NFL and finished 9-7 again in 1979. However, the Seahawks tailed off sharply the next two years, and Patera was replaced by Mike McCormack after two games of the strike-shortened 1982 season.

In 1983, McCormack was promoted to the dual role of president and general manager, and Chuck Knox left the Buffalo Bills to become Seattle's head coach. In his first season, Knox led Seattle to its first playoff appearance. Rookie running back Curt Warner provided a

Scrimmage, line of.

The Teams

○ OFFENSE
○ DEFENSE

FULLBACK
An extremely powerful runner who lines up to the tight end's side and usually gets the "bread and butter" assignments. Also expected to be a good blocker and pass receiver. Fullbacks and halfbacks are not distinguished in some offenses; they are simply designated **running backs.**

HALFBACK
The "handyman" of the team. He runs, blocks, receives, and sometimes throws passes.

WIDE RECEIVER
Usually the team's fastest receivers (pass catchers). They are "split"—stationed several yards from the interior linemen.

TIGHT END
The tight end (stationed next to the tackle) must be bigger and stronger than most receivers. Because of the extra blocking power he adds to the line, the side of the offensive formation the tight end lines up on is called the **strongside.** The side without the tight end is called the **weakside.** Defenses set up accordingly.

WIDE RECEIVER
(see below)

TACKLE
(see below)

GUARD
(see below)

QUARTERBACK
The man in charge. He calls signals, is the primary passer and ball handler, and occasionally runs the ball.

END
(see above)

CENTER, GUARDS, AND TACKLES
It is *these* five men—one center, two guards (right and left) who line up on either side of the center, and two tackles (right and left) who line up outside the guards—who make up the **interior line.**

TACKLES AND ENDS
Called the **front four** in a 4-3 set (shown here). They are the largest men on defense because their jobs are (1) stop the running attack and (2) rush the passer. Defensive linemen line up on the line of scrimmage and are permitted to use their hands against blockers.
In a 3-4 alignment, there are two ends and a middle man, called a **nose tackle;** the fourth lineman is replaced by an additional linebacker.

LINEBACKERS
The defensive team's version of the "handymen." They must pursue running plays, drop back and defend against passes, or disrupt pass plays with all-out rushes from their positions called **dogs** and **blitzes.**

CORNERBACKS AND SAFETIES
Also called **defensive backs,** they operate in the area of the defense called the **secondary.** They are required to tackle much bigger runners, yet on pass plays, they must have the speed to catch the fastest receivers. They also blitz.

CORNERBACK
(see above)

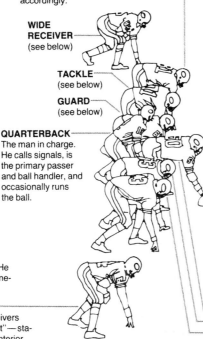

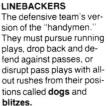

The most one-sided game in professional football was the 1940 NFL championship game between Washington, with a 9-2 record, and Chicago, which was one game behind. Chicago scored 73 unanswered points.

solid running punch to augment the sharp passing of Dave Krieg as the Seahawks scored 403 points. They finished 9-7, and, as a wild-card team, defeated Denver and Miami in the first two playoff rounds before losing to the Los Angeles Raiders 30-14 in the AFC championship game.

Seattle had a 12-4 record in 1984 and once again won a wild-card playoff berth. The Seahawks defeated the Los Angeles Raiders in the first round but lost to Miami the next week. Seattle remained in the championship race until the final weeks in both 1985 and 1986 and entered the playoffs as a wild-card team with a 9-6 record in 1987, suffering a 23-20 overtime loss to Houston in the first round. The Seahawks won their first division championship with a 9-7 record in 1988, but lost their opening playoff game to Cincinnati.

Members of the Hall of Fame:

None

Championships Won:

AFC Western Division: 1988

Overall Record:

NFL Regular Season	96	100	0	.490
NFL Postseason	3	4	0	.429
Total	99	104	0	.488

Secondary

The defensive backfield area and/or pass-coverage personnel.

Selmon, Lee Roy

b. Eufaula, Oklahoma, 20 October 1954.

When the Tampa Bay Buccaneers began play in the NFL in 1976, Lee Roy Selmon, a 6-3, 250-pound defensive end from the University of Oklahoma, was their first draft pick. In his nine seasons, he recorded 78½ career sacks and 380 quarterback pressures, both team career records. Selmon was an all-pro choice four times and All-NFC six years. In 1979, he was a consensus choice as the NFL Defensive Player of the Year. He was selected for six Pro Bowls.

Set

1. The offensive or defensive alignment.
2. The action of an offensive lineman going into a three-point stance, or the three-point stance itself.

73-0

The Washington Redskins and Chicago Bears met for the NFL championship before 36,034 fans in Washington's Griffith Stadium on December 8, 1940. Washington had beaten Chicago 7-3 three weeks earlier, but taunting remarks by Redskins owner George Preston Marshall had fired up the Bears to a fever pitch for the rematch. On the second play, Bears fullback Bill Osmanski ran around left end for 68 yards and a touchdown. The Bears scored 10 more touchdowns, three of them on interception returns, to defeat the Redskins 73-0, in the NFL's most lopsided defeat.

Bears quarterback Sid Luckman threw only six passes but completed four for 102 yards and a touchdown. Still, the game served as a showcase for the Bears' T-formation and prompted many NFL teams to make the switch to the dynamic new offense.

The Seattle Seahawks are attempting to block a Denver field goal. In 1988, the Seahawks won its first AFC Western Division championship. Since 1983, Seattle has not had a losing season, but they have only hosted two playoff games in the noisy Kingdome.

Shaughnessy, Clark

b. St. Cloud, Minnesota, 6 March 1892;
d. 15 May 1970.

Clark Shaughnessy was a star fullback at the University of Minnesota who had a distinguished college coaching career before he became involved with pro football. His first contact with the NFL came as an unofficial consultant to his friend George Halas of the Chicago Bears. Shaughnessy, who had gained national acclaim for his T- formation success at Stanford, helped to polish the Bears' attack in 1940, and they finished that season with a 73-0 win over the Washington Redskins in the NFL championship game.

In 1944, Shaughnessy, also in an advisory role, helped to teach the T-formation to the Redskins' brilliant passer, Sammy Baugh. He was named the Los Angeles Rams' head coach in 1948. In two years, he led the Rams to a 14-7-3 record and the 1949 Western Conference championship. During that season, he introduced the "three-end offense" as a regular part of his offense for the first time. As technical adviser to the Bears from 1951 to 1962, Shaugh-

nessy designed much of the multiple-formation strategy on which all modern defenses are based.

Shaw, Lawrence (Buck)

b. Mitchelville, Iowa, 28 March 1899;
d. 19 March 1977.

A former star tackle at Notre Dame, Lawrence (Buck) Shaw had 24 years experience as a college coach before he accepted his first pro football job as the head coach of the San Francisco 49ers in the All-America Football Conference in 1946. Shaw skillfully guided the 49ers for four seasons in the AAFC and the first five years after the team joined the NFL in 1950. In his nine years, San Francisco had only one losing season, and his cumulative record was an excellent 71-39-4. Shaw left the 49ers after the 1954 season and served as the head coach of the new Air Force Academy in 1956 and 1957.

In 1958, he was lured back to pro football by the Philadelphia Eagles, who had won only two games in 1957. In his third year in 1960, Shaw guided the Eagles to a 10-2 record and the NFL

Eastern Conference championship. He became the only coach to defeat Vince Lombardi in an NFL playoff game when the Eagles edged the Packers 17-13 for the NFL championship. He retired after the 1960 season with a cumulative 92-56-5 record.

Shell, Art

b. Charleston, South Carolina, 26 November 1946. Hall of Fame: 1989.

Art Shell, a 6-5, 285-pound offensive tackle from Maryland State-Eastern Shore, was a third-round draft pick of the Oakland Raiders in 1968. Shell became a fixture at left tackle in his third season in 1970. He was All-AFC six consecutive years in the 1970s and all-pro in 1973, 1974, and 1978. Shell played in eight Pro Bowl games and 23 postseason games. In his 15-season career which ended in 1982, Shell played in 238 games.

Shift

The movement of two or more offensive players before the snap; also can apply to movement by the defense.

Shotgun

An offensive formation in which the quarterback takes a long snap from center five-to-seven yards behind the line.

Shula, Don

b. Painesville, Ohio, 4 January 1930.

In his first 26 seasons as a head coach with the Baltimore Colts and Miami Dolphins, Don Shula compiled a 277-124-6 record, which placed him second behind George Halas among history's winningest coaches. Shula's teams had finished

Above: Tackle Art Shell was a vital cog in the Oakland Raiders' running game. Head coach John Madden's favorite running move involved a sweep to the left, which meant that Shell had to block out the first wave of the opposing defense, something he did superbly.

as low as third only five times. They finished first or tied for first 14 times. Shula's NFL coaching career began with the Baltimore Colts in 1963. In his seven seasons, he compiled a 73-26-4 regular-season record. His Colts won NFL Western Conference championships in 1964 and 1968. Baltimore lost the 1964 NFL championship to Cleveland but defeated the Browns for the 1968 NFL title before losing to the New York Jets in Super Bowl III.

In 1970, Dolphins owner Joe Robbie hired Shula away from the Colts. Shula coached Miami to four consecutive AFC Eastern Division championships from 1971 to 1974. The 1972 Dolphins had a 17-0 record, the only perfect season in NFL history. Their seventeenth victory was a 14-7 win over the Washington Redskins in Super Bowl VII. Miami won the Super Bowl again in 1973 with a 24-7 victory over the Minnesota Vikings. The Dolphins appeared in three other Super Bowls under Shula but lost to the NFC opponent in Super Bowls VI, XVII, and XIX. After the 1988 season, Shula's regular-season record in Miami was 205-98-2.

Shula attended John Carroll University. He played as a defensive back for seven years with the Browns, Colts, and Redskins before starting his coaching career. Before joining the Colts, he was an assistant coach with the Detroit Lions.

Left: Head coach Don Shula of Miami has been to six Super Bowls, more than anybody else. He has always been flexible, taking the best players and using a game plan that suited his personnel, rather than selecting players that could play to his style.

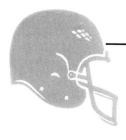

Sideline

The outer border of the playing field that runs for 120 yards from the back line of one end zone to the back line of the other. There are two sidelines on each playing field.

Signals

The number and word codes called by the quarterback in the huddle and at the line of scrimmage. Signals also are called by the defense prior to a play, usually by a linebacker.

Simpson, O.J.

b. San Francisco, California, 9 July 1947. Hall of Fame: 1985

O.J. Simpson was one of the highest-rated rookies ever when he joined the Buffalo Bills as the top pick in the 1969 draft. However, Buffalo head coach John Rauch refused to use the two-time All-America from the University of Southern California as a ball-carrying specialist, insisting he also serve on special teams. On a

kickoff return in 1970, the 1968 Heisman Trophy winner suffered a severe knee injury. Then Lou Saban, who believed in a strong running game, came along for his second term as the Bills' head coach, and Simpson's fortunes quickly took a turn for the better.

Simpson ran for more than 1,000 yards each year in the five-season period starting in 1972. He won all-pro honors and played in the Pro Bowl each year. He won four NFL rushing titles and was named NFL Player of the Year in 1972, 1973, and 1975. While many feel the 6-1, 212-pound Simpson had his best overall season in 1975, he is most remembered for the 1973 season. That year, he set an NFL single-season record with 2,003 yards rushing. After nine years in Buffalo, Simpson was traded to his home-town 49ers for his final two seasons (1978 and 1979). He wound up his 11-year career with 11,236 yards and 61 touchdowns rushing. With 14 touchdowns on receptions and one on a kickoff return, he scored 456 points on 76 touchdowns. He accumulated 14,368 combined net yards. In his first year of eligibility, Simpson was elected to the Hall of Fame.

Most Common Official Signals

When something happens on the field that involves the officials, the referee communicates what has happened to the fans, and the television audience, via a microphone and a set of hand signals.

Time out — Touchdown, field goal — Personal foul — Illegal use of hands — Illegal contact — Delay of game

Offside or encroaching — Holding — Illegal motion — First down — Pass interference — Incomplete pass, penalty refused, missed kick

Single Wing

Formerly the most popular offensive formation in football but one that is rarely used today. The tailback (or halfback) and fullback line up approximately five yards behind the scrimmage line while the quarterback serves as a blocking back and the wingback as a flanker.

Singletary, Mike

b. Houston, Texas, 9 October 1958.

In the second round of the 1981 NFL draft, the Chicago Bears selected Mike Singletary, a 6-foot, 235-pound All-America linebacker from Baylor University. Singletary became an immediate regular. He has served as the Bears' defensive captain since 1983. Through 1988, he had been named all-pro six consecutive seasons from 1983 to 1988 and had played in the Pro Bowl each year. In eight seasons, he had recovered 11 opponents' fumbles and intercepted six passes.

Situation Substitution

Substituting players with specialized skills in specific situations.

Slant

1. A charge by a defensive lineman to the left or right instead of straight ahead.
2. A running play hitting sharply off guard or tackle.

Slant-In

A quick, short pass pattern run diagonally across the middle of the field.

Smith, Jackie

b. Columbia, Mississippi, 23 February 1940.

Jackie Smith played 15 seasons with the St. Louis Cardinals from 1963 to 1977 and a sixteenth season with the Dallas Cowboys in 1978. The 6-4, 232-pound tight end from Northwestern Louisiana State was the Cardinals' tenth-round draft pick in 1963. His top season came in 1967 when he had 56 receptions for 1,205 yards and nine touchdowns. At the time of his retirement, he was the leading receiver among tight ends with 480 receptions for 7,918 yards and 40 touchdowns. Smith played in five Pro Bowls and in Super Bowl XIII with the Cowboys.

Snap Count

The signal on which the ball will be snapped.

Snap

The action of passing the ball from the center backwards to the quarterback, punter, or holder to begin a play. Also called a hike.

Sneakers Game

Overnight freezing rain turned New York's Polo Grounds into a sheet of ice for the 1934 NFL championship game between the Giants and the Chicago Bears. The Giants discussed playing in basketball shoes, but, because no sporting goods stores were open, they sent a clubhouse aide, Abe Cohen, on an emergency

O.J. Simpson was born Orenthal James Simpson, but was known throughout his career as O.J. or 'The Juice'. He was the first runner in NFL history to rush for more than 2,000 yards, gaining 2,003 in 1973.

On the frozen wastes of the Polo Grounds in New York, the Giants took on the Bears in the 1934 NFL championship game. The Giants changed into basketball sneakers at halftime and with the extra grip afforded by these soles, scored 27 fourth-quarter points to win 30-13.

mission to Manhattan College to obtain as many pairs as he could find. Cohen returned just as the third quarter began and the Giants put on the shoes. With the advantage of much better footing, the Giants overcame a 13-3 Chicago lead with a 27-point fourth-quarter outburst that swamped the previously unbeaten Bears 30-13.

Sound (Going On)

A quick variation of the snap count; the center snaps the ball on the first sound the quarterback utters.

Special Teams

The offensive and defensive units used on kickoffs, punts, extra points, and field goals.

Speedie, Mac

b. Odell, Illinois, 12 January 1920.

Mac Speedie overcame a childhood bone ailment to become a multi-sport star at the University of Utah. His play with the Fort Warren, Wyoming, army team caught the eye of coach Paul Brown, who signed him to play with the Cleveland Browns of the All-America Football

Conference. The 6-3, 215-pounder was named All-AAFC three of four years and All-NFL in 1950 and 1952. He led the AAFC in receiving in 1947, 1948, and 1949 and the NFL in 1952. Speedie left the Browns to play in Canada after the 1952 season. In seven years of American pro football, he caught 349 passes for 5,602 yards and 33 touchdowns.

Spike

When a player slams the ball to the ground after scoring.

Split

The distance a player is separated from another player.

Spot

The placement of the ball by the referee after a play or penalty.

Spot of Enforcement

The spot from which a penalty or foul is marked off; it varies depending on the situation.

Spot Pass

A pass pattern predicated on timing and coordination; the quarterback throws to a predetermined spot on the field before the receiver actually gets there.

Spread

1. An offensive formation with no running backs in the backfield.
2. The Dallas Cowboys' term for the Shotgun formation.

Squib Kick

A kickoff that is intentionally kicked low; the ball bounces along the field and can be very difficult to handle.

Stabler, Ken

b. Foley, Alabama, 25 December 1945.

Ken Stabler, a 6-3, 210-pound quarterback from the University of Alabama, was drafted by the Oakland Raiders in the second round of the 1968 AFL-NFL draft. Stabler led the AFC in passing in his first year as a regular in 1973. His last-second touchdown pass in a 1974 playoff game gave Oakland a 28-26 victory and ended Miami's quest for a third straight Super Bowl championship. Stabler was named AFC player of the year that year and again in 1976, when he guided the Raiders to the AFC title and a Super Bowl XI triumph over the Minnesota Vikings. He played in three Pro Bowls in the 1970s, but was traded to the Houston Oilers for quarterback Dan Pastorini in 1980. He was released by the Oilers and signed as a free agent by the New Orleans Saints in 1982, before retiring in 1984. His 15-year lifetime record includes 2,270 pass completions for 27,938 yards, 194 touchdowns, and a 75.1 passer rating.

Stack

When a linebacker stands directly behind a defensive lineman.

Above: Tampa Stadium, site for Super Bowl XXV in January, 1991, basks in the Florida sunshine. The Buccaneers' lack of success in recent seasons has meant slender crowds at the 74,000-seat-stadium.

Left: Joe Robbie Stadium, in the northern suburbs of Miami, Florida, is the newest stadium in the NFL. Built as a true football stadium, the seats are so designed that there is not a bad position anywhere.

Stadiums, Current

The 28 stadiums where NFL teams play today:

Team	Stadium	Surface	Capacity	First Year
Atlanta Falcons	Atlanta-Fulton County Stadium	Grass (PAT)	59,643	1966
Buffalo Bills	Rich Stadium	AstroTurf	80,290	1973
Chicago Bears	Soldier Field	Grass	66,030	1971
Cincinnati Bengals	Riverfront Stadium	AstroTurf-8	59,754	1970
Cleveland Browns	Cleveland Stadium	Grass	80,098	1946
Dallas Cowboys	Texas Stadium	Texas Turf	63,855	1971
Denver Broncos	Denver Mile High Stadium*	Grass (PAT)	76,273	1960
Detroit Lions	Pontiac Silverdome	AstroTurf	80,638	1975
Green Bay Packers	Lambeau Field (Green Bay)**	Grass	57,093	1957
	Milwaukee County Stadium (Milw.)	Grass	56,051	1952
Houston Oilers	Astrodome	AstroTurf-8	50,594	1968
Indianapolis Colts	Hoosier Dome	AstroTurf	60,127	1984
Kansas City Chiefs	Arrowhead Stadium	AstroTurf-8	78,067	1972
Los Angeles Raiders	Los Angeles Memorial Coliseum†	Grass	92,488	1982
Los Angeles Rams	Anaheim Stadium	Grass	69,007	1980
Miami Dolphins	Joe Robbie Stadium	Grass (PAT)	74,930	1987
Minnesota Vikings	Hubert H. Humphrey Metrodome	AstroTurf	63,000	1982
New England Patriots	Sullivan Stadium††	Super Turf	60,794	1971
New Orleans Saints	Louisiana Superdome	AstroTurf	69,548	1975
New York Giants	Giants Stadium	AstroTurf	76,891	1976
New York Jets	Giants Stadium	AstroTurf	76,891	1984
Philadelphia Eagles	Veterans Stadium	AstroTurf-8	65,356	1971
Phoenix Cardinals	Sun Devil Stadium	Grass	74,000	1988
Pittsburgh Steelers	Three Rivers Stadium	AstroTurf	59,000	1970
San Diego Chargers	San Diego Jack Murphy Stadium	Grass	60,750	1967
San Francisco 49ers	Candlestick Park	Grass	64,252	1971
Seattle Seahawks	Kingdome	AstroTurf	64,984	1976
Tampa Bay Buccaneers	Tampa Stadium	Grass	74,315	1976
Washington Redskins	Robert F. Kennedy Stadium‡	Grass (PAT)	55,670	1961

*   Originally named Bears Stadium
**   Originally named New City Stadium
†   Los Angeles Rams played in the Los Angeles Memorial Stadium from 1946 to 1979
††   Originally named Schaefer Stadium
‡   Originally named District of Columbia Stadium

Stadiums, Former

Stadiums used by NFL teams for 10 or more years:

Stadium	Capacity	Team	Years used
War Memorial Stadium	46,206	Buffalo Bills	1960-1972
Wrigley Field	45,000	Chicago Bears	1921-1970
Cotton Bowl	72,000	Dallas Cowboys	1960-1970
Tiger Stadium*	54,418	Detroit Lions	1941-1974
City Stadium (Green Bay)	25,000	Green Bay Packers	1925-1956
State Fair Park (Milwaukee)	32,000	Green Bay Packers	1936-1951
Memorial Stadium (Baltimore)	60,586	Baltimore Colts	1953-1983
Oakland-Alameda County Coliseum	53,825	Oakland Raiders	1966-1981
Orange Bowl	75,000	Miami Dolphins	1966-1986
Metropolitan Stadium	48,446	Minnesota Vikings	1961-1981
Yankee Stadium	64,892	New York Giants	1956-1973
Polo Grounds	52,000	New York Giants	1925-1955
		New York Titans/Jets	1960-1963
Shea Stadium	60,372	New York Jets	1964-1983
		New York Giants	1975
Franklin Field	60,658	Philadelphia Eagles	1958-1969
Shibe Park	36,309	Philadelphia Eagles	1940-1956
Busch Memorial Stadium	50,492	St. Louis Cardinals	1960-1987
Comiskey Park	35,000	Chicago Cardinals	1929-1958
Forbes Field	35,500	Pittsburgh Steelers	1933-1963
Kezar Stadium	59,636	San Francisco 49ers	1946-1970
		Oakland Raiders	1960
Griffith Stadium	36,000	Washington Redskins	1937-1960

* Originally named Briggs Stadium

Stallworth, John

b. Tuscaloosa, Alabama, 15 July 1952.

John Stallworth, a 6-2, 202-pound wide receiver from Alabama A&M, joined the Pittsburgh Steelers in 1974. Stallworth played with the Steelers for 14 years through 1987. He caught 537 passes for 8,723 yards and 63 touchdowns and ranks among the top 20 lifetime pass receivers. A long-time Steelers offensive captain, Stallworth scored the winning touchdown in Super Bowl XIV against the Los Angeles Rams on a 73-yard reception. His 12 touchdown receptions in 18 playoff games is an all-time record. He played in four Pro Bowls.

Starr, Bart

b. Montgomery, Alabama, 9 January 1934.
Hall of Fame: 1977

Quarterback Bart Starr, a seventeenth-round draft choice from the University of Alabama in 1956, didn't fare well in his first three years with the Green Bay Packers. Then Vince Lombardi was hired as the Packers' head coach in 1959, and Starr's career took a sharp turn upward. The new coach liked Starr's mechanics, his arm, his ball-handling techniques, and, most of all, his intelligence. Starr did lack one thing – confidence – but Lombardi was determined he would soon have that.

Under Lombardi's careful tutoring Starr developed into one of the NFL's greatest field leaders. In the span from 1960-67, Starr's won-lost record was 82-24-4, and the Packers won six division titles, five NFL championships, and Super Bowls I and II. The 6-1, 200-pound play-caller was the NFL's Player of the Year in 1966, the Most Valuable Player each of the first two Super Bowls, and a three-time NFL passing champion. Although he gained relatively little attention compared to some of his teammates, many who were closest to Packers football insist that Starr was the most important single member of the dynasty of the 1960s.

Starr's career totals show 1,808 completions

An overhead view of Arrowhead Stadium, home of the Kansas City Chiefs; the area also includes Royals Stadium, home of the baseball Royals. The whole facility is known as the Harry S. Truman Sports Complex.

for 24,718 yards and 152 touchdowns. He also rushed for 1,308 yards and 15 touchdowns. In his first year of eligibility, he was elected to the Hall of Fame.

In 1975 Starr was appointed coach by the Packers in a bid to bring them back to the glory of his playing days. In the strike-affected 1982 season Green Bay finished third in the NFC but lost a second-round play-off game. At the end of the following season he was dismissed.

Staubach, Roger

b. Cincinnati, Ohio, 5 February 1942.
Hall of Fame: 1985

The 1963 Heisman Trophy winner while a junior at the United States Naval Academy, Roger Staubach was a draft pick of the Dallas Cowboys in 1964. But the 6-3, 202-pound quarterback spent four years in the service before he could report to Dallas as a 27-year-old rookie in 1969. When he got his first chance to start on a regular basis in 1971, he enjoyed immediate success. Staubach won the 1971 NFL individual passing championship, NFL player of the year

acclaim, and the Most Valuable Player award in Super Bowl VI. For the next nine years, he was virtually unstoppable. Staubach won three more passing titles, was named all-NFC four times, and played in four Pro Bowls. He led the Cowboys to the biggest victories of their history, in Super Bowls VI and XII. The Cowboys have not won an NFC title since Staubach retired after the 1979 season.

Staubach was particularly effective because of his ability to run as well as pass. When he got the center snap, opposing players had little idea whether he would handoff, pass, or run. The daredevil team leader also had the uncanny ability to stage come-from-behind rallies. He engineered 23 fourth-quarter rallies that produced Dallas victories. Fourteen of them came in the final two minutes or in overtime. A typical example is the 1972 playoff game against San Francisco when Staubach threw two touchdown passes to lead Dallas from a 28-16 deficit with 70 seconds left to a stunning 30-28 triumph.

In 11 seasons, Staubach completed 1,685 passes for 22,700 yards and 153 touchdowns. He also rushed for 2,264 yards and 20 touchdowns. In his first year of eligibility, he was elected to the Hall of Fame.

Stautner, Ernie

b. Prinzing-bei-Cham, Bavaria, Germany, 20 April 1925. Hall of Fame: 1969

Ernie Stautner was a four-year regular at Boston College who had an ambition to become a pro football player. But New York Giants head coach Steve Owen told him he was too small and advised him to try another profession. The Pittsburgh Steelers decided to give Stautner a try, however, picking him in the third round of the 1950 draft. For the next 14 years, the 6-2, 235-pound Stautner was a fixture at defensive tackle, a major factor in one of the most punishing defensive units in the NFL. Always ready to play anywhere, Stautner often switched to defensive end or on to the offensive line when the occasion demanded.

Stautner migrated to Albany, New York, with his family when he was three years old. He played high school football against the wishes of his father, who was afraid he would get hurt. Stautner was extremely durable in the NFL, missing only six games in 14 seasons with the Steelers. In his first year of eligibility, he was elected to the Hall of Fame.

Steel Curtain

During the 1970s, the Pittsburgh Steelers were the dominant team in pro football, winning four

Jan Stenerud played in Super Bowl IV for the Chiefs, but when they cut him loose after 13 years, he felt he could still kick, so he joined Green Bay. After four years, the Packers said he was finished; so he traveled to Minnesota. In his first season there, he was selected for the Pro Bowl.

Super Bowls. The Steelers featured an outstanding defensive unit known as "The Steel Curtain." From 1974 to 1978, the Steelers allowed the fewest points of any NFL team four times. The Steel Curtain was at its absolute best in Super Bowl IX when it limited the Minnesota Vikings to a record- low 17 yards rushing and 119 yards in total offense.

Stenerud, Jan

b. Fetsund, Norway, 20 November 20, 1942.

Jan Stenerud was a soccer player who became an All-America place-kicker at Montana State University. He was a future draft choice of the Kansas City Chiefs in 1966, and the 6-2, 190-pound Norwegian played with the Chiefs from 1967 to 1979. In 1980, he moved to Green Bay for a four-year tenure with the Packers, then finished his career with the Minnesota Vikings in 1984 and 1985. Stenerud is the second-leading scorer in history with 1,699 points on 373 field goals and 580 extra points. He played in two AFL All-Star games and four Pro Bowls, the last one after his eighteenth season in 1984.

Stram, Hank

b. Chicago, Illinois, 3 January 1924.

Hank Stram coached for 12 years at Purdue, Southern Methodist, and Notre Dame before Lamar Hunt named him head coach of the Dallas Texans in the AFL in 1960. Stram stayed with Hunt's team, which became the Kansas City Chiefs in 1963, for 15 years. Under Stram, the Texans/Chiefs were the winningest team in AFL history with a 129-78-10 overall record. The Chiefs won AFL championships in 1962, 1966, and 1969. They lost to Green Bay in Super Bowl I, but Stram led his team to a 23-7 upset of the Minnesota Vikings in Super Bowl IV. The win evened the AFL-NFL portion of the Super Bowl series at two games apiece.

Stram had only three losing seasons in 15 years with the Texans/ Chiefs. Two years after his release by the Chiefs in 1974, Stram became the head coach of the New Orleans Saints. In two years with the Saints in 1976 and 1977, his record was 7-21. His cumulative pro record is 136-100-10. He ranks tenth in victories among all NFL coaches.

Strong, Ken

b. New Haven, Connecticut, 6 August 1906;
d. 5 October 1979. Hall of Fame: 1967

It was naturally assumed that Ken Strong, a consensus All-America at New York University in 1928, would play for the New York Giants when he turned to pro football. But the Giants' coach

Roger Staubach's cool head never was more clearly shown than late in games, when his Navy training allowed him to avoid panic. His scrambling ability gave him the sobriquet 'Roger the Dodger.'

who was sent to recruit Strong tried to sign him for $3,000 instead of the $4,000 he was authorized to offer. The 5-11, 210-pound halfback decided to cast his lot with the Staten Island Stapletons. The Stapletons folded after the 1932 season, and Strong wound up with the Giants after all.

In both 1933 and 1934, Strong was a major factor in his team's march to the NFL championship game. In 1934, he was a unanimous all-pro choice. In the championship game, he scored 17 points to pace the Giants to a 30-13 victory. In 1936, Strong jumped to the New York Yanks of the new American Football League. In retaliation, the NFL suspended Strong for five years. But after the second AFL went out of business, the NFL allowed the triple-threat offensive star to rejoin the Giants in 1939. He retired after just one season but returned four years later as a kicking specialist. Strong retired for good after the 1947 season. During his NFL career he scored 496 points.

Strong Safety

The defensive back lined up opposite the side of the offensive line containing the most players. The strong safety has the responsibility of covering the tight end on passing plays.

Strongside

The side of the offensive formation with the tight end.

Stunt

A planned rush by linebackers and defensive linemen, or by linemen alone, in which they loop around each other instead of charging straight ahead.

Stydahar, Joe

b. Kaylor, Pennsylvania, 3 March 1912;
d. 23 March 1977. Hall of Fame: 1967

When the National Football League staged its first draft in 1936, the Chicago Bears picked Joe Stydahar, a 6-4, 230-pound tackle from West Virginia University, as their number one choice. Stydahar didn't have a huge reputation, but he did have blue-chip credentials – all-East, Little All-America, and All-America honorable mention. He also played in the East-West game and the Chicago College All-Star game before joining the Bears. Fearless and large by mid-1930s standards, Stydahar became a fixture at left tackle for the powerful Bears. A rugged competitor who often shunned the use of a helmet, Stydahar was an all-pro choice each year from 1937 to 1940.

Stydahar was called into the Navy following the 1942 season, but returned in 1945 to play for two more years. During his nine years with Chicago, the Bears won three NFL championships and five Western divison titles. In Stydahar's final game in 1946, the Bears defeated the New York Giants 24-14. It also was the last

major triumph of the Bears' "Monsters of the Midway" years. In 1967, Stydahar was elected to the Pro Football Hall of Fame.

Stydahar became coach of the Los Angeles Rams in 1950, winning the NFL championship the following year. He resigned in the 1952 season and was coach of the Chicago Cardinals in 1953 and 1954.

Substitutions

Each team is permitted 11 men on the field at the time of the snap of the ball. Unlimited substitution is permitted. However, players may enter the field only when the ball is dead. Players who have been replaced are not permitted to linger on the field. Players leaving the game must be out of bounds on their own side, clearing the field between the end lines, before a snap.

Sudden Death

The overtime period that is played when a tie exists at the end of the regulation game. In regular-season NFL games, play continues until one team scores. If there is no score in the 15-minute overtime period, the game ends in a tie. In postseason NFL games, overtime play continues as long as is necessary for a winner to be determined.

Super Bowl

On June 8, 1966, when officials of the American and National Football Leagues announced the end of the costly inter-league struggle, one of the principal terms of the merger was an annual

Matt Snell (41) scored the first touchdown for the Jets in their 16-7 triumph over Baltimore in Super Bowl III. The victory had been guaranteed by Joe Namath in the week before the game, but it still was probably the biggest shock in championship football history as the Colts were 18-point favorites.

season-ending championship between the champions of the AFL and NFL. Lamar Hunt, the AFL founder and a principal merger negotiator, hit upon the idea of calling the game the Super Bowl as he watched his young daughter at play with a high-bouncing ball known as a "Super Ball." While the name was accepted by the public almost immediately, the first title game between Kansas City and Green Bay on January 15, 1967, officially was called The AFL-NFL World Championship Game. The name Super Bowl did not appear on game tickets until Super Bowl IV.

After lopsided wins by the Packers in the first two games, critics insisted the AFL was too weak for the NFL and the Super Bowl had no competitive viability. However, the New York Jets and Kansas City Chiefs, with big upsets of the Baltimore Colts and Minnesota Vikings in Super Bowls III and IV, respectively, silenced such talk.

The Super Bowl has become one of the world's premier sports events. Super Bowl games have accounted for the 10 most-watched television sports events of all time and 8 of the 10 most-watched television programs of any kind. In the United States, almost 50 percent of all the nation's television sets are tuned to every Super Bowl. Super Bowl XXII also was seen in 55 countries.

Supplemental Draft

A maximum of two supplemental drafts is held by the NFL for the selection of players who become eligible between the time of the regular draft and the start of the regular season. A lottery drawing determines the selection order, with the team with the poorest record getting 28 chances, the team with the second-worst record 27 chances, and so forth. A team that selects a player in a supplemental draft loses its choice in the corresponding round of the next regular draft.

Swann, Lynn

b. Alcoa, Tennessee, 7 March 1952.

Lynn Swann, a 6-foot, 180-pound super-smooth wide receiver, was the top pick of the Pittsburgh Steelers in the 1974 NFL draft. The former University of Southern California All-America spent much of his rookie year as a punt-return specialist but became a heavy duty pass-catcher in his second season. Swann's finest performance came in Super Bowl X when he caught four passes for 161 yards and a touchdown and named Most Valuable Player. He holds Super Bowl career records for receptions (16) and reception yardage (364).

The Super Bowl Series

Season/ Super Bowl	Winner, Loser,	Score	Most Valuable Player
1966, I	Green Bay Packers (NFL)	35	Bart Starr, QB
	Kansas City Chiefs (AFL)	10	Green Bay
1967, II	Green Bay Packers (NFL)	33	Bart Starr, QB
	Oakland Raiders (AFL)	14	Green Bay
1968, III	New York Jets (AFL)	16	Joe Namath, QB
	Baltimore Colts (NFL)	7	New York
1969, IV	Kansas City Chiefs (AFL)	23	Len Dawson, QB
	Minnesota Vikings (NFL)	7	Kansas City
1970, V	Baltimore Colts (AFC)	16	Chuck Howley, LB
	Dallas Cowboys (NFC)	13	Dallas
1971, VI	Dallas Cowboys (NFC)	24	Roger Staubach, QB
	Miami Dolphins (AFC)	3	Dallas
1972, VII	Miami Dolphins (AFC)	14	Jake Scott, S
	Washington Redskins (NFC)	7	Miami
1973, VIII	Miami Dolphins (AFC)	24	Larry Csonka, RB
	Minnesota Vikings (NFC)	7	Miami
1974, IX	Pittsburgh Steelers (AFC)	16	Franco Harris, RB
	Minnesota Vikings (NFC)	6	Pittsburgh
1975, X	Pittsburgh Steelers (AFC)	21	Lynn Swann, WR
	Dallas Cowboys (NFC)	17	Pittsburgh
1976, XI	Oakland Raiders (AFC)	32	Fred Biletnikoff, WR
	Minnesota Vikings (NFC)	14	Oakland
1977, XII	Dallas Cowboys (NFC)	27	Randy White, DT
	Denver Broncos (AFC)	10	Harvey Martin, DE
			Dallas
1978, XIII	Pittsburgh Steelers (AFC)	35	Terry Bradshaw, QB
	Dallas Cowboys (NFC)	31	Pittsburgh
1979, XIV	Pittsburgh Steelers (AFC)	31	Terry Bradshaw, QB
	Los Angeles Rams (NFC)	19	Pittsburgh
1980, XV	Oakland Raiders (AFC)	27	Jim Plunkett, QB
	Philadelphia Eagles (NFC)	10	Oakland
1981, XVI	San Francisco 49ers (NFC)	26	Joe Montana, QB
	Cincinnati Bengals (AFC)	21	San Francisco
1982, XVII	Washington Redskins (NFC)	27	John Riggins, RB
	Miami Dolphins (AFC)	17	Washington
1983, XVIII	Los Angeles Raiders (AFC)	38	Marcus Allen, RB
	Washington Redskins (NFC)	9	Los Angeles
1984, XIX	San Francisco 49ers (NFC)	38	Joe Montana, QB
	Miami Dolphins (AFC)	16	San Francisco
1985, XX	Chicago Bears (NFC)	46	Richard Dent, DE
	New England Patriots (AFC)	10	Chicago
1986, XXI	New York Giants (NFC)	39	Phil Simms, QB
	Denver Broncos (AFC)	20	New York
1987, XXII	Washington Redskins (NFC)	42	Doug Williams, QB
	Denver Broncos (AFC)	10	Washington
1988, XXIII	San Francisco 49ers (NFC)	20	Jerry Rice, WR
	Cincinnati Bengals (AFC)	16	San Francisco

Series Record
AFL 2, NFL 2
AFC 10, NFC 9
AFL/AFC 12, NFL/NFC 11

Swann was named all-pro in 1975 and 1978 and All-AFC in 1977. He was voted to the Pro Bowl three times. In nine seasons, he had 336 receptions for 5,462 yards and 51 touchdowns.

Sweep

A run around end.

Swing Pass

A short pass thrown quickly to a back on either side of the quarterback.

★ ★ ★ ★ ★ ★ ★ ★ ★ ★ ★ ★ ★ ★ ★

T-Formation

An offensive formation in which the quarter-back lines up directly behind the center and the running backs line up in a straight line behind the quarterback, thus forming a "T." If there are three running backs in the line, the formation is called a full house. If there are two running backs, it is called a Split-T.

Tackle

1. To stop a ball carrier and force him to the ground.
2. The offensive line positions outside the guards but inside the ends.
3. The defensive line positions in the middle of a four-man line.

Vinny Testaverde was the first pick of the 1987 draft, but because of its record Tampa Bay did not have the time for him to develop on the sidelines. In 1988, 7.5% of his passes were intercepted. Testaverde has admitted to color blindness.

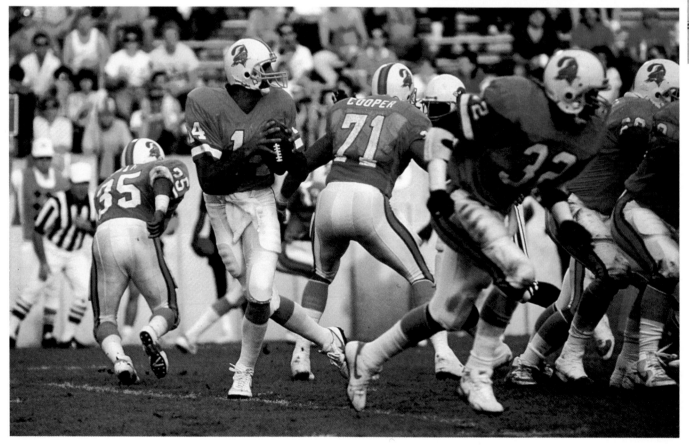

NFL

Tampa Bay Buccaneers

The Tampa Bay Buccaneers' franchise was established in the National Football League in 1974 with Hugh F. Culverhouse, a Jacksonville, Florida, attorney and real-estate investor, as the principal owner. The Tampa City Council agreed to expand Tampa Stadium from 46,500 to 72,000 seats. John McKay, who had won four national collegiate championships at the University of Southern California, signed a five-year contract as head coach. With the first pick in the NFL draft in 1976, the Buccaneers chose Lee Roy Selmon, an All-America middle guard from Oklahoma. They took his brother Dewey, a defensive tackle, in the second round. Tampa Bay was assigned to the AFC Western Division in 1976 and then moved to the NFC Central Division the next season.

In 1976, the Buccaneers became the first team in NFL history to finish 0-14 and the first to go winless since the 1960 Dallas Cowboys. In 1977, Tampa Bay lost its first 12 games to run its losing streak to 26 in a row before defeating the New Orleans Saints 33-14 on December 11.

More than 8,000 fans were on hand to greet the team when it arrived home at the Tampa airport. A week later, Tampa Bay made it two straight with a 17-7 victory over St. Louis.

The Buccaneers won five games in 1978, then stunned the football world in 1979 by winning the NFC Central Division with a 10-6 record. They defeated the Philadelphia Eagles 24-17 in their first playoff game before losing to the Los Angeles Rams 9-0 in the NFC championship game. Lee Roy Selmon was named the NFC's Defensive Player of the Year, and running back Ricky Bell rushed for 1,263 yards. Doug Williams, a young quarterback from Grambling, proved to be a dangerous long-distance passing threat.

In 1981, Tampa Bay defeated the Detroit Lions 20-17 in the season's final game to win its second NFC Central Division championship in three years. However, in the first playoff game, the Buccaneers were overwhelmed by the Dallas Cowboys 38-0. In the strike-shortened 1982 season, the Buccaneers' 5-4 record put them in the playoffs again but they lost to Dallas 30-17 in the first game. McKay gave up his

Above: Doug Williams quarterbacked Tampa Bay, leading the Buccaneers to the brink of consistent success.

Above left: Lynn Swann was appropriately named; there have been few more graceful receivers in football. He was a favorite receiver of Terry Bradshaw's, and he holds the records for both number of receptions and yards gained by a receiver in Super Bowls.

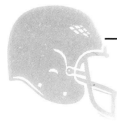

coaching duties after the 1984 season and was replaced by Leeman Bennett. Under Bennett, Tampa Bay finished 2-14 in both 1985 and 1986. In 1987, Ray Perkins was hired away from the University of Alabama to coach the team.

Members of the Hall of Fame:
None

Championships Won:
NFC Central Division: 1979, 1981

Overall Record:

NFL Regular Season	57	138	1	.293
NFL Postseason	1	3	0	.250
Total	58	141	1	.293

Tarkenton, Fran

b. Richmond, Virginia, 3 February 1940.
Hall of Fame: 1986

In 18 seasons in the National Football League, Fran Tarkenton, a 6-0, 185-pound quarterback from the University of Georgia, amassed yardage totals that stagger the imagination. His career totals were 47,003 yards passing and 3,674 yards rushing for a total of 50,677 yards – almost 29 miles or 500 football fields. Tarkenton's career was divided into three distinct sections. He started in the NFL as a third-round draft choice of the Minnesota Vikings in 1961. Six seasons later, he was traded to the New York Giants, for whom he played for five years. In 1972, Tarkenton came back to Minnesota, the second time he had been the principal figure in a multi-player trade between the Vikings and Giants.

Tarkenton had a spectacular pro debut in the 1961 season opener, coming off the bench to throw four touchdown passes and run for a fifth in a 37-13 upset of the Chicago Bears. Tarkenton gained major attention in the 1960s for his scrambling style that saw him dodge and dart past tacklers all across the field before he passed or ran.

In his second tenure in Minnesota, Tarkenton proved that he could lead a winning team, something he had not done in his first two stops. From 1973 to 1978, Minnesota enjoyed a 62-22-3 record, won six consecutive NFC Central Division championships, and advanced to the Super Bowl three times. In addition to his massive yardage totals, Tarkenton accounted for 374 touchdowns, 342 by passing and 32 by rushing.

Tatum, Jack

b. Cherryville, North Carolina, 18 November 1948.

Jack Tatum, a 5-11, 205-pound All-America safety from Ohio State University, was selected by the Oakland Raiders in the first round of the 1971 NFL draft. In 1972, Tatum earned a spot in the record book by returning a fumble 104 yards for a touchdown against Green Bay. Tatum was an All-AFC selection in 1975, 1976, and 1977, and played in the Pro Bowl after each of those seasons. In eight years with the Raiders and one with the Houston Oilers, he had a lifetime total of 37 interceptions, which he returned for 736 yards.

Taylor, Charley

b. Grand Prairie, Texas, 18 September 1941.
Hall of Fame: 1984

The first-round draft pick of the Washington Redskins out of Arizona State in 1964, Charley Taylor began his pro football career as a big-yardage halfback who was also a threat as a pass receiver. His goal was to be a great running back. Thus, he was unhappy when Redskins head coach Otto Graham moved him to split end midway through his third season in 1966. However, the position change turned out to be his ticket to the Hall of Fame. In his first start as a full-time wide receiver, the 6-3, 210-pounder caught eight passes for 111 yards against Baltimore. He wound up the season as the top NFL receiver with 72 catches for 1,119 yards and 12 touchdowns.

Taylor led the NFL in receiving again in 1967. He averaged 60 receptions a year until he was sidelined by injuries in 1971. Taylor played through 1975, sat out 1976 with injuries, and came back for a final year in 1977. He wound up his career with 649 catches – best ever at that time – for 9,140 yards and 79 touchdowns. He also scored 11 touchdowns rushing. Taylor was all-pro three years, playing in eight Pro Bowls.

Taylor, Jim

b. Baton Rouge, Louisiana, 20 September 1935.
Hall of Fame: 1976

When the Green Bay Packers dominated the NFL in the 1960s, Jim Taylor, a 6-0, 216-pound battering-ram fullback from Louisiana State University, was the man they looked to for tough yardage in tight situations. He was the prime disciple of head coach Vince Lombardi's "run to daylight" doctrine. He caught short swing passes, and blocked with rugged determination.

The Green Bay fullback, who became the first player from the Packers' dynasty years to be elected to the Hall of Fame, rushed for more than 1,000 yards five consecutive seasons beginning in 1960. He reached his zenith in 1962, when he had a career-high 1,474 yards

and was named the NFL Player of the Year. In the 1962 NFL championship game, he carried 31 times for 85 yards and scored the only touchdown in a 16-7 victory over the New York Giants. Taylor played nine years in Green Bay, then wound up his career with the New Orleans Saints in 1967. In his 10 NFL seasons, he rushed for 8,597 yards and 83 touchdowns. He also had 225 pass receptions for 1,756 yards and 10 touchdowns.

Taylor, Lawrence

b. *Williamsburg, Virginia, 4 February 1959.*

Linebacker Lawrence Taylor, a 6-3, 243-pound All-American from the University of North Carolina, joined the New York Giants as their first-round draft choice in 1981. Taylor has been named all-pro seven straight seasons and selected for the Pro Bowl each year. In 1986, he became only the second defensive player in history to be honored as the NFL's Most Valuable Player. Taylor has recorded 99 sacks in his first eight years.

Taylor, Lionel

b. *Kansas City, Missouri, 15 August 1936.*

Lionel Taylor, a graduate of New Mexico Highlands, began his pro football career as a free-agent linebacker with the Chicago Bears in 1959. In 1960, he joined the Denver Broncos of the AFL. With the Broncos, the 6-2, 205-pounder became a prolific pass catcher, leading the AFL in receiving in five of its first six seasons. Taylor caught 92 passes in 1960 and 100 in 1961, both pro football records at the time. He played with the Houston Oilers in 1967 and 1968. In his career, Taylor caught 567 passes for 7,195 yards and 45 touchdowns. He was named All-AFL in 1960, 1961, and 1965, and played in two AFL All-Star games.

Tee

A small, hard rubber stand used to suspend the ball in an upright position on a kickoff.

Television Time Out

The number of breaks in play for television time outs was reduced from 22 to 16 in 1986. The breaks are designed to allow the covering network to insert three 30-second commercials. Generally, breaks will take place after scores and changes of possession.

Thorpe, Jim

b. *Prague, Oklahoma, 28 May 1888;*
d. *28 March 1953. Hall of Fame: 1963*

Late in the 1915 season, the fabled Sac and Fox Indian athlete, Jim Thorpe, signed with the Canton Bulldogs for $250 a game. The 6-1, 190-pounder who had been an All-America at the Carlisle Indian Institute, proved to be both an exceptional football player and an unparalleled gate attraction. With Thorpe leading the way, the Bulldogs claimed unofficial world titles in 1916, 1917, and 1919. While Thorpe's feats tend to be exaggerated with the passing years, there is no question he was superb in every way. He could run with power and speed, pass and catch passes, punt long distances, and kick field goals, either by dropkick or placekick. He blocked with authority and was a bone-jarring tackler on defense. If he had a weakness, it was his relaxed approach to the game. Thorpe

Jim Taylor was a compact, punishing fullback and a vital part of the Packers' philosophy of 'run to daylight.' He holds Green Bay's game, season, and career rushing records.

Indians, Oorang Indians, Toledo Maroons, Rock Island Independents, and New York Giants. He played one game with the Chicago Cardinals in 1928.

Thorpe was given the Indian name, Wa-tho-huk, meaning Bright Path. Outstanding at almost any sport he tried, Thorpe gained his greatest fame by winning the decathlon and pentathlon events at the 1912 Olympics only to have his medals taken away because he had earned $15 a week playing minor league baseball one summer. Thorpe played major league baseball from 1913 through 1919. But he liked football best and left his mark on that sport before his death. In 1950, *Associated Press* named him the greatest American athlete of the first half of the twentieth century.

Three-Four

A defensive formation that features three down linemen and four linebackers.

Tight End

The player on the end of the offensive line who usually lines up next to the right tackle. His responsibilities call for him to block on running plays and to be a potential receiver on passing plays. Some teams often play with two tight ends.

Time Out

A halt to game action called by either team or the referee. Each team is allowed to call three charged time outs per half.

Tittle, Y.A.

b. Marshall, Texas, 24 October 1926.
Hall of Fame: 1971

Y.A. Tittle's 17-year pro football career began with the Baltimore Colts of the All-America Football Conference in 1948. The Colts moved to the NFL in 1950 but folded after one season. The 6-0, 200-pound quarterback from Louisiana State University was acquired by the San Francisco 49ers, with whom he performed with distinction for 10 years. Then, in 1961, at the age of 34, he was traded to the New York Giants, with whom he enjoyed four exceptional seasons.

With the Colts and 49ers, Tittle had never played on a championship team, but he did with New York. Early in 1961, he shared quarterbacking duties with Charley Conerly, but, as the Giants moved nearer to the Eastern Conference crown, Tittle gradually became the man in charge. In 1962, Tittle threw 33 touchdown passes and had a career-high 3,224

Lawrence Taylor's career has been a big hit, often on some unsuspecting ball carrier. He is a multi-talented sportsman, and could probably have had a successful career in profesional basketball, too.

claimed it made no sense to practice something he knew he could do supremely well.

Thorpe served as the first president of the American Professional Football Association after it was organized in Canton in 1920. Although his magic name was of inestimable value to pro football, Thorpe's best athletic days were behind him when he joined the Bulldogs at age 27. His last outstanding season came with the 1919 Bulldogs. In the first six seasons of the NFL from 1920 to 1925, Thorpe saw service with six different teams – the Bulldogs, Cleveland

yards. In 1963, he completed 60.2 percent of his passes for 3,145 yards and a record 36 touchdowns. The Giants won the NFL Eastern Conference title all three years. Tittle was the NFL's Most Valuable Player in 1961 and 1963. He wound up his career with 33,070 yards and 242 touchdown passes. He also rushed for 1,245 yards and 39 touchdowns. Named all-pro in 1957, 1962, and 1963, he also played in six Pro Bowls.

Touchback

When a ball is whistled dead on or behind a team's own goal line (e.g. on a kickoff that goes into the end zone), or if the defense takes over possession in its own endzone. The ball is put in play on that team's 20-yard line.

Touchdown

A six-point scoring play that occurs when one team crosses the other team's goal line with the ball in its possession.

Trafton, George

b. Chicago, Illinois, 6 December 1896;
d. 5 September 1971. Hall of Fame: 1964

George Trafton, a 6-2, 235-pound center who played briefly at Notre Dame, was one of the most skilled performers in the NFL during his 13-season career from 1920 to 1932. Although he had the moves of a halfback to go with his size and strength, Trafton also had the reputation as one of the toughest players in the league. He was one of the first centers to rove on defense and the very first on offense to

★ ★ ★ Triple Crown ★ ★ ★

Until free substitution was permanently instituted in the NFL in 1950, players performed on both the offensive and defensive units. Only three, however, won the so-called "Triple Crown," three individual statistical championships in one year:

1943	**Sammy Baugh**	Forward passing (1,754 yards, 23 touchdowns); punting (45.9-yard average); interceptions (11).
1945	**Steve Van Buren**	Rushing (832 yards); scoring (110 points); kickoff returns (28.7-yard average).
1946	**Bill Dudley**	Rushing (604 yards); punt returns (14.2-yard average); interceptions (10).

center the football with only one hand.

Performing at a time when teams were founded and disbanded the same season and players shifted from club to club in helter-skelter fashion, Trafton played his entire career with just one team, the Chicago Bears, who began as the Decatur Staleys in 1920.

Training Camp

Summer training camp usually begins two weeks before the first preseason game for NFL teams. Most training sites are located at a college or other satisfactory practice facility either in the team's home city or in a small town within driving distance.

Trap

A running play in which a defensive lineman is enticed across the line of scrimmage, then is blocked by a pulling guard or tackle.

The right guard slants into the right defensive end, exposing the defensive tackle (75). The left guard (61) pulls behind the center, who takes on the other defensive tackle.

2. The uncovered defensive tackle moves across the line into the trap area and, as the quarterback hands off, is hit by the pulling left guard.

3. The running back makes his cut off the trap block. The right tackle slants into the middle linebacker (58), clearing a running lane into the secondary.

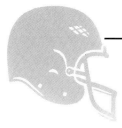

Trippi, Charley

b. Pittston, Pennsylvania, 14 December 1922. Hall of Fame: 1968

A two-time All-America from the University of Georgia, Charley Trippi was signed to a four-year, $100,000 contract by the Chicago Cardinals in 1947. Not only was the multi-talented Trippi a major prize in the fierce inter-league war with the All-America Football Conference, but his acquisition completed the "Dream Backfield" of Cardinals' owner Charles W. Bidwill, Sr. Although Bidwill did not live to see it, Trippi became the game-breaker in a talented group that included Paul Christman, Pat Harder, Marshall Goldberg, and, later, Elmer Angsman.

Trippi was at his absolute best in the 1947 NFL championship game. He gained 206 total yards and scored touchdowns on a 44-yard run and a 75-yard punt return as the Cardinals defeated the Philadelphia Eagles 28-21. The 6-0, 185-pounder could play anywhere. A halfback his first four seasons, he switched to quarterback in 1951 and 1952. He was a halfback again in 1953 and then played in the defensive backfield in 1954 and 1955. Trippi totalled 3,506 yards rushing, 130 receptions for 1,321 yards and 11 touchdowns receiving, and 2,547 yards and 16 touchdowns passing in his nine-year career.

Charley Trippi was the big-game player that Charles Bidwill needed. His best day for the Cardinals was in the 1947 NFL championship game against Philidelphia, when he gained 206 total yards and scored twice for Chicago.

Tunnell, Emlen

b. Bryn Mawr, Pennsylvania, 29 March 1925; d. 23 July 1975. Hall of Fame: 1967

Emlen Tunnell suffered a broken neck when he was a freshman at the University of Toledo and was told he would never play football again. Both the Army and Navy considered him unfit for service, but he did spend three years in the Coast Guard. After the war, Tunnell won a spot on the University of Iowa football team. Because the Hawkeyes had him tagged for the defensive unit and he preferred offense, Tunnell quit. He then contacted the New York Giants, who offered him a $5,000 contract, making him the first black player on the team. Tunnell was the first black player to be elected to the Hall of Fame.

Ironically, the Giants also wanted Tunnell to play defense. An outstanding special teams player, the 6-1, 200-pounder became known as the Giants' "offense on defense" during his 11 years in New York from 1948 to 1958. In 1952, Dan Towler of the Los Angeles Rams led NFL rushers with 894 yards, but Tunnell accounted for 923 yards on punt returns, kickoff returns, and seven interceptions. He averaged 17.8 yards each time he touched the ball. Tunnell, who played safety at the back of the Giants'

famed Umbrella defense, was a threat to force a turnover on every play. In 14 seasons – he spent his final three years in Green Bay – he intercepted a then-record 79 passes. He was a four-time all-pro pick, playing in nine Pro Bowls.

Turner, Clyde (Bulldog)

b. Sweetwater, Texas, 10 November 1919. Hall of Fame: 1966

Clyde (Bulldog) Turner, a 6-2, 235-pound Little All-America from Hardin-Simmons University, was the first-round draft choice of the Chicago Bears in 1940. Turner excelled as a premier center-linebacker for the next 13 seasons. Beginning in 1940, the Bears won four NFL championships in seven years and Turner earned all-pro honors six times. The Giants' Mel Hein had been the all-pro center eight consecutive years but Turner broke Hein's string in his second season, when he was only 22.

On offense, Turner was a flawless snapper and an exceptional blocker who could also play guard or tackle. A linebacker blessed with outstanding speed, he had eight interceptions in 1942 to lead the league and set a single-season record. He wound up his career after the 1952 season with 16 interceptions, which he returned for 289 yards and two touchdowns. In an emergency situation in 1944, Turner even became a ball carrier. He culminated his fullback debut with a 48-yard touchdown run.

Turner spent one year as coach of the New York Titans in 1962, a year before they changed their nickname to the Jets.

Turnover

The term for any play in which the offensive team loses the ball to the defensive team. A turnover may come on a fumble or on a pass interception.

Two-Minute Offense

A time-conserving, quick-play (usually passing) attack primarily used in the last two minutes of a game or half. Also called a "two-minute drill" or a "hurry-up offense."

Two-Minute Warning

The notification given to both benches by the officials that two minutes remain in a game or half. It is a time out, not charged to either team.

Tyrer, Jim

b. Newark, Ohio, 25 February 1939;
d. 15 September 1980.

Jim Tyrer, a 6-6, 280-pound All-America at Ohio State, was a third-round choice of the Dallas Texans in the 1961 AFL draft. Tyrer played with the Texans, who later became the Chiefs, for 13 seasons. He finished his career with the 1974 Washington Redskins. A fixture at left tackle on the Texans/Chiefs offensive line, Tyrer was a seven-time All-AFL selection and an All-AFC choice in 1970-71. He played in seven AFL All-Star games and two Pro Bowl games. In 1969, he was named to the AFL's all-time team.

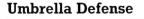

Umbrella Defense

In 1950, the high-powered Cleveland Browns were shut out once and scored a total of only 21 points in three games against the New York Giants. The architect of the Giants' defense was head coach Steve Owen, who devised a new formation, soon to be acclaimed as the "umbrella defense." It was basically a 6-1-4 alignment with the two ends dropping back to cover on passing plays. From this, the 4-3-4 defense and many other modern tactics developed.

Unbalanced Line

An offensive formation with a lineman shifted to overload one side of the line.

Undershift

A defensive formation in which all or some defensive linemen shift one position toward the weakside of the formation.

Uniform Numbers

The jerseys of all players must be numbered according to their positions as follows: Quarterbacks and kickers, 1-19; running and defensive backs, 20-49; centers and linebackers, 50-59; defensive linemen and interior offensive linemen, including centers, 60-79; wide receivers and tight ends, 80-89. Defensive linemen and linebackers also may be numbered 90-99.

Unitas, Johnny

b. Pittsburgh, Pennsylvania, 7 May 1933.
Hall of Fame: 1979

Johnny Unitas was a ninth-round draft pick of the Pittsburgh Steelers in 1955, but he was cut before he could even throw one pass in a preseason game. After playing semi-pro football in Pittsburgh for $6 a game for a year, Unitas signed as a free agent with the Baltimore Colts in 1956. In the fourth game, the regular quarterback, George Shaw, was injured and Unitas took over. Although his first pass was intercepted and returned for a touchdown by the Chicago Bears, he quickly developed into a star. Unitas was all-pro five times and NFL Player of the Year three years. He played in 10 Pro Bowls and was the game's Most Valuable Player three times. Unitas played with the Colts for 17 years, then finished with the San Diego Chargers in 1973.

Unitas saved the day for the Colts many times over the years but it was his clutch performance in the 1958 NFL championship game that made him a folk hero. With two minutes remaining, he completed four consecutive passes on a 73-yard drive to set up a tying field goal. Then, in overtime, Unitas engineered an 80-yard march to beat the New York Giants 23-17.

Unitas's most outstanding feat was his 47-

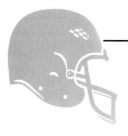

game streak in which he threw at least one touchdown pass, a record that has lasted for 30 years without being seriously threatened. His career statistics show 2,830 pass completions for 40,239 yards and 290 touchdowns. He also rushed for 13 touchdowns. Unitas was elected to the Hall of Fame in his first year of eligibility.

Johnny Unitas was arguably the greatest quarterback in NFL history. Great quarterbacks are always compared with Unitas, but nobody ever compares him with anybody.

United States Football League

David Dixon, a New Orleans antique dealer, conceived the idea of a pro football league that would play in the spring in major cities around the nation. He envisioned a salary cap with a handful of stars to bolster rosters filled with players from local colleges. On May 11, 1982, the United States Football League was born. ABC Sports contracted to televise 22 games, and ESPN agreed to a 34-game TV package. Twelve franchises, nine of them in NFL cities, were awarded. However, the salary cap scheme quickly evaporated.

The USFL began play in March, 1983, with the Boston Breakers, New Jersey Generals, Philadelphia Stars, and Washington Federals in the Atlantic Division; the Birmingham Stallions, Chicago Blitz, Michigan Panthers, and Tampa Bay Bandits in the Central Division; and the Arizona Wranglers, Denver Gold, Los Angeles Express, and Oakland Invaders in the Pacific Division. Attendance was encouraging at first but sagged badly as spring turned into summer. By July, when Michigan defeated Philadelphia 24-22 for the first USFL championship, many clubs were in serious financial difficulty.

The USFL expanded from 12 to 18 teams in

1984, then dropped back to 14 teams in 1985.

The league announced it would play in the fall beginning in 1986. It became apparent in the 1985-1986 offseason that no major television network contract was forthcoming, and the USFL, which had suffered cumulative losses of more than $200 million, decided to cease operations and base all its hopes on the successful outcome of its $1.69 billion antitrust suit against the NFL.

In July, 1986, a jury in the U.S. District Court in New York awarded the USFL just three dollars in damages. Two years later, an appeals court upheld the original verdict.

Unsportsmanlike Conduct

A penalty assessed for any act that is contrary to the generally understood principles of sportsmanship.

Up Back

1. A blocking back on a kick play who lines up just behind the linemen.
2. The receiver(s) set in front of the deep receivers on kicks.

Upshaw, Gene

b. Robstown, Texas, 15 August 1945.
Hall of Fame: 1987

Until Gene Upshaw was the number one draft choice of the Oakland Raiders in 1967, pro football guards usually were stocky – strong but not too mobile and standing only 6-1 or 6-2. Upshaw, who stood 6-5 and weighed 255 pounds, started a trend. The Texas A&I University product was extremely fast, intelligent, and dedicated to working as hard as necessary to become the best at his position. The Raiders were particularly dangerous with their powerful sweeps around left end. As the left guard, Upshaw had the responsibility of leading the blocking.

In his 15-season career that lasted until 1981, the highly-skilled athlete was all-AFL/AFC eight times. He played in the 1968 AFL All-Star Game, six AFC-NFC Pro Bowls, 10 AFL/AFC title games, and Super Bowls II, XI, and XV. Upshaw was picked by the Raiders for the specific purpose of neutralizing big defensive tackles such as the Kansas City Chiefs' Buck Buchanan. Upshaw played an incredible 307 preseason, regular-season, and postseason games.

Upshaw became the only modern player who performed exclusively as a guard to be elected to the Hall of Fame. Upshaw is currently the executive director of the NFL Players Association.

Van Brocklin, Norm

b. Eagle Butte, South Dakota, 15 March 1926;
d. 1 May 1983. Hall of Fame: 1971

Norm Van Brocklin, a former University of Oregon All-America, enjoyed great success in his 12-year pro career that began with the Western Division champion Los Angeles Rams in 1949 and ended with the NFL champion Philadelphia Eagles in 1960. A multi-talented performer, "The Dutchman," as he was nicknamed, led the NFL in passing three times and in punting twice. The 6-1, 190-pound quarterback once passed for a record 554 yards in a single game. His 73-yard touchdown pass clinched the Rams' 1951 NFL title victory over the Cleveland Browns. His career record shows 1,553 completions for 23,611 yards and 173 touchdowns. Van Brocklin also scored 11 touchdowns rushing and had an excellent 42.9-yard career punting average. He played in eight Pro Bowls.

Early in his tenure with the Rams, Van Brocklin was forced to share quarterback duties with another Hall of Fame inductee, Bob Waterfield. Even after Waterfield retired, Van Brocklin still had to share playing time with other passers. But in 1957, he was traded to Philadelphia, where head coach Buck Shaw gave him a free hand with the offense. Behind "The Dutchman," the Eagles finished second in 1959 and won the championship in 1960. Van Brocklin was a unanimous all-pro pick and the Most Valuable Player in the NFL championship game. In the Pro Bowl a month later, he ended his career with a three-touchdown outburst.

Immediately after his playing career ended, Van Brocklin was named as the first coach of the Minnesota Vikings, a post he held until the end of the 1966 season. In 1968 he was hired by the Atlanta Falcons as their coach, but was released midway through the 1974 season.

Van Buren, Steve

b. Le Ceiba, Honduras, 28 December 1920.
Hall of Fame: 1965

Steve Van Buren once was turned down for football as a high school sophomore because he weighed only 125 pounds. Even during his days at Louisiana State University, Van Buren played blocking back for two years and blossomed as a superior ball carrier only in his senior season. His NFL career with the Philadelphia Eagles

Guard Gene Upshaw is about to blast aside a New York Jets linebacker to allow the Oakland Raiders' running back space. With Art Shell and Jim Otto on either side of Upshaw, the ball carrier normally could find lots of daylight.

from 1944 to 1951 was far more distinctive. The 6-1, 200-pounder, who lined up at halfback but had the battering ram tendencies of a fullback, won four NFL rushing titles, and surpassed 1,000 yards in both 1947 and 1949. In 1945, he won an unusual triple crown with individual championships in rushing, scoring, and kickoff returns. Van Buren was named all-pro as a rookie and four more times in his first six seasons.

Van Buren was a major contributor to both Eagles championship victories in 1948 and 1949. In the snowy 1948 title game against the Chicago Cardinals, he scored the only touchdown in a 7-0 victory. The next year, playing in the rain against the Los Angeles Rams, he rushed for a record 196 yards as the Eagles won 14-0.

W

Waivers

A process of releasing a player either to be claimed by another club or to become a free agent.

Walker, Doak

b. Dallas, Texas, 1 January 1927.
Hall of Fame: 1986

Although Doak Walker had been a three-time consensus All-America and the 1948 Heisman Trophy winner at Southern Methodist University, many pro football scouts felt he was too small to play in the NFL when he joined the Detroit Lions in 1950. The 5-11, 173-pound halfback quickly erased any doubt he belonged in the NFL. He led the league in scoring with 128 points, was named Rookie of the Year and all-pro and was selected to play in the Pro Bowl. Walker continued to star for five more seasons, winning all-pro honors three more times and being named to four more Pro Bowls. He was a major star in Detroit's 1952 and 1953 championship seasons.

The versatile Texan's career shows entries in every possible statistical category – rushing, passing, receiving, punt and kickoff returns, punting, placekicking, and even interceptions. In just six years, he scored 534 points. His 24-yard scoring pass helped Detroit to a 31-21 victory over the Los Angeles Rams in a 1952 Division Playoff Game. A week later in the NFL championship game against Cleveland, his 67-yard run was the game-winner in the Lions' 17-7 victory. In the 1953 NFL championship game, also against the Browns, Walker scored a touchdown and kicked the winning extra point in a 17-16 victory. He retired after the 1955 season, when he again led the league in scoring.

Walsh, Bill

b. Los Angeles, California, 30 November 1931.

In 1979, San Francisco owner Edward J. DeBartolo, Jr., named Bill Walsh as the eleventh head coach of the 49ers. In 1988, Walsh retired after his tenth season in the job, the longest tenure of any coach in team history. His 102-63-1 record was the best of any San Francisco coach. Under Walsh, the 49ers won six NFC Western Division championships in eight years and NFC championships in 1981, 1984, and 1988. In January,

1982, San Francisco defeated the Cincinnati Bengals 26-21 in Super Bowl XVI and Walsh was named the NFL coach of the year. Three years later, the 49ers defeated the Miami Dolphins 38-16 in Super Bowl XIX. In Super Bowl XXII, the 49ers beat the Bengals again, this time 20-16. Walsh's teams also reached the playoffs in 1983, 1985, 1986, and 1987. Walsh is a graduate of San Jose State. His 25-year pre-49ers coaching career included head coaching stints at San Jose State and Stanford University and assistant coaching jobs with the Oakland Raiders, Cincinnati Bengals, and San Diego Chargers.

Ward, Arch

b. Irwin, Illinois, 27 December 1896;
d. 9 July 1955

Arch Ward was the long-time sports editor of the *Chicago Tribune* who played a prominent role in the creation of the College All-Star game series that lasted from 1934 to 1976. In both 1940 and 1941, he was recommended for the National Football League commissioner's job but turned it down. In 1944, he organized the All-America Football Conference that began play in 1946.

Warfield, Paul

b. Warren, Ohio, 28 November 1942.
Hall of Fame: 1983

Paul Warfield played high school and college football in his home state. When he finished his career at Ohio State, he was the first-round draft choice of the Cleveland Browns in 1964. For the next six seasons, he performed spectacularly as a big-play wide receiver for the perennially contending Browns. In 1970, he was traded to the Miami Dolphins. In the next five seasons, the flashy 6-0, 188-pound speedster averaged 21.5 yards per reception for a Miami team that compiled a perfect 17-0 record in 1972 and won Super Bowls VII and VIII. Tempted by a large contract, Warfield played out his option in Miami and jumped to the Memphis Southmen of the World Football League in 1975. When that league folded, Warfield moved back to the Browns for the 1976 and 1977 seasons.

Warfield played primarily for ball-control teams. In Miami's perfect season, the Dolphins rushed 613 times while passing only 280 times. Warfield made only 29 receptions. Yet many consider him to have been the key element in the unprecedented season. As a result of his teams' personalities, his career totals fall far short of those of many less-talented receivers. He made 427 catches for 8,565 yards, 85 touchdowns, and a dazzling 20.1-yard average. In his first year of eligibility, Warfield was elected to the Hall of Fame.

Washington Redskins

The Washington Redskins began in 1932 when George Preston Marshall headed a four-man syndicate that was awarded a National Football League franchise for Boston. Originally named the Braves because they used Braves Field, home of the National League baseball team, they changed their name to Redskins when they moved to Fenway Park in 1933. Led by two outstanding rookies, halfback Cliff Battles and tackle Glen (Turk) Edwards, the Redskins finished with .500 records their first three seasons. Under new coach Ray Flaherty in 1936, they defeated the New York Giants 14-0 on the last day of the season to win the Eastern Conference championship. But Marshall was so unhappy over the poor crowds in Boston that he moved the NFL championship game to the Polo Grounds in New York, where nearly 30,000 people watched Green Bay defeat his team 21-6.

In 1937, Marshall moved his team to Washington, where he organized a team band and produced the first elaborate halftime shows. That same year, Marshall signed a rookie passer named Sammy Baugh, who teamed with Battles and end Wayne Millner to lead the Redskins to another Eastern championship. More than 10,000 Washington fans rode a special train to New York to watch the Redskins clinch the title with a 49-14 win over the New York Giants. In the 1937 NFL championship game, Baugh threw three long touchdown passes to defeat the Chicago Bears 28-21. The Redskins won their next Eastern championship with a 9-2 record in 1940, but the Chicago Bears won the NFL title 73-0, the most lopsided score in NFL history.

Two years later, in the 1942 title game, Flaherty, coaching his last game with the Redskins, gained revenge with a 14-6 victory that ruined the Bears' perfect season. In 1943, with Arthur (Dutch) Bergman as head coach, Baugh won individual NFL championships in passing, punting, and interceptions but the Redskins lost to the Bears 41-21 in the NFL championship game. Dudley DeGroot was the head coach when the Redskins won their sixth Eastern title in 10

years in 1945 but lost to the Cleveland Browns 15-14 in the NFL championship game.

The Redskins only had one losing season during their first 15 years in the NFL but they only had three winning seasons in the 22-year period from 1947 to 1968. Beginning with Turk Edwards in 1946-1948, the team tried nine coaches with little success until Vince Lombardi took charge in 1969. Led by quarterback Sonny Jurgensen, running back Larry Brown, and end Charley Taylor on offense, and defensive backs Pat Fischer and Brig Owens on defense, the 1969 Redskins finished with a 7-5 record, their first winning season since 1955. But, before the 1970 season, Lombardi died of cancer.

In 1971, George Allen became the head coach. Allen's philosophy that "the future is now" prompted him to trade draft choices for seasoned veterans and the policy paid immediate dividends. In the next seven seasons, Allen compiled a 69-35-1 record. His teams won wild-card playoff berths in 1971, 1973, 1974, and 1976, and the NFC championship in 1972. Quarterback Bill Kilmer was a major force in the 1972 season when the Redskins won 11 of 14 games. In the NFC championship game, they defeated Dallas 26-3. In Super Bowl VII, the Redskins lost 14-7 as Miami completed a 17-0 season.

Allen resigned after the 1977 season but the Redskins started another winning era when Joe Gibbs became head coach in 1981. Washington won eight of nine games in the strike-shortened 1982 season, defeated Dallas 31-17 for the NFC championship, and whipped Miami 27-17 in Super Bowl XVII. Paced by quarterback Joe Theismann, fullback John Riggins, receiver Charlie Brown, and placekicker Mark Moseley, the Redskins scored an NFL record 541 points in 1983. They had a 14-2 regular-season record, defeating San Francisco 24-21 for the NFC championship, but lost to the Los Angeles Raiders 38-9 in Super Bowl XVIII.

Washington won the Eastern Division in 1984 but lost to the Chicago Bears in the first playoff game. The Redskins were a wild-card team in 1986 and advanced to the NFC championship game before losing to the New York Giants, 17-0. In 1987, the Redskins had an 11-4 record, and then defeated Chicago and Minnesota for their third NFC championship. With Doug Williams throwing a record four touchdown passes in the second quarter, the Redskins defeated the Denver Broncos 42-10 in Super Bowl XXII. Gibbs has a 92-42 record in eight seasons as head coach of he Redskins.

Marshall died in 1969, and, in 1974, Jack Kent Cooke became the majority stockholder of the Redskins. Today he serves as the club's chairman of the board.

Mike Webster has a local problem with an Atlanta nose tackle during a replacement game. Very few players have been on more winning teams that the 15-year Pittsburgh center.

Kelvin Bryant, 24, follows the lead block of 'Hog' Joe Jacoby (66). Washington's starting offensive line in Super Bowl XXII of Jacoby, McKenzie, Bostic, Thielemann, and May weighed in excess of 1,400 pounds.

Members of the Hall of Fame:

(15) Cliff Battles, Sammy Baugh, Bill Dudley, Glen (Turk) Edwards, Ray Flaherty, Ken Houston, Sam Huff, David (Deacon) Jones, Sonny Jurgensen, Earl (Curly) Lambeau, Vince Lombardi, George Preston Marshall, Wayne Millner, Bobby Mitchell, Charley Taylor.

Championships Won:

Super Bowl: XVII, XXII
NFL (before 1970): 1937, 1942
NFC: 1972, 1982, 1983
NFL Eastern Conference: 1936, 1937, 1940, 1942, 1943, 1945
NFC Eastern Division: 1972, 1983, 1984, 1987

Overall Record:

NFL Regular Season	382	330	26	.535
NFL Postseason	16	12	0	.571
Total	398	342	26	.537

Waterfield, Bob

b. Elmira, New York, 26 July 1920;
d. 25 April 1983. Hall of Fame: 1965.

Bob Waterfield enjoyed an exceptional rookie season in 1945 when he quarterbacked the Cleveland Rams to the NFL championship. The UCLA graduate was a unanimous all-pro choice and the league's Most Valuable Player, the first

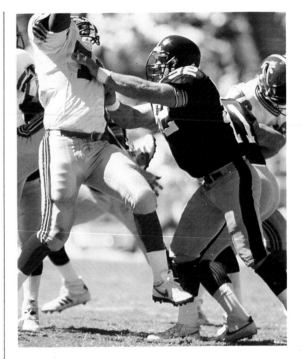

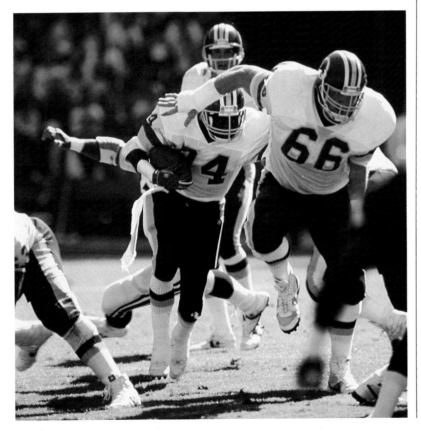

rookie ever to win the award. Early in 1946, owner Dan Reeves moved the Rams from Cleveland to Los Angeles. For the next seven seasons, Waterfield was a brilliant field general and precision passer who put points on the scoreboard in massive doses. Waterfield also was a dangerous runner and sensational punter and placekicker. In addition, he intercepted 20 passes while playing defense his first four seasons.

The 6-2, 200-pound Waterfield was at his best in the clutch. In the 1945 NFL championship game, he threw 37- and 44-yard touchdown passes. Earlier that year, in a crucial game against Detroit, he completed 10 passes to Jim Benton for a stunning 303 yards. In a playoff game against the Bears in 1950, he came off the bench to throw three touchdown passes despite a severe case of the flu.

Waterfield divided his playing time with another Hall of Fame quarterback, Norm Van Brocklin, his final five years, then retired after his eighth season in 1952. His lifetime record shows 11,849 yards and 97 touchdowns by passing, 13 rushing touchdowns, a 42.4-yard punting average, and 573 points scored. A two-time NFL individual passing champion, he was named all-pro three times.

The Los Angeles Rams named him coach in 1960, but he resigned halfway through the 1962 season.

Weakside

The side of the offensive formation without the tight end.

Webster, Mike

b. Tomahawk, Wisconsin, 18 March 1952.

In 1988, center Mike Webster played his fifteenth season, the longest tenure of any player in Pittsburgh Steelers' history. He was the last active Steelers player on all four winning Super Bowl teams. The 6-2, 254-pounder from the University of Wisconsin was the 125th player selected in the 1974 NFL draft, but he did not miss a game until his thirteenth season in 1986, when injuries forced him out of four games. Webster was a Steelers captain in 1988 for the ninth consecutive year. Going into 1988, he had been a seven-time all-pro choice and a nine-time Pro Bowl selection.

Weinmeister, Arnie

b. Rhein, Saskatchewan, Canada, 23 March 1923. Hall of Fame: 1984

Arnie Weinmeister, a 6-4, 235-pounder from the University of Washington, was the dominant defensive tackle in pro football during his two seasons in the All-America Football Conference and four years in the NFL. He played with the New York Yankees in 1948 and 1949 and then with the New York Giants from 1950 to 1953. Weinmeister was named all-AAFC in 1949 and all-pro all four seasons in the NFL. He played in four Pro Bowls.

Weinmeister had the size, aggressiveness, and dedication expected of a superior defensive tackle. He also had exceptional speed. Giants coaches continually intimidated fleet-footed rookies by matching them in 100-yard dashes against the ace defensive tackle, who almost always won. He also possessed the unique ability to diagnose enemy plays, then to range from sideline to sideline to bring down the ball carriers in the open field.

White, Byron (Whizzer)

b. Fort Collins, Colorado, 8 June 1917.

Byron (Whizzer) White, an All-America halfback at the University of Colorado in 1937, was signed to a $15,800 contract, one of the biggest to that time by Art Rooney, the owner of the Pittsburgh Pirates. White agreed to play when he learned he could postpone his acceptance of a Rhodes scholarship. He led the NFL in rushing with 567 yards as a rookie in 1938, then left for Oxford the next year. The outbreak of World War II forced him back to America in 1940. Detroit paid Pittsburgh $15,000 for his negotiating rights, and White became a member of the Lions in 1940. He gained 514 yards to win his second NFL rushing championship. In his third and last pro season in 1941, White won

a third individual championship by returning 19 punts for 262 yards.

White is now a Justice on the United States Supreme Court.

Reggie White has maneuvered behind tackle Mark May (73) and has wrapped up Kelvin Bryant. Philadelphia's defensive lineman is one of the most dangerous pass rushers in the NFL, and is the cornerstone of head coach Buddy Ryan's defense.

White, Randy

b. Wilmington, Delaware, 15 January 1953.

Randy White was an All-America tackle and the 1974 Outland Trophy winner at the University of Maryland. He was the Dallas Cowboys' first-round pick and the second player selected in the 1975 NFL draft. During his first 13 years in the NFL, the 6-4, 265-pound White, who still is active, was showered with numerous honors. He was named all-pro eight consecutive years from 1978 to 1985 and played in nine Pro Bowls. White was named the Co-Most Valuable Player after the Cowboys' 27-10 win over Denver in Super Bowl XII. In 13 seasons, he recorded 112½ sacks.

White, Reggie

b. Chattanooga, Tennessee, 19 December 1961.

Reggie White, an All-America defensive end from the University of Tennessee, began his pro football career with the Memphis Showboats of the United States Football League in 1984 and 1985. When the USFL folded, the Philadelphia Eagles, who had selected White in an NFL supplemental draft in 1984, signed the 6-5, 285-pounder. Even though he played 18 games in the USFL early that year, White saw action in 13 games with the Eagles in 1985. In his first 51 games with the Eagles, White recorded 52 sacks. In 1987, he had an NFL-leading 21 sacks in 12 non-strike games. He was named all-pro in 1986 and 1987 and invited to the Pro Bowl after the 1987 season. White was named the 1987 NFL Defensive Player of the Year.

Paul Warfield, along with Larry Csonka and Jim Kiick, left Miami after the Dolphins' perfect season to join the short-lived World Football League. The speedy receiver, whose figures are not a fair reflection of his ability, was elected to the Hall of Fame in 1983.

Wide Receiver

Usually the two or more players who line up furthest from the center on either side of the line. This is a general term for the flankers (who must line up a yard behind the scrimmage line) and the split end (who must be up on the line). They are the players who ordinarily are expected to go downfield for passes.

Willis, Bill

b. Columbus, Ohio, 5 October 1921.
Hall of Fame: 1977

In Bill Willis's first scrimmage after he joined the Cleveland Browns in 1946, he was stationed across the line from veteran center Moe Scarry. On four consecutive plays, Willis charged at the instant of the snap, flattened or eluded Scarry, and crashed into the quarterback. Head coach Paul Brown watched a few more plays to be certain everything his new recruit did was perfectly legal. After practice, he signed the Ohio State product to a $4,000 contract. The 6-2, 215-pound Willis was one of the smallest linemen in the Browns' camp but he also drew attention because he was one of the first two black players to sign with an All-America Football Conference team.

At first, Willis, played both offense and defense but it was as a middle guard on defense that he won lasting acclaim. Lightning quickness was his trademark but opponents in-

sist he was a hard-hitting tackler as well. In seven of his first eight seasons he was all-league, three times in the AAFC and four in the NFL. Willis also played in three NFL Pro Bowls. He retired after the 1953 season.

Wilson, Larry

b. Rigby, Idaho, 24 March 1938.
Hall of Fame: 1978

Larry Wilson, a graduate of the University of Utah, joined the St. Louis Cardinals in 1960 as a halfback. He could not win the starting job, so Cardinals' defensive coordinator Chuck Drulis moved him to safety. Drulis was planning a daring new maneuver – soon to become famous as the safety blitz – and he felt Wilson was the person to make the play work. The tactic called for the safety to burst through the offensive line on the snap, time his charge perfectly, and tackle the quarterback before he had time to react.

Wilson handled the safety blitz so well he acquired the nickname of the play's code-name, "Wildcat." For the next 13 years (through 1972), Wilson harassed NFL offenses not only with his blitzes but with outstanding pass coverage. He intercepted 52 passes, which he returned for 800 yards and five touchdowns. Wilson also had the reputation of being the toughest player in pro football. The 6-0, 190-pounder ignored an endless string of injuries to stay in the lineup. In a game against Pittsburgh,

Wilson, playing with two broken hands, intercepted a pass for the go-ahead touchdown. A six-time all-pro choice, Wilson played in eight Pro Bowls. In his first year of eligibility, he was elected to the Hall of Fame.

Wilson was named as St. Louis' interim coach for the last three games of the 1979 season, but he did not continue the following year.

Winslow, Kellen

b. St. Louis, Missouri, 5 November 1957.

The San Diego Chargers selected Kellen Winslow, a consensus All-America tight end from the University of Missouri, in the first round of the 1979 NFL draft. Winslow missed nine games of his rookie season with a broken leg but returned in 1980 to become one of the major offensive threats in pro football. He had 89 receptions in both 1980 and 1981, and 88 receptions in 1983. The 6-5, 250-pound Winslow was all-pro in 1980, 1981 and 1982. He played in five Pro Bowls, his last coming after the 1987 season, then retired in 1988. Winslow caught 541 passes for 6,741 yards and 45 touchdowns.

Wishbone Offense

An offense – pioneered by University of Texas coach Darrell Royal in the late 1960s – that employs a mobile, running quarterback and three running backs. The Wishbone has not been popular in the NFL because most pro coaches tend to minimize runs by quarterbacks.

Wojciechowicz, Alex

b. South River, New Jersey, 12 August 1915.
Hall of Fame: 1968

Alex Wojciechowicz, the pivotman of Fordham University's famous "Seven Blocks of Granite" forward wall and a two-time All-America, was the Detroit Lions' first-round draft choice in 1938. In his first week, he earned the "iron-man" tag that would follow him through his 13-season career by playing in four games in seven days. The Chicago College All-Star Game was followed in rapid succession by the New York All-Star Game, a Lions intrasquad scrimmage, and the Detroit-Pittsburgh preseason opener. By the time the regular season began, Wojciechowicz was firmly entrenched as a regular. On offense, he was a play-every-down center who became famous because of his wide stance over the ball – five feet, four inches! On defense, the 6-0, 235-pound Wojciechowicz was a sure-tackling linebacker with good range in the secondary. In 1944, he intercepted seven passes, a Lions record for several years.

After 8½ seasons in Detroit, Wojciechowicz was waived midway through 1946. The Philadelphia Eagles immediately claimed him. Head coach Earle (Greasy) Neale installed him as a linebacker in the defensive unit that would bring the Eagles three divisional and two NFL championships in the next three seasons. Wojciechowicz retired after the 1950 season.

Wood, Willie

b. Washington, DC, 23 December 1936.
Hall of Fame: 1989

Willie Wood, a 5-10, 190-pound defensive back from the University of Southern California, was a free-agent acquisition of the Green Bay Packers in 1960. Wood was named an all-pro safety seven times in eight years from 1964 to his final season in 1971. He played in eight Pro Bowl games. Wood started for the Packers in five NFL championship games and Super Bowls I and II. His 50-yard return of an interception in Super Bowl I was the turning point in a 35-10 victory over the Kansas City Chiefs. In 12 seasons, he intercepted 48 passes for 699 yards and two touchdowns. He also returned 187 punts for 1,391 yards.

World Football League

In 1973, Gary Davidson, who had been a co-founder of both the American Basketball Association and the World Hockey Association, founded the World Football League. Twelve franchises were awarded for the 1974 season. The WFL schedule called for no preseason games but 20 regular-season games, beginning in July.

No one paid much attention to the WFL until March 31, 1974, when John Bassett, Jr., of the Toronto Northmen (who soon became the Memphis Southmen) announced he had signed Larry Csonka, Jim Kiick, and Paul Warfield of the Super Bowl-champion Miami Dolphins to a three-year, $3 million package starting from 1975. By June 4, WFL teams claimed the signing of 59 NFL players who were playing out their options so that they could join the WFL in 1975.

The WFL began play in July, 1974, with 12 teams (the Florida Blazers, New York Stars – later Charlotte Hornets, Philadelphia Bell, and Jacksonville Sharks in the East; Memphis, Birmingham Americans, Chicago Fire, and Detroit Wheel in the Central; Southern California Sun, Hawaiians, Portland Storm, and Houston Texans – later Shreveport Steamer, in the West) but virtually every team in the WFL experienced severe financial problems almost immediately. Four teams either folded or changed cities. The Birmingham Americans defeated Florida 22-21 for the 1974 WFL championship, but their

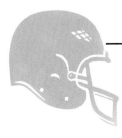

uniforms were repossessed after the game.

Under new commissioner Chris Hemmeter, the WFL adopted many cost-cutting procedures in the offseason. The San Antonio Wings entered the WFL, but Detroit and Florida dropped out, and a two-division set-up was used with Memphis and Birmingham (who were renamed the Vulcans) joining the East division, and Chicago (who became the Wind) and San Antonio joined the West; Portland changed its name to Thunder, and Jacksonville became Express. Chicago folded on September 2, and, with the exception of Memphis and Birmingham, every other team faced imminent financial ruin. Twelve weeks into its second season, the WFL disbanded on October 22, 1975. All players were released from their contracts, and most former NFL players were back in their old league by 1976.

Y

★ ★

Yard Line

The numerical designation of the line across the playing field, perpendicular to the sidelines that denotes distance from the end zones. There are 99 yard-line designations on the football field (Team A: 1-yard line to 49-yard line; 50-yard line; Team B: 49-yard line to 1-yard line).

Yary, Ron

b. *Chicago, Illinois, 16 August 1946.*

Ron Yary, a two-time All-America tackle at the University of Southern California, was selected

by the Minnesota Vikings in the first round of the draft in 1968. The 6-6, 255-pound Yary was a fixture on the Vikings' offensive line for the next 14 years; he played his fifteenth NFL season with the Los Angeles Rams in 1982. The durable tackle missed only six of 213 regular-season games. Yary played in seven Pro Bowls. He was an all-pro or All-NFC selection six times from 1970 to 1978.

Youngblood, Jack

b. *Jacksonville, Florida, 16 January 1950.*

In 1971, the Los Angeles Rams drafted Jack Youngblood, a 6-4, 242-pound All-America defensive end from the University of Florida, on the first round. In his 14-year career, Youngblood missed only one of 203 games, that lone miss coming in his final season in 1984. In the 1979 NFC playoffs, Youngblood fractured a leg in the first game but wore a plastic brace and played every defensive down in the NFC championship game and Super Bowl XIV. Youngblood was named All-NFC six times and selected for seven consecutive Pro Bowls from 1973 to 1979.

Z

★ ★ ★ ★ ★ ★ ★ ★ ★ ★ ★ ★ ★ ★ ★ ★

Zone

An assigned area of pass defense.

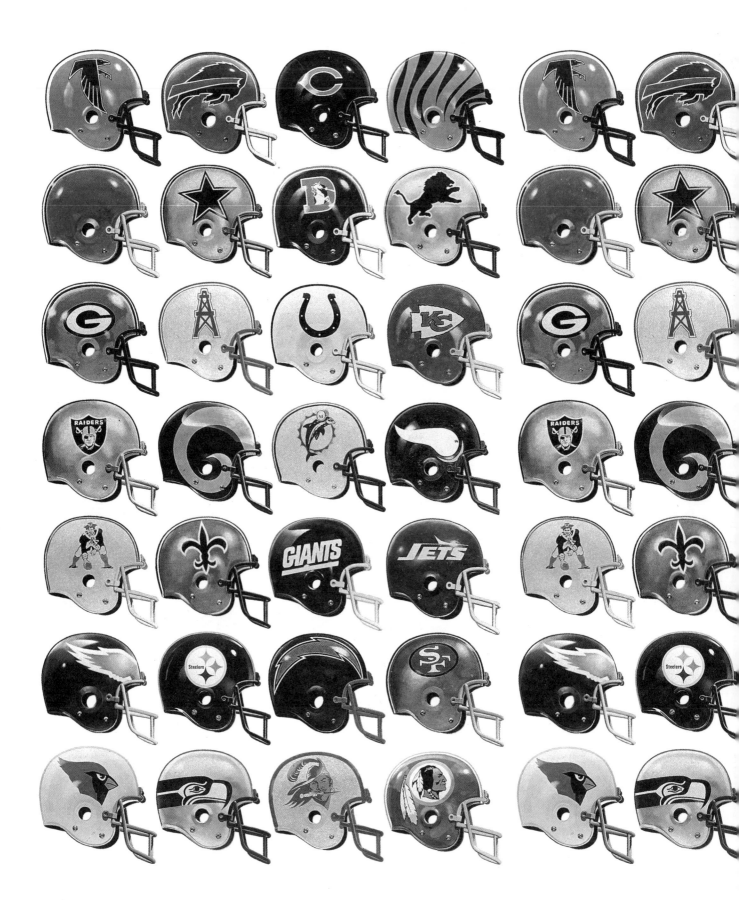